# LEAVES AND FRUIT

# LEAVES AND FRUIT

BY

SIR EDMUND WILLIAM GOSSE

*Essay Index Reprint Series*

**BOOKS FOR LIBRARIES PRESS**

**FREEPORT, NEW YORK**

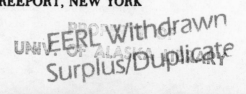

First Published 1927
Reprinted 1970

STANDARD BOOK NUMBER:
8369-1505-4


LIBRARY OF CONGRESS CATALOG CARD NUMBER:
70-105017


PRINTED IN THE UNITED STATES OF AMERICA

TO
LYTTON STRACHEY
WITH AFFECTIONATE
ADMIRATION

# PREFACE

THOSE kind readers who have been sitting every Sunday
for the last eight years beneath my imaginary pulpit do
not need that I should defend to them the choice of my text.
It is, indeed, whimsical in the extreme, and I have to admit
that my own taste is indulged by it and not the advice of
my parishioners. Unknown auditors write, in the kindest
of terms, to beg me to be something other than my mood
dictates. They wish me to be frivolous while I am reading
Epictetus; they propose Bacon as a subject when I am
thinking of Ninon Lenclos. But by dint of gazing inter-
minably over the vast expanse of literature, I have gradually
and unconsciously come to regard with equal interest all
forms of passionate expression, whether grave or gay, profound or superficial. I ask of books only that they should
be amusing, that is to say, competently enough executed
to arrest an intelligent observer. My little essays on them
are so many pieces of broken looking-glass held up to catch
the figures and gestures of life as they pass by. It is for
my readers to say whether the mirror is clear or tarnished;
at all events I do not think it is dimmed by prejudice.

E. G.

*August* 1927.

# CONTENTS

# A SONG TO DAVID

# A SONG TO DAVID

LITERARY history offers us no phenomenon more odd or more unaccountable than the appearance in 1763 of the quarto poem in 516 lines called " A Song to David." That a work of surpassing originality should appear at a moment when the canon of verse seemed to be conventionally fixed is interesting, but not remarkable, since this is how poetry is perpetually being renewed. Nor is it particularly wonderful—though indeed strange enough—that not one single human being in that highly intelligent and inquisitive age should have perceived its merit or have attached any importance at all to it, since prophets are apt to speak in a key so high that, like some birds and crickets, nobody hears them. But what is really miraculous is that the wonderful piece was the work of an active versifier who had been composing odes and effusions for twenty years, and was to write more, in neither case producing anything that was not entirely conventional.

It is true that since the merit of " A Song to David " has been recognised many critics have searched Smart's other works for traces of genius, and have produced what they fondly hoped would pass. No less sensitive an expert than Mr. Oliver Elton is among them. I confess that I myself have delved and brought up fragments from " The Hilliad " or " The Hop-Garden." But here and now I recant, and I protest that there is nothing, not a line, in the whole of Smart's other writings which possesses permanent value or would ever be glanced at if the one great

3

lyric had been lost, as it so nearly was. This is the miracle of " A Song to David," that it is an inestimable jewel buried in a dust-heap.

That the middle of the eighteenth century displayed a genuine capacity for song of a sedate and measured kind is now generally admitted. The elegiac writers between 1730 and 1770 have their warm admirers, but even Mr. Iolo Williams will admit that their range was narrow and that they walked rather than leaped or ran. In 1763 Pope had been dead for nineteen years, but his authority was rarely questioned; " The Messiah " still marked the way in which a bard should approach a sacred theme, and this was the way in which Smart had endeavoured to celebrate the Deity in many a dreary prize-poem. The most celebrated metrical artists of the day were Young and Gray, since Collins and Thomson were dead. All these had been poets of permanent value, so far as I can see unequalled then elsewhere in Europe for their peculiar gifts, but they illustrated a convention. By their side, Christopher Smart cultivated the same convention in his odes and descriptive pieces, though very tamely. In the didactic order, Smart doubtless admired, and perhaps tried to emulate, the magnificent " Vanity of Human Wishes " of his friend, Mr. Samuel Johnson.

But what was remarkable about " A Song to David," and what renders it a miracle, is that it has no affinity whatever with these contemporary masterpieces, whether in tone, in language, or in disposition. The one thing that all the other eighteenth-century bards avoided was ecstasy. Even Gray, who is splendid and vociferous, is never ecstatic. At his most elevated moments Gray never forgets the decencies of language, the limits of what is " proper to poetry." His hair is uplifted, but his feet are on the ground. Now, the main feature of " A Song to David " is ecstasy. The author abandons himself and

floats into the empyrean on the wings of the wind. No
wonder that it passed unobserved, and that when Hunter
collected Smart's posthumous writings he specifically refrained from including " A Song to David," on the plea
that it bore " too many melancholy proofs of the estrange-
ment of Smart's mind " to be fit for publication.

Let us, for whom madness is no longer a bar to fame,
examine this unique product of Bedlam. It is not precisely an ode or a hymn, it is rather what some old Italian
poet might have called a *trionfo*, a Triumph. It celebrates
the splendour and beauty of the created world, in small
things as well as great, the whole diapason of existence
combining to laud and magnify the Creator. In per-
forming his task the poet, who had been translating the
Psalms into very dull verse, adopts the companionship of
David much as Dante leans upon that of Virgil. He
expatiates on the virtues of the Psalmist :—

> Great, valiant, pious, good and clean,
> Sublime, contemplative, serene,
>   Strong, constant, pleasant, wise !
> Bright effluence of exceeding grace;
> Best man ! the swiftness and the race,
>   The peril and the prize.

He takes each of the qualities here mentioned, and
shows how each was exemplified in the character and acts
of King David :—

> His Muse, bright angel of his verse,
> Gives balm for all the thorns that pierce,
>   For all the pangs that rage;
> Blest light, still gaining on the gloom,
> The more than Michal of his bloom,
>   The Abishag of his age.

In these opening stanzas there lingers a little of the
conventional eighteenth-century verbiage, but with the
thirtieth a change comes over the theme. We listen no
longer to the direct praise of David, hyperbole soaring
over hyperbole, but the poet lifts us above the mortal

Psalmist to the immortal mystery which inspires the Psalm; we have a succession of stanzas in praise of the Seven Pillars of the Lord, and each is like a fresh blast upon the trumpet. We begin to detect a certain incoherence of expression, a certain loss of hold upon the logic of speech, but this is condoned by an audacity which was probably out of Smart's reach when his brain was not somewhat disordered. The poet then resumes the triumphal praise of David, now presented as the central figure in a choir of transcendent practitioners, adoring God in the perfection of his works :—

> For ADORATION all the ranks
> Of angels yield eternal thanks,
> And DAVID in the midst.

Thus, in the fifty-first stanza, the word is reached to which all has been leading up, the mysterious word " Adoration," which from this moment incessantly recurs with the blare of some brass instrument in an orchestra. And the writing from this point onward has an orchestral effect, as of a choral symphony, unseen figures of angelic ancestry joining in a loud unison of voice, harp, and clarion. Like the seraphim of Milton, the verses sing, and singing in their glory move. In all the manifestations of created life, in the small as in the great, the poet perceives the universal anthem. It is voiced by sounds, by colours, by forms, by the elements, by the agencies of nature. Whether in the nocturnal splendour of the starry sky, whether in the richness of the ripening almond; whether in the perfume of the quince or in the roll of the ocean, the whole creation sings its hosanna to the Highest :—

> For Adoration seasons change,
> And order, truth and beauty range,
>    Adjust, attract and fill
> The grass that polyanthus cheques;
> And polish'd porphyry reflects,
>    By the descending rill.

Nothing is too modest to be chronicled, nothing too gran-
diose. The planets move in their ring, Orion brandishes
his sword in worship, while no less—

> For Adoration, beyond match,
> The scholar bulfinch aims to catch
> The soft flute's ivory touch;
> And, careless on the hazel spray,
> The daring redbreast keeps at bay
> The damsel's greedy clutch.

It is in these illustrative stanzas, without doubt, that
the poet reveals the disorganisation of his reasoning powers.
In his rapture he sometimes loses the thread of his utter-
ance; the zeal of his ecstasy wafts him away from logic,
but never from essential beauty. There are odd divergencies
from grammatical sequence :—

> For Adoration ripening canes
> And cocoa's purest milk detains
> The western pilgrim's staff;
> Where rain in clasping boughs inclos'd,
> And vines with oranges dispos'd
> Embow'r the social laugh.

It is easy to see how this would exasperate Dr. Johnson and scandalise the long-suffering dons of Pembroke
College. What, they would say, is the verb associated
with " canes," and what is the " pilgrim's staff," and why
is he a " western " pilgrim, and how does the milk in the
cocoa-nut " detain " him? What is the grammatical
relation of the " rain " to Adoration, and what is the
" social laugh " which is " embower'd " by vines and
oranges? This is not the way in which poetry was practised by Mr. Pope and is still inculcated by Dr. Richard
Hurd. The poor man is mad, and that is the end of it.
No, that was not the end of it! We see and feel the fervour,
the richness, the force partly concealed by the discordant
language, and we are moved by them as the faultless

grammar of other bards of that age has completely ceased
to move us.

Presently the tumult of the symphony declines, and the
flute is heard above the trumpet. The poet's vision is
filled with images of delicate beauty pervading the world
of men, and all uniting in their tribute to the Supreme
Being. In the midst of his gentler rapture the singer is
recalled to his original guide, since he perceives " the
shepherd-king upon his knees." The vision recalls to his
mind the resonances of adoration which David, who was,
in essence, " the Lord's own heart," summed up in his
deathless psalmody. Once more the transport breaks
forth and the brass instruments are dominant. The poem
closes in a burst of adoration :—

> Glorious the northern lights a-stream ;
> Glorious the song, when God's the theme ;
>   Glorious the thunder's roar ;
> Glorious hosanna from the den,
> Glorious the catholic amen ;
>   Glorious the martyr's gore.
>
> Glorious, more glorious is the crown
> Of Him that brought salvation down,
>   By meekness call'd Thy Son ;
> Thou at stupendous truth believ'd,
> And now the matchless deed's achiev'd,
>   Determined, dared, and done.

When we close this high-pitched and magniloquent
poem we naturally inquire how far Smart's peculiar condition of brain accounts for its general character. That
he was insane seems to be unquestioned, but his disorder
was certainly periodic, and his attacks were soon over.
In college, where they gave a great deal of annoyance to
" scholastic pride," these relapses were brief, and were
usually borne with by the dons, but in 1751, and again in
1761, Smart became so obstreperous that he was in each
case removed to Bedlam. We are told few particulars,
except that he scandalised Cambridge by constantly falling

on his knees in the street to say his prayers. Johnson
told Dr. Burney that he did not think Smart ought to be
shut up. " His infirmities were not noxious to society;
he insisted on people praying with him; and I'd as lief
pray with Kit Smart as with anyone. Another charge
was that he did not love clean linen; and I have no passion
for it." The poet does not seem to have been unhappy
in confinement; he dug in the garden of the madhouse,
and grew fat. Probably alcohol, in which Smart always
exceeded, had produced toxic symptoms which the pro-
hibitions of Bedlam relieved. The richness of vocabulary
in his great poem seems to show that his verbal memory
was not impaired, as it commonly is by these recurrent
attacks. A silly contemporary story was that Smart
scratched the whole of " A Song to David " with a key
on the walls of his cell. Anyone who credits this tale
may try to perform the feat of scribbling 516 verses on the
whitewash of a small room. Evidently the poem was
composed when the violence of Smart's dementia had
passed away, merely leaving the brain excited and under
incomplete control.

The old problem of the alliance between madness and
genius is raised in this instance, as in that of Blake and
other mystics. We may note that this particular kind of
disturbance usually takes a religious form, either in pious
rapture, or, as in the case of Cowper, in acute melancholia.
The good fortune for literature was that Christopher
Smart, whose mind was habitually occupied with Biblical
imagery, happened to be seized with poetic afflatus at the
moment when he was recovering from a paroxysm of
insanity of the exalted type. His imagination was still
glowing with a religious megalomania, but the fit was so
far subdued that he could write like an artist and within
the bounds of decorum. Perhaps no work exists which is
poised more perilously than " A Song to David " on the

line which divides madness from sanity. There is just
enough distraction left to break down the barrier of " good
taste," to induce a recklessness of speech, an abandonment
to emotion, which were foreign to the discipline of that
age and an outrage against the canons of composition.
It was barely decent to point to the way in which " the
scalèd infant clings to the mermaid's pap " as an instance
of worship, and very sad to admit so obvious an hallucina-
tion as that " opposing spirits " may be seen " tilting in
the pink and mottled vault." This was no way to express
mental experience in 1763. We are broader in our grammar
and perhaps looser in our logic. We detect in " A Song
to David " a miracle of uncovenanted lyric art.

# MONTAIGNE

# MONTAIGNE

How impossible it is to say anything new about Montaigne! No words can be found which add to the charm that all wise men and women have discovered in the "Essays" for three centuries and a half, a charm which will not evaporate nor decline so long as civilisation lasts. How can anybody dare to paint the lily of Mme. de Sevigné's appreciation :—

"I have found entertainment in a volume of Montaigne that I did not think I had brought with me. Ah! the charming man! What good company he is! He is an old friend of mine, but by dint of being old, he is new to me. I cannot read without tears what the Maréchal de Montluc says of the regret that he felt in not having imparted himself to his son, and in having left him in ignorance of what tenderness he felt for him. Read this page, I beg you, and tell me what you find in it. It is in a letter to Madame d'Estimac about the love of fathers to their children. Mon Dieu! How full this book is of good sense."

The passage in which Mme. de Sevigné delighted at Livry occurs in the Eighth of the Second Book of the Essays. "Ah! the charming man," and what an excellent occasion for us to read once more the delicious and humane sentences, wandering over the page like the wind across an Æolian harp! What music, what tenderness, what grace, what sound French common sense! This essay,

too, is particularly characteristic of the author. It is one
of those which appeared somewhat curtly and baldly in
the original edition of 1580, and received additions, corrections, and revisions until the end of Montaigne's life.
Moreover, it is one of the essays in which he supplies most
interesting notes of his own character. It is here that he
tells us that he started " this idle thought of writing " to
relieve his " weariness of the solitude " into which he
retired in 1571 when, having completed the pious task of
publishing the works of his beloved dead friend, Etienne
de la Boétie, Montaigne shut himself up for nine years in
the tower of his ancestral château. Here, too, it is that
he tells us of his behaviour to his own children, and how
he tried, by familiar talk, to secure their confidence and
to break down the barrier of age. It was the almost
universal habit at that time for parents to think it needful
to preserve discipline by adopting " a harsh and contemptuous austerity " towards their children. Not so
our divinely perspicacious essayist. Here, too, are reflections about women which supply food for the eternal
query, Was Madame de Montaigne a real helpmeet or was
she not? The essay is typical of its author, *ondoyant et
divers*.

Shut up in his castle, surrounded by his books, it would
have been natural for Montaigne to lose himself, as many
of his reflecting contemporaries lost themselves, in mere
idle scholarship, flinging their souls, worn out with intellectual lassitude, into the arms of the Ancients. At first
he thought to confine his thoughts to the department of
Roman history, and he is found annotating the texts of
Cæsar and Sallust. But though he retained a curious
partiality for the former historian, seeing in him a " perfection and excellence " greater than that of any other
writer, yet he soon grew tired of this class of studies, which
we may suppose too objective for his native taste. So,

about the year 1573, having gained release from conventional opinion in the society of his library—which gave him all he wanted and nothing which he did not want—we find Montaigne turning away from the military historians to the easier company of Cicero and Plutarch, where he met with the purely personal quality which appealed to him; and in this way the liberty of scholarship protected him against becoming barrenly a mere scholar.

Montaigne had lived an active life of public responsibility, in the course of which his sole, but most precious intellectual entertainment, had come from endless talks with La Boétie. When his friend died prematurely, and when Montaigne shut himself up in his solitude, we cannot doubt that it was the mental stimulus of La Boétie's conversation which he missed the most, nor that it was the need of a confidant which led him to make his earliest efforts in literature, his first crude and fragmentary "essays," take the form of letters to an imaginary person. It is not easy, however, to know at what moment he saw clearly before him the great central fact that the whole world of readers was his natural confidant. "My book," he was wont to say long afterwards, "is agreeable because it contains nothing whatever except an account of my own life and my behaviour." He was slow, however, in realising the importance of this fact. Looking back afterwards, with his marvellous power of self-knowledge, he perceived that his early essays *sentent à l'étranger*—that is to say, that they might be written by somebody else, that they are not so peculiar to himself as to describe no other person, while yet appealing to the sympathy of everyone.

Students of the text of Montaigne, with all the precious additions and annotations before them, grow steadily conscious of the way in which he embroidered his reflections with instances taken from his personal experience. He did this with more and more courage until the end, adding jewel after jewel to the surface of his style. Montaigne was not yet sixty years of age when he was carried away by an attack of quinsy, from which modern skill might probably have relieved him. It is not extravagant to hold that few deaths have been more disastrous to literature than his, since ten years more of health would have given Montaigne the opportunity to plunge deeper than ever before into the unplumbed depths of human sensation. M. Paul Bonnefon, to whom every lover of Montaigne owes a debt of gratitude, has shown in close detail how merrily the essayist, towards the close of his life, mocked at, and rejected, the advice of those who desired him to refrain from drawing attention to himself. Far from acting as Pasquier and others recommended, Montaigne sought to throw light into any corner of his soul that his previous study had happened to neglect. It is impossible to believe that the priceless copy in the Bordeaux library contains the sum of Montaigne's revisions. He would have gone on adding to the fabric if he had lived till 1610, when his age would only have been sixty-seven.

The strange way in which the " Essays " were built up must strike every careful reader, and accounts for the fact that almost without exception the longest chapters are the most interesting and the most significant. It seems probable that, as Montaigne sat reading and dreaming among his books in the tower, an idea or an anecdote would strike his attention, and he would jot down a note of it. This note might become the nucleus of an Essay, but it would depend on chance or whim whether it would develop. It was like a seed planted in the earth; it might shoot or it might not. Probably the essayist kept his first drafts on separate sheets of paper, so as to give himself room for their possible expansion. His method may be studied, I think, by comparing those sketches which never fructified, yet were not entirely dismissed, with the chapters that grew into the foliage and blossom of complete composition. Take, for instance, in the Second Book, the brief essay called " Business To-morrow." This begins with a reflection on the merit of Amyot's translations from the Greek, and a suggestion that " this good man " should tackle Xenophon, and then it refers to several anecdotes in Plutarch; and closes, abruptly, with a characteristic warning against forcing conduct, under all circumstances, to follow a stringent rule. The thing is a chain of ideas jotted down while reading Plutarch. It is a seed which failed to fructify.

This strange element of growth, with its inherent imperfection of form, may have had something to do with the welcome given to Montaigne in England so soon as the character and nature of his genius were observed on this side of the Channel. The " Essays " have always had a stronger effect on English literature than on any other, perhaps even more than on French, although, of course, it would be absurd to pretend that they have been read here so eagerly or with so much appreciation as in France. Montaigne was the earliest " trivial " author of Europe, and wherever his spirit was welcomed it was as the enemy of dogmatism and pedantry. England, about 1595, was peculiarly prepared to resist the scholastic spirit. Montaigne, who liked to think that his family, the Eyquems, were English by extraction, did not live to see his name or work recognised in this country, but their influence is found to be busy at the opening of the seventeenth century. The principle of the " Essays " was in direct opposition to the theory of modern expression so obstinately held by Bacon, who, nevertheless, was very plainly fascinated by their form.

What Shakespeare knew of Montaigne is more interesting to us. We have the indubitable evidence of " The Tempest," and perhaps that of " Hamlet." But it is

c

disconcerting to find the serious Gonzalo dismissing Montaigne's charming description of the ideal Commonwealth
as a " kind of merry fooling." Yet this was, no doubt, the
grudging way in which the individualism of our enchanting
sceptic was received in England at the close of Elizabeth's
reign. The spirit of the Essayist was amusing and delightful, it was even tempting; it revealed new vistas, down
which the fancy could not resist a temptation to wander.
But it was frivolous, and in its degree vaguely revolutionary. It must be welcomed with caution. So far as I have
observed, the earliest definite English comment on the
style and matter of Montaigne came from the pen of that
graceful and sympathetic writer, Samuel Daniel, himself
definitely conservative in taste, and desirous of returning
to the old Senecan standards. The ode in which Daniel
discusses the new French writer is very interesting, and
has never received due attention. Praising the " Essays "
in warm terms, Daniel nevertheless remarks :—

> And let the critic say the worst he can,
>   He cannot say but that Montaignë yet
> Yields most rich pieces and extracts of men,
>   Though in a troubled frame confus'dly set.

The want of system, the " troubled frame," is present
to the sense of the singularly accomplished mind of Daniel,
but does not prevent him from acknowledging merits
which neither Shakespeare nor Bacon seems to have been
willing openly to recognise, although they both succumbed
to their charm.

The three illustrious Elizabethans may have met Montaigne not in the original, but in the version of John Florio.
an Italian born in London, bred in Paris, and trained at
Oxford. This extraordinary person, of whom we would
fain know more than we do, was the main *officier de liaison*
between England and the literatures of France and Italy.
He was reader in foreign languages to Queen Anne, and

his dictionaries were widely circulated. His translation
of Montaigne, after having been kept on the stocks for
several years, was published in folio in 1603, and took hold
of England immediately. It has introduced the spirit of
Montaigne to thousands of English readers. The editor
of the version now before me, Miss Grace Norton, and the
translator, Mr. Ives, speak of Florio with great disdain,
which no doubt they can justify by instances. Miss
Norton finds Florio " tiresome," " clumsy," and often
" unintelligible." I can readily understand that, in the
course of a very searching comparison with the original,
she has frequently been irritated by Florio's lapses. But a
rendering which should be exact at every point was not
called for from an Elizabethan translator, and I cannot
follow Mr. Ives in depreciating the style of Florio. It
seems to me to show no trace of the foreigner, and to be
faithful, in the majority of instances, to the spirit of the
French.

If, however, I plead for mercy and suggest that Florio
should be shown a little indulgence, I do not pretend for a
moment that a new standard translation was not called
for. It is surprising that it has been so long awaited.
The version of Mr. Ives seems to me masterly to a very
high degree; it was worth waiting for, and completely
supersedes all precursors. Wherever I open it I find small
indications that it is an improvement upon them. Montaigne was fond of quoting Latin poetry, and Florio felt it
to be his duty to translate these citations in rhymed
English, which would be the most contemptible ever
printed if Burton's similar quotations in the " Anatomy "
were not even worse. Mr. Ives wisely gives prose versions
in notes. Montaigne, living in an age when speech was
free, frequently trenches upon subjects of delicacy. He is
never morbid or offensive, but he is sometimes outspoken.
At such moments, without any emphasis, Mr. Ives simply

allows his author to retain his old French speech until he
ceases to be indiscreet.  No method could be more praiseworthy.

The temper of Montaigne has always been powerfully
attractive to women, even from the time of his earliest
interpreter, that pathetic and polemical enthusiast, Mlle.
de Gournay.  In our own day, the late Miss Edith Sichel
distinguished herself by her work in the same field.  But
no one, not even the redoubtable sibyl who claimed to be
the Essayist's adopted daughter, has brought more zeal,
patience, and good judgment to the task of annotation than
Miss Grace Norton.  For years past she has been the
leading American authority on the text of Montaigne.
In the present edition, she has contributed to each essay
a prefatory note, often of considerable length, in which
she gives exactly the information required to complete the
pleasure of the ordinary reader.  It is seldom that we
have the satisfaction of welcoming a work of such importance as this version of Montaigne's " Essays," carried
through with such modest and yet complete success.   I
hope that a cheaper reprint of this admirable work
may eventually take its place as the authorised English
translation.

# SHAKESPEARE IN ARDEN

# SHAKESPEARE IN ARDEN

THE Master of Jesus College, Cambridge, Mr. Arthur Gray, has written a little romance of literary life which, whether we accept the base of it or no, will be read with pleasure and approval, so modest is it, so well informed, so calculated to stimulate the imagination. We have here no embroidery on the preposterous theories which have darkened the biography of Shakespeare. Mr. Gray treats with merited contempt the babblings of the Baconians, and has no doubt about the genuine existence of the poet born in Stratford. He is soberly conservative, nor even touched by the scepticism of Sir George Greenwood, who is forced to see in the author of " Hamlet " another man of the same name. The Master of Jesus, however, is inclined to throw overboard the scraps of tradition which cling around the early life and have been accepted, in the emptiness of the scene, even by such careful writers as Sidney Lee. His attack is on Stratford, not on Shakespeare, and he treats the old familiar tales of Aubrey, Davenant, and Betterton as the foolishness of gossip, invented long after date to feed a curiosity which was hardly awakened until after 1680. He claims that South Warwickshire left no mark on the juvenile mind of Shakespeare, and that we must look for early impressions to the extreme north of the county.

It is admitted that between the birth in 1564 and the purchase of New Place in 1597 there is a gap in Shakespeare's residence in Stratford which is filled up by none but slight and traditional allusions. That he attended the grammar school, that he left it prematurely to enter the wool business, that he was apprenticed to a butcher, that he departed hurriedly for London to escape punishment for deer-stealing are incidents in what Mr. Gray calls " a monstrous fabric of fable, gossip, inference, and pure surmise." Mr. Gray, we must not forget, has a " surmise " of his own to put forward, with which all these legends are incompatible. Perhaps this makes him a little too ready to sweep away the information collected and arranged by Rowe in 1709, a century, we must, however, recollect, after the events. I am inclined to believe that biographical legends, if not manifestly spiteful, are seldom without a basis of authority. Mr. Gray hardly lays sufficient weight on Sir Aston Cokain's assertion, in 1658, that antiquaries already chose Stratford-upon-Avon as the centre of Shakespeare's activities. Nevertheless, it is impossible to deny that the Master of Jesus is destructive of the legends which discover in the plays direct references to the neighbourhood of Stratford. He points out, very acutely, that Rowe, while saying that Shakespeare was bred " for some time at a free school," does not state that it was the Stratford grammar school, as is always taken for granted. He points out reasons why the famous identity of Shallow and Sir Thomas Lucy, with the whole picturesque Charlecote episode, are far from being so " perfectly credible " as Sir Walter Raleigh believed. I cannot go here into the arguments of the Master of Jesus with regard to Charlecote, but I am much impressed by them, and if we give up Charlecote and the " luces-louses," the vestiges of South Warwickshire in the plays do, certainly, become very thin.

The question of the education of Shakespeare gives the Master of Jesus some concern, as indeed it does all the biographers. Sidney Lee, never doubting that the poet was brought up at Stratford, devoted many pages to the grammar school of that town, and to its character in

Tudor times. Without precisely saying so much, he artfully insinuated that Shakespeare had a part in all this
training. Wherever he was taught, he seems to have left
school at the age of thirteen, a much more mature time of
life, it must be remembered, three hundred years ago
than it is to-day. A bright boy could acquire, in 1577,
a very competent acquaintance with what the end of
the sixteenth century called knowledge. Ovid might be
at his finger-tips, and, like Polonius, he might find Seneca
not too heavy and Plautus not too light. The education
of that age demanded in the first place an accurate verbal
memory, and we cannot too often remind ourselves how
large a portion of what seems so dazzling in Shakespeare's
accomplishment was the result of a memory retentive, no
less than selective, beyond all experience. The difficulties
raised regarding Shakespeare's extraordinary, though easily
exaggerated, width of acquaintance with the technical
details of professional practice cease to be incredible when
we consider the tenacity of his memory. With his preter-
natural gifts of imagination and wisdom he combined
what was perhaps the most precious advantage of all—he
never forgot anything. What geniuses we all should be,
even without Shakespeare's art, if our minds retained every
atom of fact which ever entered them !

It has always seemed to me very idle to doubt whether
the provincial boy of the legends could have blossomed
into the man who wrote " Hamlet " and " Midsummer
Night's Dream." Mr. Gray is not quite so happy in discussing Shakespeare's education as he is elsewhere, although
he is very ingenious in showing that the true parallel to
Shakespeare in this matter is Dickens. But I do not
know why Mr. Gray says that " to thrust Chatterton into
the company of Shakespeare is ridiculous." On the
contrary, I think the parallel of Chatterton extremely
suggestive. If the Master of Jesus thinks the collocation

" ridiculous " because of Chatterton's inequality of talent, I would remind him that the Bristol boy, when he died, had produced work in quality as well as quantity greater —far greater—than that produced by any other English author at the age of less than eighteen years. No one can even guess what Chatterton would have become, but no more striking case of untutored juvenile genius is on record. Quite recently, however, we have had an instance to the point. A young Irish dramatist, on whom not Lord Oxford alone finds the stamp of " genius," has been introduced to public notice with the statement that, such were the disadvantages of his birth, he did not learn to read till he was sixteen. The plays of this author, nevertheless, are particularly "literary"; they are studded with allusions which display the working of a cultivated memory. The Master of Jesus seems to go too far when he says that Shakespeare could not have met with books in Stratford; several of the inhabitants are known to have had libraries. But it was necessary for the Polesworth theory to represent Stratford as the very Abdera of letters.

Where then, if not in Stratford, did the boy pick up the "little Latin and less Greek" with which all the biographers credit him? The Master of Jesus has a bold reply: it was at Polesworth Hall, in the service of that erudite and enlightened country gentleman, Sir Henry Goodere. After the suppression of the monasteries in 1538, the Abbey of St. Edith of Polesworth was sold to Francis Goodere, a London merchant. The grandson of this gentleman, Henry, was born in 1571, being thus seven years younger than Shakespeare; he was ultimately knighted, and he fills a place in the literary history of his age which would be seen to be very important if we only possessed a fuller record of it. From an early age he cultivated literature and enjoyed the company of the poets; in particular, Michael Drayton, who was by a few

months the senior of Shakespeare, lived as page in the
family of the Gooderes. Let me explain at once that
Mr. Gray's hypothesis is that Shakespeare did the same,
and that he was brought to Polesworth at an early age,
lived there several years, and proceeded thence—not from
Stratford—when he ultimately came up to London. Mr.
Gray dates the transference 1572 for reasons of his own;
" then or later," he says, " little William was packed off
to Polesworth." I would only interpolate that his patron
must have been the father, not the son; infants of one
year do not, as a rule, appoint their own pages. It is easy
to fall into confusion about the Gooderes, and when Mr.
Gray remarks that Polesworth Hall was the plot where all
the Muses were " imparadised," we are not sure that he
distinguishes the friend of Drayton from the friend of
Donne.

Polesworth is a little ancient town in the north-east
corner of Warwickshire, on the tail of the forest of Arden.
It consists, as Mr. Oliver Elton has described it, of " a
street of ruddy-roofed, black-and-white cottages," with a
church, school, and vicarage attached, all a legacy of the
Abbey of Benedictine Nuns founded in the reign of Stephen.
Under Henry VIII. the Gooderes destroyed the cloisters
and built a manor-house on the site; this, very unfortunately, was demolished sixty years ago. A ruined chancel,
too, has now disappeared; Mr. Gray ingeniously surmises
that it inspired Shakespeare to write of " bare, ruin'd choirs,
where late the sweet birds sang." The building still exists
which appears to have been used for the schoolroom in
the sixteenth century. Mr. Gray thinks that a certain
John Atkyns, who taught Drayton here until 1578—a
" mild tutor "—taught the gentle Shakespeare also. At
Polesworth were to be found, between 1570 and 1580,
books, a society of cultivated gentlefolk, " an education
that encouraged poetic gifts," and a hint of patronage

when school was over.  What had Stratford to compare
with all this?  Nothing, says Mr. Gray, who shrinks, not
unaccountably, from the butcher's shop and the " un-
luckiness in stealing rabbits." Once admit that the
amenities of Polesworth lay between Stratford and London
and the paradox ceases to be alarming.  No wonder that
Shakespeare became what he grew to be if he was nurtured
in the warm elegance of the most cultivated country-house
in England.  So he becomes page to Sir Henry Goodere
and companion of the wits who " oft at Polesworth by the
fire have made us gravely merry." It is a charming
dream, but on what fact is it founded?

One point which the Master of Jesus makes is very
ingenious, even if it can hardly be called evidence.  There
are two references in the plays to a place called Wincot in
" The Taming of the Shrew," and Woncot in the second
" Henry IV."; these are regarded as the same, and have
commonly been identified with Woodmancote, in the
Cotswolds.  But Mr. Gray rejects this identification, and
remarks that this Gloucestershire Woncot is fifty-four
miles from Stratford.  He is sarcastic at the idea of Shakespeare's " trudging this distance, to and fro, on what
visit?" But he has found that there is a Wincot in
Arden, in Polesworth parish, close to Pooley Hall, where
the Cockains lived, and he has noted that Sir Aston Cockain
distinctly stated that Shakespeare much appreciated Wincot
ale.  In a world of faint suggestions this does seem to
me to be a definite touch.  Any page-boy could walk to
Pooley Hall, taste the Wincot ale, and return unwearied.
Another little topographical emendation appears to be
even more brilliant.  In " Henry IV.," Shallow asks,
" How a good yoke of bullocks at Stamford Fair?" But
neither Shallow nor his counsin Silence could have any
curiosity about what went on at Stamford, eighty miles
from Stratford.  But in the Quarto of 1600 the name is

" Samforth," which means nothing. The Master of Jesus
makes the really exhilarating suggestion that Shakespeare
wrote " Tamworth," a market town only four miles from
Polesworth, already famous in Elizabeth's reign for its
cattle fair. Mr. Gray's suggestions with regard to Sutton-
Coldfield, to Barston, and less persuasively to Greet, do
not amount to much, but have a certain cumulative
value.

Desirous to yield to the supposition of the Master of
Jesus, the complete silence of Michael Drayton affects me
painfully. If the Polesworth theory is correct, it involves
that the two poets were closely associated as pages, as
schoolboys, and as adolescent companions. But, as a
matter of surviving fact, or even inference, we do not see
them together until that unlucky final night when Ben
Jonson and Drayton had " a merry meeting," when Shakespeare drank so hard that he died of a fever then con-
tracted. This is one of several stories, rejected by commentators of the graver sort, designed to show that our
Prince of Poets was no prohibitionist. But even if this
particular legend be true, it does not prove a boyish intimacy
with the author of " Idea." The only definite relationship
that I can trace is that Shakespeare's son-in-law cured
that excellent poet, Master Drayton, of a tertian fever
by the administering of a syrup of violets. If Shakespeare
had taken this delicate remedy he might have survived
the merry meeting. But Drayton, who had an almost
over-weening admiration for the literary profession, and
delighted in celebrating its proficients, could hardly have
spent his boyhood with the greatest of poets and not have
mentioned him. If Spenser could celebrate young Eagle-
heart, the gentle Aetion, in 1594, can we conceive Spenser's
breathless disciple refraining from all mention of his
school-fellow and fellow-page? Or can we believe that
Shakespeare would be silent about the Gooderes while

Drayton overflowed with gratitude? Yes, we can conceive both these things, for everything in the personal life
of Elizabethan literature is so perplexing and so obscure
that we are ready to accept any unlikely conjecture, short
of believing that a single very busy lawyer composed all
the books that the other men published. But although
the dream that Shakespeare was bred in Arden can hardly
be confirmed or denied, the Master of Jesus has woven
round it a very charming little tapestry, full of illuminating
analogies.

# THE PHŒNIX NEST

# THE PHŒNIX NEST

As a rule the fictitious animals invented by our ancestors not only give us a poor opinion of their taste, but prove them to have been wholly unobservant. A creature with the head of a cock set upon a serpent's body could impress nobody, because we should say of it what the Western farmer said when he was shown a rhinoceros : " I don't believe it." But among all the silly wyverns and cockatrices, outrages upon natural form, there is one bewitching exception; the fancy which created the Phœnix was a charming one. This radiant Arabian bird, whose nest was drenched in delicious perfume, and starred with heavenly dew, might be absurd, but it was never contemptible. When it reached its apogee, it lighted its own funeral pyre, and was exhaled to heaven in a cloud of odour. But as soon as the spicy sacrifice was complete, out of its ashes rose a new Phœnix, which was the old one, since, as Petrarch said, there is but one in the world, nor shall it ever find a mate.

The celebration of the Phœnix was characteristic of the close of one literature and the revival of another, and our chief authority about its habits comes from Claudian and Lactantius, poets of the Latin eclipse, and from the paganised dreamers of the Renaissance. The name of the immortal bird was borrowed by the very interesting anthology of which a reprint is before me, and I am tempted to inquire why? The titles of Elizabethan books are fantastic, but there can generally be discovered some reason for them. In the meantime, let us examine " The Phœnix Nest " of 1593.

D

It is one of the rarest of important books, for not more than five copies of it are believed to survive. Mr. Hugh Macdonald, in his valuable preface to the reprint, tells all that is certainly known of its history, and this is very little. It was compiled by R. S., but who this may have been is left to the dimmest conjecture. He was a gentleman of the Inner Temple, and Mr. Macdonald, with the list of students admitted towards the end of the sixteenth century before him, gives us twenty-three names, all equally inconspicuous, to choose from. It is not likely that R. S., whoever he was, did more than act as a secretary by collecting and copying the verses. "The Phœnix Nest" has the peculiar interest of being the "only source of a number of beautiful and interesting poems," and in this respect claims much closer attention than the other contemporary anthologies, such as "England's Helicon," which depended upon printed sources.

A very important fact is that where the texts in "The Phœnix Nest" can be compared with those in published volumes, there are not merely frequent variations, but these are almost always clear improvements. The point of this is that "The Phœnix Nest" appears to carry authority with it, and to represent not the copyings of an admirer, but versions prepared for it by the authors themselves. This indicates, in my judgment, a collected effort consciously combined by a set of friends; in fact, a species of manifesto semi-privately put forth by a sort of club. I do not see in "The Phœnix Nest," as I do in most of the Elizabethan anthologies, the enterprise of a publisher who takes advantage of the defenceless state of literary copyright, but the deliberate act of a group of poets. It is obvious that if we could prove the existence of such a bond it would be very interesting.

Forty-five years ago I started the conjecture that Lodge was responsible for the arrangement of this book. Mr.

Macdonald does not pay me the compliment of mentioning this suggestion, which, indeed, scarcely seems to me to-day so well founded as it did in 1882. It is true that Lodge, in the induction to his " Phillis " of 1593, says, " I that have lived a Phœnix in love's flame," but not much can be made of this, even with regard to the fact that Lodge is by far the most abundant contributor to " The Phœnix Nest." If we could be sure that immediately at the close of his long voyage to South America, while making acquaintance with what his poet-friends in England had done during his absence, Lodge collected specimens of their lyrical work and added it to a much larger proportion of the sonnets he himself had written on shipboard, printing the whole with a certain purpose, this would complete the story, but we are in the mist of conjecture.

One or two facts, however, reward examination. Of the authors known to be represented in " The Phœnix Nest," all were still alive in 1593, except Greene and Watson, but these had died only the year before. If, then, R. S. took a reasonable time in collecting the specimens, especially if he had a reason for awaiting Lodge's imminent return from Patagonia, his work, but for Lodge, might well have been completed in 1592, when all the authors were still alive. Mr. Macdonald justly remarks that the contents of this anthology " are less varied in style than those of most of the Elizabethan anthologists," and this suggests that some one poet was the leading spirit in the selection. I still think that Lodge was that director, and I am confirmed by the Lodge-like character of the anonymous pieces. The collector of such an anthology is always inclined to include poems which are in sympathy with his own ideals of style.

Let me now return to the question why the particular title, " The Phœnix Nest," was given to this volume. I think it was connected with the start of English poetry in 1593. To our eyes, bewildered by the outburst of dramatic and epic verse in the last days of Elizabeth, it seems as though poetry had never been so flourishing. But we must recollect how subterranean most of it was, how little appreciated or perceived by the public. The great protagonist of verse, Sir Philip Sidney, had been careful never to print his poems; his famous " Defence of Poetry," which became the creed of his successors, remained unpublished, like his " Arcadia," till long after his death. It was passionately, but almost clandestinely, studied in manuscript by all the Arcadian youth of Oxford and Cambridge. But to Sidney himself the effort to create a poetical literature had come to seem in vain. Even of Spenser, he had seen nothing printed, except " The Shepheard's Calendar," and he mourned that England had grown " a hard step-mother " to poets. " Poetry," he said, " had fallen to be the laughing-stock of children." On the other hand, to the poets themselves Sidney had appeared as the morning star who was to herald a millennium of poetical appreciation. He delayed in breaking through the clouds of publicity, but his genius would be all the more brilliant when it shone out. And then, after the field of Zutphen, he incontinently died. He had published nothing, and the Phœnix, that is to say the poetical art of England, had gone up to Heaven in an aromatic cloud.

But the characteristic of a Phœnix is that when it is burned up and gone, it is on the very brink of revival. From the ashes of its nest, the Arabian wonder is newborn. The idea of the compilers of this anthology was, in my opinion, that although the Phœnix, Poetry, had blazed on the funeral pyre of Sidney, it was reincarnated in the lyrical work of the young men who had taken heart of grace to pursue their art since their hero's death. The state of literature had rapidly changed; " Astrophel and

Stella " was now published, and the " Arcadia," which had been so nearly sacrificed to a dying scruple, was in everybody's hand. The dead voice was discovered upbraiding the density of English appreciation :—

" That Poesy, embraced in all other places, should only find, in our time, a hard welcome in England, I think the very earth laments it, and therefore decks our soil with fewer laurels than it was accustomed."

So Sidney was found to have said, in a treatise even in 1593 still unpublished, but here are his own Raleigh and Dyer, his adoring Matthew Roydon, his gifted satellites Greene and Lodge, Peele and Watson, Breton and A. H., assuring him that he was mistaken, and proving to him, by the fulness of beautiful lyric talent in this book, that Poetry is restored at last, and the Phœnix reinstated in her odorous nest. That at least is the theory which I have the temerity to advance.

Although it is Poetry itself, and not the genius of Sidney, which takes the place of the Phœnix in this " nest of spiceries," the image of the author of " Astrophel " is present throughout. It animates the zeal of the poets and inspires their verse. No one can now for a moment parallel the genius of Sir Philip Sidney with that of Shakespeare or even of Spenser, but in his lifetime, and for a long time afterwards, his power over the young was far greater than theirs. He was the protagonist, the patron, the proto-martyr, and the contents of the anthology before me, various as they are, have this in common, that they all seem to be directed to the thought of Sidney.

A curious fact is that, where all else is metrical, a piece of bald prose intervenes at the very outset. Mr. Hugh Macdonald remarks of " A Dead Man's Right " that it " is out of place in ' The Phœnix Nest,' " but he offers no conjecture as to how it got there. It is a defence of the Earl of Leicester, Sidney's uncle, Robert Dudley, whom the poet had defended in prose and regarding whose character he was known to hold very strong views. I suggest that " A Dead Man's Right," written apparently soon after 1588, embodies those views as recollected by Matthew Roydon or some other faithful disciple. At any rate, the only reason we can give why this prose tract is not entirely " out of place " is that it completes the Sidneian character of the book.

It is followed by a very long and exasperatingly unequal elegy or " friend's passion " by Matthew Roydon. This was universally admired as " the immortal epitaph of his beloved Astrophel," but scarcely anything is known of Roydon or of his connection with Sidney, with whom he was evidently intimate, since he says :—

> When he descended down the mount,
>   His personage seemed most divine;
> A thousand graces one might count
>   Upon his lovely cheerful eyne;
> To hear him speak and sweetly smile
> You were in Paradise the while.
>
> A sweet attractive kind of grace,
>   A full assurance given by looks,
> Continual comfort in a face,
>   The lineaments of gospel-books;
> I trow that countenance cannot lie
> Whose thoughts are legible in the eye.

The writer of these lines should have been at the top of his profession, but unhappily he had neither taste nor reserve. An attempt to describe with realism the circumstances of his hero's mortal wounding could hardly have been made more flat than it is. He feigns that the God Mars was jealous of the starry gleams of Sidney's coat of armour (which, as a matter of fact, he had rashly thrown off), and held them to be a challenge :—

> In this surmise he made with speed
>   An iron cane, wherein he put
> The thunder that in clouds doth breed;
>   The flame and bolt, together shut,
> With privy force burst out again;
> And so our Astrophel was slain !

It is as the concealed protagonist of pure poetry against Puritanism that the spirit of Sidney, often obscurely, sometimes inaccurately, but always with enthusiasm, animates " The Phœnix Nest." Aubrey says, harshly, that Sir Philip Sidney was " cloyed and surfeited " with the praise of poetasters, but this hardly explains the continuance of that feeling long after his death. The fact rather seems to be that by instinct the lyric poets felt that Sidney had been their friend, their instigator and defence, and that when he came to his untimely death he left them without a protector. But Poetry was alive, even though the prince of poets was departed, and " The Phœnix Nest " is a manifesto. Among features of the volume on which it would be pleasant to dilate, it is not right to overlook the evidence it gives of the extraordinary freedom in versification which the whole of this group of writers had learned from Sidney. Lodge exemplies this to a remarkable degree, and there are here anonymous pieces, probably not the work of famous hands, which show how powerful his influence was. Here is an instance from a poem, once absurdly attributed to Sir Walter Raleigh, but now abandoned to anonymity, which exhibits the extraordinary liberty of movement, at the cost sometimes of thought and sincerity, which English lyrical verse by 1593 had gained, through Lodge, from Sidney :—

> Sweet violets, Love's paradise, that spread
>   Your gracious odours, which you couchèd bear
>     Within your paly faces,
> Upon the gentle wing of some calm-breathing wind
>     That plays among the plain,
> If by the favour of propitious stars you gain
> Such grace as in my Lady's bosom place to find,
>     Be proud to touch those places.

This is not very valuable in itself, but it shows how completely and in how short a time the dangers from which English prosody had suffered from the innovations of classicists such as Gabriel Harvey and the Senecans, heresies to which Spenser himself had once inclined, had passed away and left English lyric verse with a new honey melting on the tongue.

# ENGLAND'S HELICON

# ENGLAND'S HELICON

NOTHING could be further from my thoughts than to belittle that activity of English scholarship which has been displayed, more keenly than ever before, during the past quarter of a century. But there is another side to the question of restoring old literature. The main thing, of course, is to provide exact texts and illuminating notes, and by no one is this done better than by Mr. Hugh Macdonald in such a reprint as that which now lies before me. It may also, however, be permissible to think of what used to be called " the general reader," who should not be frightened away by the particularity of textual criticism. " England's Helicon " is a very famous book, on which a succession of learned men—none, I believe, more learned than Mr. Hugh Macdonald—have expended an infinitude of pains. I will not pretend to compete with them to-day, nor discuss what relation A. B. held to J. B., nor whether L. N. was N. L. But I will try to give an impression of what this beautiful book meant to its first readers, and what it means to us to-day, who really are occupied with the character and attitude of the contents, and not with the mysteries of its production.

" England's Helicon," then, was an anthology of pastoral poetry, all comparatively recent at the time of its publication. It was the best and nearly the latest of the collections of lyrical verse made at the close of Elizabeth's reign. The late A. H. Bullen was the first to draw particular attention to the fashion for albums of contemporary poetry which raged in these last years of the century. Almost all these collections had charming names, although not all of them deserved to be thus scented and belaurelled. " Davison's Poetical Rhapsody " was considered by Bullen, who reprinted the whole series of them, the most valuable of our old anthologies. But that, again, was the scholar's view; there is much more in the " Rhapsody " which can be traced to no other scource, while, if " only a bare list of the first lines of the poems " had been preserved, we could succeed in restoring " England's Helicon " from other printed sources. This makes the task of annotating it less absorbing, but takes nothing away from the pleasure of the general reader, who finds more enjoyable verse in " England's Helicon " than in the " Rhapsody."

I find it amusing to ask myself what my own feelings would have been if, at my present age, I had opened " England's Helicon " in 1600, and perhaps the answer to this question may serve to place the book in some perspective. The first thing, then, which would have struck me would have been the amazing development, both of fancy and of language, which had taken place since not merely my childhood, but my middle years. Barbarism of thought, clumsiness of style, dullness of appreciation had been the marks of everything produced in England after the isolated and ineffectual miscellany of " Songs and Sonnets," brought out by Tottel in (I continue my parallel) my thirty-third year. Would England ever begin to possess a poetry of her own? It had seemed just possible in 1557.

Within twelve months Elizabeth replaced her sour sister on the throne, but for a long time there was no visible improvement in literature. Oddities, pedants, vile translators jostled one another in a limbo of mediocrity. I should hear, in my retirement, of " sonnets sweetly sauced " by Sackville, but neither I, nor anyone else, could ever see them. It would, however, cause me at least a great sensation, when I was nearer sixty than fifty, to meet with a momentous little volume by the new genius Edmund Spenser, called " The Shepheard's Calendar," and to find it full of thrilling melody and delicate artificial imagination. Then would burst forth a choir of songsters, Watson and Sidney and Lyly, with one prodigious gust of music following another, Shakespeare on the heels of Marlowe, poet upon poet crowding the stage and making it re-echo with choral exuberance. To anyone born long ago in the dead time, when the voice of England was an exhausted whisper—to any such person still capable of receiving sharp æsthetic impressions, the suddenness of the change would be almost insufferable, like an outburst of tropical vegetation after the earliest rain. Splendid phrases were dashed recklessly about, intrepid images were flung away half formed, a poetry that was like Venus rose from the waves, rained upon by gilliflowers and carnations, a Venus exquisitely coiffed and elaborately sandalled leaping in Pagan apotheosis out of a melancholy Puritan ocean. The old survivor from Queen Mary's reign, in whose ears the jingle and the jangle of the so sorely misnamed " Paradise of Dainty Devises " still echoed, like the notes of some broken down pianola in the distance, would doubt the evidence of his senses.

This, then, is the light in which we have to regard " England's Helicon." But a modification immediately presents itself. This is part of English literature as it had suddenly developed in twenty astonishing years, but only part. The impression this anthology gives is wilfully eclectic, and to form from it alone an idea of what poetry seemed to the reader of 1600 would be false. Everything violent and ugly is here withdrawn. Tragic drama, in its sudden explosion, had been dissolute and bloody, satire had snarled at good things and bad alike, poetry had been didactic, pious, even topographical, often ponderous and fanatical. The editor of " England's Helicon," whoever he was,

silently eliminated all these elements, sacrificing them without reserve to his sense of pure beauty.   There is nothing
here which could not be warbled by an enamoured swain,
seated under an oak-tree by a crystal fountain, in the
serenest of weather, while waiting for Amaryllis, who,
dressed in green, will appear at length and fill him with
despair by laughing at him.   It is particularly to be
observed that this note of sentimental gaiety, tenderly
perverse   or   melodiously   wanton,   inspires   the   whole
anthology :—

> Through yonder vale as I did pass
>   Descending from the hill,
> I met a smirking bonny lass,—
>   They call her Daffodil.
>
> And all the shepherds that were nigh
>   From top of every hill
> Unto the valleys loud did cry,
>   " There goes sweet Daffodil ! "

These pieces represented a peculiar twist in the Elizabethan temperament, which held that " the most exquisite
vein of a witty poetical head is showed in the sweet sobs of
shepherds and nymphs."   In that rough chamber, pastoral
was a cupboard where the swashbuckler kept his intellectual
sweetmeats.

Why did the vision of the idle and amorous shepherd thus
fascinate the Elizabethan fancy ?   The illustrated edition
of Spenser's " Shepheard's Calendar " merely increases our
perplexity.   Here, in landscape that is exclusively English,
we find characters of two classes, aged tenders of the flock
quite miserably tattered and torn, and elegant youths in
sombreros and tight hose, who swagger about swinging
hooks eight feet long, and pressing laurel wreaths on one
another's foreheads.   Meanwhile men who are not shepherds, but just contemporary peasants, are making hay,
walking in procession to church, reaping corn, or mending
bagpipes. So that here is at once expressed that inconsistent Elizabethan attitude regarding pastoral which

animates all the writers of the time and finds in " England's
Helicon " its choicest selection.   The poets go back to
Sicily, and yet remain in Sussex, paying a long visit to Italy
on the road.   They mingle a fantastic idealism which goes
vaguely back to Theocritus through Sannazaro, with an
attempt at rustic realism which is grotesque.   The result
is a strange inconsistency, a mixing of scenery and images,
a delicate truth of description beside what is merely queer
and forced.   Robert Greene, who cuts a fine figure in
" England's Helicon," is inspired to write :

> When tender ewes, brought home with evening sun,
>     Wend to their folds,
>     And to their holds
> The shepherds trudge when light of day is done,

and then (a warning to such as try to be funny in pastoral):—

> Thy lips resemble two cucumbers fair,
>     Thy teeth like to the tusks of fattest swine;
> Thy speech is like the thunder in the air :
>     Would God thy toes, thy lips, and all were mine.

A note of breathless incoherence, or of lyrical intoxication, is mingled with all this queer celebration of the
shepherd and his maid.   This is more illogically expressed
in the lesser than in the greater poets, who naturally, even
during a sudden rise of temperature, retain the habit of
self-control.   But the " minors," in their agitation and
ecstasy, are always on the point of losing their heads.   An
instance may be found in the " edillions " of Edmund
Bolton, a writer about whom very little appears to be known,
but who is a frequent contributor to " England's Helicon "
and a very characteristic one.   It is often far from easy to
know what Bolton is talking about, but never doubtful
that he is in a genuine high pastoral frenzy :—

> For here and there appear forth towers,
>     Among the chalky downs;
> Cities among the country bowers,
>     Which smiling sunshine crowns;

> Her metal buskins, decked with flowers,
>   As th' earth when frosts are gone,
> Besprinkled are with Orient showers
>   Of hail and pebble-stone;
> Her feature peerless, peerless her attire,
> I can but love her love, with zeal entire.

Whom is Edmund Bolton addressing, and what does he exactly mean? Is the Cosma of his song a shepherdess, or Queen Elizabeth, or England itself?

> A little world her flowing garment seems,
> And who but as a wonder thereof deems?

There is no logical answer to these queries, and all that we can be sure of is the ecstasy, the intoxication of the poet. He is inebriated with colour and melody and rapture; he does not know quite what he is saying or singing, but he feels the sunlight in his eyes and the perfume of spring in his nostrils; he is drunken with beauty.

The appearance of " England's Helicon " in 1600 marks the critical moment when this thoughtless intoxication came to its height. There followed a generation of great poetry, but it was more sober, more logical, and also in a cumulative degree weightier and harsher than the late Elizabethan had been. The music was there, but it was codified, it ceased to burden every bough. No one any more indited melodies at once so innocent and so sumptuous as those that had been warbled by nameless poets in the boscages of " England's Helicon."

The original editor of this anthology, whoever he may have been, was a man of taste. At a time when creative genius far outstripped critical judgment, so that whether the poets wrote well or ill there was nobody to say what goodness was and what badness, he had a clear sense of workmanship. This is shown by the clever way in which he picks out the best " cowslips of Jerusalem and cloves of Paradise " from the rough nosegay of Michael Drayton, who appears to have had no restraining taste whatever. He detects unerringly the good things in Lodge and Greene, and especially in Nicholas Breton, lovely lyrics which succeeding ages long ignored. In particular, this highly competent editor realises the extreme inequality of Sir Philip Sidney's verse, and preserves " No, no, no ! my dear, let be " and " Ring out your bells " and " My sheep are thoughts," while rejecting so much that is flat and empty in the verse of the " Arcadia." He is also a man of spirit, as is shown by his impudent and humorous address " to the Reader, if indifferent," in which he treats the question of literary copyright in a manner which must shock the Incorporated Society of Authors.

" Now, if any stationer shall find fault that his copies are robbed by anything in this collection, let me ask him this question, Why more in this than in any divine or human author ? "

To which dauntless challenge there could be no reply.

# EPICTETUS

# EPICTETUS

EVER since, in his edition of 1535, Trincavelli introduced Epictetus to modern Europe, the influence of the Phrygian sophist has been maintained.  Scores of texts of the " Enchiridion " have made it familiar through four centuries, and the " Discourses " have been hardly less minutely studied.  An interesting summary might be compiled showing the variety of ways in which the mind of Epictetus has made its impact upon serious persons of every shade of conviction.  He has been quoted with approval by Christians and with sympathy by atheists; he seems to have something to say to everyone who regards human life with gravity.  There would be much in his teaching to illustrate the pantheism of Spinoza, while readers familiar with Pascal know how frequent are the references to Epictetus, not only in the " Entretien " but in the " Pensées."  But it was later and in England, when the conventional orthodoxy was beginning to break up at the opening of the eighteenth century, that the influence of the great sophist began to be paramount.  His doctrine was absorbed by Shaftesbury and the Deists, and used by the bishops to refute the errors of those very writers.  In short, all moralists started from Epictetus, and no conception of idealistic morality could boast of any breadth if it ignored him.

The general reader has no excuse for not following the thought of Epictetus, since hardly any writer of antiquity has been more amply and satisfactorily translated.  In the present generation probably it is the annotated version

of Mr. P. E. Matheson which has introduced most English
readers to the "Discourses" and to the "Enchiridion."
Mr. Oldfather, who is very generous to his predecessors in
the preface to his "Loeb" translation, speaks of this as
"a most fluent and graceful version," which it certainly is.
But he also praises Elizabeth Carter's "vigorous and idio-
matic reproduction," and this gives me pleasure, because it
was in that that I first made acquaintance with Epictetus.
1 am grateful to Madam Carter, and wish that Mr. Matheson,
who does not (I think) mention her, had been inclined to do
her justice.

Elizabeth Carter was an extraordinarily interesting
personage. She was born in 1717, in easy circumstances,
into a clerical family which encouraged learning. Although
she was a slow, she was an extremely persistent scholar, and
she taught herself with unremitting zeal, concentrating her
mind on Greek, "to which noble language," her nephew
Montagu Pennington assures us, "she was particularly
partial." To this end she wound a wet towel about her
hair, chewed coffee and green tea, and sat with an alarum
at her elbow, thus inducing headaches from which she never
recovered. Yet she was anything but a prig; her favourite
exercise was dancing, and Dr. Johnson said that she could
"make a pudding as well as translate Epictetus, and work
a handkerchief as well as compose a poem." She once
put aside her Greek while she made twelve shirts. In spite
of the green tea, she lived to be ninety, a charming and
versatile old maiden lady, something of a "romp" to the
last.

It was the famous Secker, then Bishop of Oxford, who set
Madam Carter on her task. She had ventured to correct
him on a point of textual criticism (I. Cor. 7), and when he
had attempted to defend himself she had proved her point.
Secker was a great admirer of the Stoic, and thought that
he should be snatched from the Deists, and that no one living

could do it so well as Elizabeth Carter.  She doubted her powers, but began in 1749 and carried through the task by 1752, although the version was not published until 1758, when, to her surprise, and even to Secker's, it enjoyed an immense popular success.  Madam Carter's " Epictetus " was on every toilet-table.

Her correspondence with Secker, which was printed after her death, provides a point of criticism which is worthy of attention.  When she submitted the first draft to the Bishop, he very acutely objected to the Addisonian style.  He remarked that it was not suited to the plainness and brevity of the Greek, and he plainly told Elizabeth Carter that she was making Epictetus too " polite," was dressing him in a laced coat, when a rough jerkin became him best.

This was very sound criticism, and Elizabeth Carter had the good sense to take it.  She made her Epictetus speak in homely terms, and that is doubtless why her translation can still be read with so much pleasure.  I must apologise for dwelling a little on Madam Carter, because recent editors pay not the slightest attention to her.  Considering that for nearly one hundred years her version withstood the battle and the breeze, and was the sole guide of the English general reader, I think she deserves at least as much notice as a host of German pedants squabbling over the text of him whom they call " Epiktet."

The form in which the " Diatribes " or Discourses of Epictetus have come down to us is very interesting.  The philosopher is not known to have written anything, and he owes his reputation to the ardour of a disciple, Flavius Arrian, who recorded his lectures and conversations.  Mr. Oldfather dwells on the fact " that Arrian's report is a stenographic record of the *ipsissima verba* of the master," and remarks that this is " really unique in literature." Unique, he must mean, in ancient classical literature.  He says that it is " settled " that Arrian took down the discourses in shorthand. I do not know what can have " settled " this point. It is evident that we have the actual words of Epictetus, because Arrian says so, but as very few of the Discourses, in their present shape, would take ten minutes to broadcast, it is surely obvious that Arrian did not put down everything that the lecturer said on any one occasion. He must have omitted all but what specially interested him, and why are we forbidden to suppose that he trusted to his memory?

What Mr. Oldfather says on this matter is curious and invaluable. It would seem that regular instruction in the classes consisted of the reading and explaining of passages from the Stoic classics, particularly from Chrysippus. I suppose that Epictetus would briefly summarise these discussions, which would mainly be held among the pupils themselves, and that when the master intervened Arrian would write down or commit to memory what he said. But it is very interesting that no other evidence of the actual impact of a philosopher's mind upon his scholars should be preserved.

Arrian was himself a gifted philosopher. He was living, a very young man, at Nicopolis when Epictetus, who was driven out of Rome by Domitian in the year 89, took refuge in Epirus. Arrian was long afterwards promoted by Hadrian to be legate of Cappadocia. By that time, if Epictetus was still alive, he must have been a very old man, for he was born about the year 55. Arrian's preface is charming, and insists on the fact that what follows is not an elaborate literary composition, like the dialogues of Plato and perhaps of the lost early Stoics, but aims at nothing so much as a rendering of the exact language of Epictetus, " the frankness of his speech." He says that when you listened to the lecturer you could not help feeling exactly what Epictetus wanted you to feel, and all Arrian desires is that he may have the skill, in reproducing the words, to repeat that magical effect.

His success appears to have been considerable. There is nothing in his record of the " Discourses " of a rhetorical or ornamental nature, but a plain man of extreme vigour of thought expands in homely language the thoughts that occur to him. The general subject-matter of the " Discourses " is so austere, often even so sublime, that I think it has blinded most readers to the variety of tone, and even to the humour of the lecturer. We are not in the habit of regarding Epictetus as cultivating any mood but the deadly serious, yet I think he must have intended to be deliberately funny in many of his instances. He was not afraid occasionally to be what we think unseemly. I shall never be persuaded that he did not intend his pupils to laugh when he talked about the discomfort of tourists who catch cold at Olympia, or compared the unfaithful husband to a baked sucking-pig. He was an unflinching individualist, and much of the hold with which he still grasps our attention is due to the value which he sets on the antinomies of life.

A bard of the eighteenth century expressed the view of his age when he wrote—

> Come, Epictetus, arm my breast
> With thy impenetrable steel
> No more the wounds of grief to fee.
> Nor mourn by others' woes depressed.

This conception of the Stoic doctrine as a hopeless and immobile passivity, rewarded only by a mechanical peace of mind, is entirely false, but particularly so because it ignores the central importance given by Epictetus to conduct. If we are to feel nothing and do nothing, speculation about conduct becomes absurd. But here, it is true, we can but observe a certain inconsistency. The passive attitude was recommended; pity, as Mr. Matheson puts it, was viewed with suspicion; while friendship and affection, if admitted at all, were to be closely restricted.

Pascal, much tempted to take the same course, blamed Epictetus for telling his pupils to withdraw into the recesses of their own being, since there alone could they find rest. But the Phrygian philosopher would not leave them there, stabilised in an Oriental self-contemplation, but would fain bring them out into active relation with other men. Mr. Oldfather defines in a very lucid manner the inconsistency of the Stoic teaching, the result of which on our modern minds is " an almost incredible mixture of Theism, Pantheism, and Polytheism " developed into a system of conduct whch no human being could intelligibly follow. And yet, fragment by fragment, this confused theory of existence presents to us elements of the most winning and stimulating moral beauty.

The first aim of Epictetus is to be calm. His complaint against the Galileans, as he called the Christians of the first century, was that they were turbulent. You cannot be calm until you have purged your soul of all its desires and all its aversions. Then you may hope to attain serenity, for you will be acting in harmony with nature. When absolute serenity has been reached we discover that we are carrying about a living soul in a dead body, but here again the inconsistency of the Stoic formula is discovered. It could not be a motionless condition, a *nirvana*, which Epictetus recommended, since no one is more anxious than he to guard against mental petrifaction. He dreads the advance of old age, which deprives the faculties of their elasticity, and, while he preaches the contemplative habit he excludes inactive sloth. While the soul must steadily accept with pensive resignation everything which occurs, it must retain its absolute responsibility in action and never cease to strive after positive moral perfection. But what a difficult scheme it all is, if we try to adapt it to practical modern conduct !

Perhaps the aspect of Epictetus which is of most permanent value is the paramount importance that he placed upon the development of the will. Indeed, so far as the Stoic perceives, there is nothing good or bad except the will. God has given each man or woman the power to choose, to determine his or her path. He has laid no embargo upon the will of any individual. This is doubtless what Pascal was thinking of when he said that Epictetus showed mankind that it was on the wrong road, and that there was another, entire dependence on God who is without us, and yet within us. Pascal complained that Epictetus failed to take his listeners along the right road, " c'est celui de vouloir ce que Dieu veut." But this seems an unjust charge, founded on a difference in the definition of " God." Indeed, as Mr. Oldfather points out, it was in Epictetus, coming at the end of the long procession from the Stoa, that the religious possibilities of the school were furthest developed.

He is still an object of legitimate, though rather vague, enthusiasm in our modern world of thought, though there are probably few general readers of his " Discourses " who will blindly subscribe to-day to what Justus Lipsius said of their author :—

" So help me God, what a keen and lofty spirit ! a soul aflame, and burning with love of what is honourable ! There is nothing in Greek their like, unless I am mistaken; I mean with such notable vigour and fire. . . . When a man has made some progress in true philosophy, it is amazing how Epictetus stirs him up, and, though he is always touching some tender spot, yet he gives delight also. . . . I never read that old man without a stirring of my soul within me."

The English reader now has the advantage, in the invaluable Loeb Library, of possessing a version of the " Discourses " with the Greek text printed opposite. He is in a position to do full justice to one of the most disinterested of authors, and the very prototype of pure Stoic independence.

# FATHERS OF THE CHURCH
## EUSEBIUS AND BASIL

# FATHERS OF THE CHURCH
## EUSEBIUS AND BASIL

WHEN I was Librarian to the House of Lords, I was once rebuked by a learned prelate (now with God) for buying a certain collection of the Apostolic Fathers. The Bishop considered that the pagan writers of Greece and Rome, whom I took a pride in collecting, were suitable for their Lordships' use, but not the Christian Fathers. The text of Apuleius was welcome, but let not St. Augustine enter. I could not then, and do not now, agree with my ecclesiastical mentor, in whose prejudice I seem to perceive a remnant of old-fashioned scholasticism. If a statesman may turn to Tacitus, why not to Eusebius? There is, indeed, lingering at the back of many minds a dim sense that what is Christian cannot be literature. This prejudice is incident even to bishops and other episcopal persons. Matthew Arnold displayed it when he held up " The Golden Treasury " and " The Book of Praise " for scornful contrast. Nor is this feeling without some excuse. The range of non-Christian interest is so much wider, more independent and more various than what the dogmas of the Church can offer that it is natural to find the former more amusing than the latter. But even a martyr, if he wrote books, may be the object of legitimate curiosity.

The inestimable Loeb Library, to which we cannot too often express our gratitude, is of my way of thinking. It welcomes Galen by the side of " Daphnis and Chloe," and Lucian marches shoulder by shoulder with Clement of

Alexandria. All are equally welcome so long as they illustrate the temperament and character of antiquity. We are beginning to perceive that this is the aspect in which all readers, except grammarians and textual critics, should regard the Ancients. The authors have come to be more interesting than what inspired them to write; for instance, though I cannot pretend to care about the doctrine of the Eternity of the Co-existent Logos, I am filled with anxiety to know all that can be gleaned about the remarkable men for whom it was the central interest of life. Unfortunately, and this is the sore disappointment of classical biography, the incidents of authorship were rarely preserved, or have been tragically lost.

We take the case of Eusebius, the most eminent historian of Christian antiquity, the leading man of letters in an age of adventurous transitions, a participant in all the most theatrical changes of statecraft, and we are baffled by a pitiful lack of information. We long to know all about the man who was perhaps the most accomplished literary figure of the fourth century, but who is nearly fifty years of age before we meet with him at all. We ought to be acquainted with his youth, his training, his convictions, and his friendships, and perhaps these were told by Acacius, his disciple and successor in the see of Cæsarea, who wrote a life of Eusebius, but that biography is wholly lost. Enough remains, however, to whet out appetite, and to justify some important conjectures.

The eminent historian of the early Church was probably born in 260. He called himself Eusebius Pamphili, to indicate that he was the disciple, perhaps originally the slave of Pamphilus, an Egyptian philosopher who settled in Cæsarea, and who was famous for the extent and wealth of his library. It is thought that the surviving writings of Eusebius must be the work of his old age, and no date in his life has been preserved earlier than 309, when he was imprisoned, but not tortured, during the Diocletian persecution. Possibly his confinement, which lasted until the edict of toleration in 311, encouraged him to write, for his output is found to be prodigious. A disagreeable fanatic called Potammon accused Eusebius, twenty years later, of having betrayed the faith during the persecution. There is no confirmation of this charge, which probably only indicates that Eusebius was a moderate, true to his religion, but unprepared to go to extremes in its defence.

The blank refusal of the Christians, at the beginning of the fourth century, to yield in the smallest degree to the laws and practices of the State is a feature of the struggle too often neglected. The temper of the militant Christians was odious; the amiable Pliny blames their " inflexible obstinacy." They were bitter anti-militarists in a coterie of nations to whom war was a necessity, and they offered a sullen resistance to the great object of successive rulers, the unification of the Empire. They delighted in secret association, which Rome peculiarly feared and abhorred. The famous persecution, promulgated by the edict of February 3, 303, and begun when the soldiers burned the bibles in the cathedral of Nicomedia, was the result of Christian pin-pricks which had finally become intolerable. Peace and latitude had encouraged the arrogance of the Churches, and in many provinces the Christians took an ingenious pleasure in exasperating and insulting the magistrates. Sentimentality about Christian martyrs needs to be tempered by an acknowledgment that most of them were insufferable.

No doubt the intellectual leaders would have been willing to check the violence of these extremists, but the pent-up flood of pagan anger broke out and swept them all away. The story is better told by Eusebius than by anyone else, and he does not deny the corruption which long prosperity had wrought in the Church. Cyprian had thought it proper

F

to evade the lions of Carthage, and we contemplate the solemn flirtation of Origen with the Empress Mammæa. This story, by the way, is told by Eusebius, but not in the volume before me to-day. The publishers of the Loeb Library, doubtless for good reasons, have the habit of issuing their authors in fragments. We have here one volume of Eusebius and one of Basil, and may wait months for the continuations. It is only fair to warn inquisitive readers that they will not find what is of special interest to them in the present instalment, which brings us only down to the reign of Commodus. Professor Lake, who perhaps did not know in what form his translation would appear, gives us no hint of this fact. For the account of events in which Eusebius himself took a part, and particularly for the action of Constantine up to his reception into the Church upon his death-bed, we must wait until the Loeb Library reaches the seventh and eighth books of the " Ecclesiastical History." In the meantime we can repose upon Gibbon.

If the early life of Eusebius is dim, that of Basil stands out clearly in the light. Dr. Deferrari, who is a recognised authority on this Saint, excuses himself for giving but " a bare outline of Basil's crowded career." The general reader would perhaps prefer more biography and less about the Subordinationist Controversy, which is a very dry bone to-day. Basil himself, in one of his letters, speaks of living in the " mournful days of boundless controversy," which his later years were spent in rebuking and dispelling. The Edict of Milan brought political peace to the Christian world, but opened the floodgates of heresy and private faction. The rage of Arius had worse results than the fury of Maximin. Dr. Deferrari, in his learned intro-duction, dwells upon the finally triumphant orthodoxy of Basil in strict technical fulness. But the non-theological reader will slip away to the Letters themselves, in which a precious humanity is revealed. Of these over 300 are preserved, by marvellously good luck, and though many of them are rather homilies or pastoral epistles than friendly communications, enough of the latter exist to display the beautiful character of the man. Those in the present volume date from 357, when Basil was about twenty-eight, to 370, when he was elected Archbishop of Cæsarea. He was the second son of a wealthy landowner in the Pontus and of his wife, Emmelina, a very remarkable woman, mother of three saint-bishops, a nun and a monk. To our ears this enumeration may sound unattractive; in the fourth century it meant the highest social and moral eminence in the most prominent sphere of activity.

Basil was a sickly child, and all through life he suffered, as his letters testify, from ill-health. He was nursed on a country farm by a family of peasants, to whom (a curious touch of the times) Basil's father presented several slaves in token of his gratitude for the care taken of his son. Basil went to school at Cæsarea and Constantinople, and finally attended the pagan university of Athens, where he made friends with a fellow-student, the Emperor Julian, afterwards unkindly surnamed the Apostate. Athens was still the centre of the intellectual life of the world, and Basil left it steeped in the humanities. In after years, when he was completely an ecclesiastic, he retained his familiarity with the pagan classics, and in one of these letters he quotes a verse from Sophocles, attributing it, doubtless by a slip of the pen, to Solomon.

He had spent five brilliant years at Athens, when the death of his father called him back to the Pontus to administer his vast estates. For two years more he occasionally lectured as a sophist in the capital of Cappadocia, and here his Christian vocation revived. He resigned his professorial chair, deputed his estates to his mother and his younger brother, was baptised and " gave himself to God." The earliest letter we possess seems to belong to a time when he was still fascinated by the teaching of the pagan philosopher, Eustathius, whom he pursued, as with humorous exaggeration he describes, through Egypt, Syria, and to the borders of India. But this was a passing mood, and about 358 Basil withdrew to the family estate of Annesi, on the Iris, where he founded a religious community. In a long letter to his dearest friend, Gregory Nazianzen, he describes minutely the plan of his monastic cell, where, however, he lived without austerity, in great material comfort. It is noticeable that his household in the *cœnobium* included many male and female servants. But the extravagant zeal of the Arians, with whom he found himself more and more in divergence, called him back to Cæsarea, although he continued, in theory at least, to identify the monastic rule with the ideal Christian life.

The human side of St. Basil is very agreeably indicated in his familiar letters to his friends. Dr. Deferrari remarks that in the middle of the fourth century the letter was beginning to perform the service now furnished by the newspaper. Basil's letters are largely public documents, intended to be passed from hand to hand, and read aloud in the churches, but there are, especially in the earlier years, private letters as well. These are often as graceful as those of Pliny, and perhaps more sincere. Basil is remarkable, if not unique, for his passionate enjoyment of natural scenery; this is displayed in his epistles to Gregory Nazianzen. Readers of Cardinal Newman will remember what he says of Basil's description of his country house in Pontus. The letter containing this beautiful celebration of the forests and mountains, the ravines and cascades, the song-birds and flowers of his exquisite retreat, is supposed to have been written in 360. We see in it that St. Basil was then not too austere to collect around him guests in hunting-parties, nor able to reject the attraction of the

fruit and game on his estate, although he adds, " for me the
most pleasing fruit it nourishes is tranquillity." Holy as
was his life, Basil had no touch of the brutal fanatic. We
find him, even in the middle years, still affected by songs
and lyre-music, by the clatter of clog-dances, by the voice
of buffoons, and by the clamour of an enormous crowd,
though he resolutely put those temptations behind him.
He grew more and more serious as his work in the Church
became more responsible. The famous letter, or homily,
on the Monastic Life is attributed to 364; it is a counsel of
perfection, towards which, no doubt, the writer was more
and more strenuously urged by circumstances.

Gradually, rebuking frailty and fighting heresy, St. Basil
lost something of his gentler amenity. He was conscious
of what he called " inhumanity," a tendency to judge
harshly, and if the long and terrible letter " to a Fallen
Virgin " is authentic, he became capable of a cruel bigotry
of expression. The present volume of letters brings us up
to the year 370, when, at the age of about fifty-five, he
was elected Archbishop of Cæsarea. He died nine years
later, after composing the most celebrated of his works,
the " De Spiritu Sancto." When we reach this point we
find ourselves plunged into the whirlpool of the Arian
controversy, where in a murky abysm the horrors of
" homoousion " hurtle with the fallacies of " hypostasis."
We have a terrible vision of " troops of bishops galloping
along the highways " to rouse against St. Athanasius " the
abhorrence of the East," and of St. Basil growing hard and
harsh as he looks down upon the odious swarm.

One last warning I must venture to give. Not knowing,
of course, that their books would appear simultaneously,
Dr. Lake and Dr. Deferrari equally expatiate on Eusebius.
But it is not the same Eusebius of whom they speak, although contemporaneous, and although each, in his time,
bishop of Cæsarea. In fact, I make out that there were

at least a dozen Eusebii of considerable distinction, all flourishing together in the middle of the fourth century. This sets a trap for wandering feet in the jungle of the Arian controversy, where it is not always easy to know which Eusebius is referred to, even by the lucid periods of Gibbon.

# THE AGONY OF THE
# MIDDLE AGES

# THE AGONY OF THE
# MIDDLE AGES

How many rare and priceless treasures, like Dante's angels and Raffaele's sonnets, have disappeared from the face of the earth for ever? The question is as vain as that celebrated inquiry as to what music the Sirens sang. It is raised once more by the adventure of the memories of Pero Tafur, which have escaped complete destruction by a miracle. The original manuscript had long been lost, and this valuable record has been preserved only in a copy made some two centuries ago, and hidden in a library at Salamanca. Here it was discovered in 1874, and printed by a learned Spanish antiquary. Hitherto, although it has been described and quoted, no version of it has been available for English readers, and thanks are due to Mr. Malcolm Letts for the industry and zeal with which he has translated and annotated a document of unique interest, which must have offered considerable difficulties to its editor.

It was well worthy of his skilful care, since it is a picture of the state of Europe, east and west, at the most critical moment of its history, when all the Continent, except perhaps Burgundy and the great mercantile cities of Flanders, was overwhelmed by misery, disease, and unrest, when the old order was everywhere changing, and when the distracted Empire of the East was, as Gibbon says, "rocking to its fall." A cool and deliberate observer, without prejudice, without excitement, Pero Tafur noted the symptoms of decay. This record, which was unknown to the English historian of the " Decline and Fall," confirms in a striking way his eloquent summary of events. It should be read in connection with Gibbon's final volume.

Pero Tafur was a Spaniard of good family. He was born in Cordova about 1410; the Council of Pisa had just been convened; Popes were ignominiously falling; Europe was given up to rapine and confusion; the split between the Western and the Eastern Churches was threatening the very existence of Christianity. Tafur, as he grew up endowed with wealth and enterprise, became consumed with curiosity to see for himself the wonders of the world, and, undismayed by the terrific risks and discomforts of travel, he started on a grand tour of his own. He was driven by a violent *wanderlust* to see men and manners in their crudity, and it may be noted that he did not realise, as we may realise for him, how dreadful was the condition of the countries he visited. He was able to contemplate the sorrows of individuals with complete detachment, and he was no sentimentalist. He describes, during his journey through Palestine, how he saw a German gentleman drowned in the Jordan, and an officer's head chopped off in Jerusalem, and " a squire of France "—in the act of gallantly helping a lady to climb the mountain where our Lord was tempted of the Devil—slip and be smashed on the rocks below. Tafur mentions these incidents of travel calmly, without emotion, and proceeds to investigate Job's dunghill, a main attraction to mediæval tourists. We gain by what may seem to be Tafur's insensibility, since if he had been more sensitive, he would certainly have succumbed to the miseries of the route. There was no Blue Train to Constantinople in 1435.

The traveller started from San Lucar on board a troop-ship which was taking some soldiers back to Genoa after an unsuccessful attempt to drive the Moors out of Gibraltar.

The voyage was terrific, and for the first and only time Tafur, who had perhaps never been to sea before, lost heart. He arrived in Genoa shattered with sea-sickness, fatigue, and depression, " and this was the first time," he says, " that I began to know God." With the return of health, however, his piety declined, and he appears to have been no little of a Laodicean. Even his credit with the merchants failed him at first, but the Doge took him under his protection.

Proceeding through Italy, he found the unfortunate Pope Eugenius IV. in exile at Bologna; this was the " contumacious successor of St. Peter " who had been ignominiously driven from the Vatican by the arrows of Rome. Tafur made no reference to any painful incidents in the Pope's career, but accepted from him a Bull of plenary absolution and a licence to go to Jerusalem. At Venice he learned that no boat would start for the Holy Land for three months, and Tafur therefore passed over the Apennines to Rome, of which he gives a minute description. Rome, " which used to be the head of the world and is now the tail," was in the most miserable condition of squalor and decay, and the Spanish traveller notes the contempt which the population of the city showed for the monuments of past Roman glory. That " stupendous destruction " of ancient buildings which excited the indignation of Petrarch was in full blast, and no Roman was ashamed of breaking a last statue or razing an abandoned temple to the ground. Tafur adds a remarkable instance of the desolation of the city, when he says :—

" Rome, though depopulated, has more inhabitants than any other Christian city in the world, but there are parts within the walls which look like thick woods, and wild beasts, hares, foxes, wolves, deer, and even (so it is said) porcupines breed in the caves."

From Rome Tafur recrossed the Apennines by a leisurely route, and it is noticeable that he found the small cities of Italy in a condition of greater prosperity than the capital. The country between Viterbo and Assisi " is so thickly inhabited that cities, towns, and castle seem all joined together," and at Gubbio the pious Count of Urbino (who afterwards only just escaped being canonised) overwhelmed him with caresses and with three sets of towels. Ravenna was already partly deserted, but Rimini was in all its glory, and thence Tafur sailed to Venice, which, from his account, must have been at that date the most flourishing city of Italy. But on this occasion the Spanish traveller merely passed through it, anxious to accomplish his journey to Jerusalem. Sailing through the Adriatic, his ship was borne down upon by a fleet of Aragonese vessels, but she " displayed our pennons for Jerusalem, and when they saw these they left us at once and sailed away "; there was still a crusader's magic about the holy city. All this Dalmatian coast, and the greater part of Greece, were then Venetian, but at Rhodes the traveller entered the juris-diction of the Knights Hospitallers, who reigned there with great magnificence, and Tafur's account of the island principality is very curious. They sailed on to Cyprus, where they did not land on account of the bad air and water of Paphos, and they reached Jaffa on the fourth day, proceeding without further adventure to the Holy Sepulchre.

Tafur's adventures in Palestine must not delay us, since they do not offer anything of especial novelty. But as an instance of the reckless courage with which he pursued his curiosity I cannot refrain from quoting the account of his penetration, disguised as a Moslem, into the Mosque of Omar, from which Christians were excluded. That exclusion makes his description of the monument parti-cularly valuable :—

" That night I bargained with a renegade, a native of
Portugal, and offered him two ducats if he would get me
into the Temple of Solomon, and he consented.  At one
o'clock in the night I entered, dressed in his clothes, and saw
the Temple, which is a single nave, the whole ornamented
with gold mosaic work.  The floor and walls are of the
most beautiful white stone, and the place is hung with so
many lamps that they all seemed to be joined together.
The roof above is quite flat, and is covered with lead.
They say, in truth, that when Solomon built it, it was the
most magnificent building in the whole world. . . .  If I
had been recognised there as a Christian I should have been
killed immediately.  Not long ago this Temple was a
consecrated church, but a favourite of the Sultan has
prevailed upon him to turn it into a mosque.  The renegade
who had escorted me now returned with me to Mount Zion,
where the friars were mourning for me as one already dead,
since I had not come at the appointed time."

The intrepid adventurer unwillingly abandoned his plan
for a visit to India, and returned to the Levant, where I
must not follow him in detail through Syria, Cyprus, and
Egypt.  He was fascinated by the King of Cyprus, who,
although not seventeen years of age, was very tall and fat,
with legs of the same size at the garter and at the thigh.
He must have looked odd on horseback, but Tafur admired
his grace in the saddle.  His Majesty gave him a leopard,
which seems a troublesome travelling companion.  From
Nicosia our Spaniard went back to Rhodes with letters
from the King of Cyprus and was very well received by the
Grand Master, who, however, died that same night—
fortunately, since Tafur is able to give a detailed account
of the election of a successor, a ceremony not otherwise
recorded.

He then went to Chios and to Troy, and, at last, in

November, 1437, found himself in Constantinople. All
these little voyages were attended by terrible alarms from
Venetian, Turkish, Castilian, and Catalan ships, which were
little better than pirates, and were ever on the look-out for
whom they might devour. The courage involved in
putting out to sea on the chance of meeting these hornet-
galleys is amazing, but Tafur was sustained by the in-
domitable perseverance of the born traveller for whom
discomfort, or even death, has no terrors. He was twice
wrecked between Cyprus and Constantinople, and the
second time, when the ship sank under him, he was only
saved by clutching a piece of wreckage and clinging to it.
In all these vicissitudes it is difficult to see how he retained
the leopard or any other property, but no sooner does he
land than he seems to be rich again and to have everything
comfortable about him.

On this final occasion some friendly Castilians saved him,
and in their charge he landed at Pera. Thence, after paying
his compliments to the Spanish colony, he demanded an
interview with the Emperor of Constantinople, John VIII.;
it is difficult to distinguish one flitting Palaeologus from
another, but this ineffectual despot was, like his ancestor
John I., " well disposed to embrace, to believe, and to obey
the Shepherd of the West." He proceeded to believe, and
then to embrace Pero Tafur, who surprisingly confided to
the Imperial ear that he himself was no Spaniard by
extraction, but of the Emperor's own blood—porphy-
rogene, in fact. The two became very intimate, and the
Emperor set all his antiquaries to work hunting up a
pedigree for Tafur, who he proposed should settle down in
Constantinople and marry his imperial sister, but " the
people were bestial and the food did not agree with me."
So he was soon on the road again, this time for Tartary.
Meantime, and on a second visit, he made a close study of
Constantinople itself, and this is of extraordinary interest,

as a description of the city in its very latest years before the capture and partial destruction of it by the Turks. Tafur went to High Mass in the church of St. Sophia, in company with two emperors and an empress, and his account of the interior, as well as his general record of the appearance of the dying metropolis of the East, is graphic and valuable. The second Emperor with whom he went worshipping was the ruler of Trebizond, and the face of Tafur was now turned to Asia Minor.

The romantic name of Trebizond has always singularly fascinated me, and I was in hopes of finding Tafur describing it minutely, but he neglects to do so, although the cordiality of his reception in the Court of John IV. Commenus must have furnished him with opportunities. John IV. had recently made an orphan of himself by murdering his father, whose body he buried with great pomp. Tafur, with his usual coolness, rebuked this Christian parricide for having married the daughter of a Turk, and so cutting himself off from Christendom. The despot was quite meek, and said that he hoped to make a Christian of her. Tafur imperturbably replied : " My Lord, they say rather that the Turks gave her to you so that she could turn you into a Moor." This was a bold saying to a man who had just slain his own father, but the Emperor merely ordered that Tafur should be well fed and sent back in safety to Constantinople. This seems to have been the prince whom Gibbon depicts impressing three vermilion crosses on the Golden Bull. But I am not sure; I wish someone would write a chronicle of the Empire of Trebizond; no province of history is more obscure and mysterious. The very size and form of the city are given with startling variations. Tafur estimated that it had 4,000 inhabitants; Gibbon quotes Peyssonel as reporting that at this very time it had 100,000. Which estimate was correct?

Space fails me to accompany Pero Tafur any further.

He saw Venice again, and with peculiar vividness; he crossed the Alps into Germany; he explored Flanders and penetrated Poland, "for ever roaming with a hungry heart." Of England he seems to have known no more than he did of China. At last, in 1439, his travels abruptly land him at Cagliari, in the island of Sardinia. Mr. Letts thinks that he returned to his own country in March or April of that year. He settled down as a married alderman at Cordova, where he died about 1484. His record of the shattered civilisation of the Near East is extremely valuable, and Tafur writes with a mixture of the ancient and the modern which is almost as appropriate to that age of transition as Herodotus would be, expanded by Pierre Loti.

# ROCHESTER

# ROCHESTER

IN the wildest part of Woodstock Park there stands a
lonely seventeenth-century building in which, according to
local tradition, John Wilmot, Earl of Rochester, died on
July 26, 1680. The scene was doubtless more smiling then
than it is now, when the briars and fern brush up against the
grim purlieus of the house. But in its present desolation,
far from human neighbours, it seems a fitting hearth
prepared for that fiery spirit to expend its last glow in before
it faded into ash. Here the favourite of kings, the most
dissolute of poets, the leading reprobate of the age, made a
salutary end in the arms of the Church, his libertine pride
dissolved in the most humble penitence. The world enjoys
these violent revulsions, and Rochester, who had been the
type of depravity at Court and the terror of well-doers,
was no sooner dead in his sequestered hermitage than
respectability began to shout his praises. His reputable
decease, in the words of Waller, " relieved the afflicted
world," and Rochester's " fair soul " was made the text
of a hundred sermons. But alas! his disgraceful verses
remained, and they were read in secret when the deathbed
repentance was forgotten.

Through that affecting final scene the young earl, for he
was only thirty-three when he died, was attended by a
gifted ecclesiastic, not much older than himself; this was
the Rev. Gilbert Burnet, lately chaplain to the King, and
dismissed from his office, so it was said, for remonstrating
with Charles II. on his profligacy. Out of favour with the
Court, he was the darling of the true-blue Protestant

churchmen, and it was understood that, if he had so chosen, he could have been Bishop of Chichester; later on he became a great figure as Bishop of Salisbury. Burnet had published, in 1679, a " History of the Reformation," which was widely read, and, among others, by Rochester, whose bodily sufferings had now turned his thoughts to religion. In the midst of his riotous life he had always held a dim background of piety; he was a devil that believed and trembled. Now that the shades were gathering, he invited Burnet to be his guest in that dark house in the park, and he gave himself up to pious reflections. He related his past crimes to his sympathetic confessor. Like converted prize-fighters at revival prayer-meetings, he expatiated with unction on his past misdeeds. Burnet was not to spare him, nor to conceal his sinfulness from the world. He offered himself up as the supreme example of the sinner saved, " suffering his faults to be exposed for the benefit of others." He exaggerated his offences, as repentant sinners do. He lay on his bed, a miserable victim " to all the excesses of Riot," and he whispered things which Burnet, though no prude, declined to repeat. The result was a volume of " Passages of the Life and Death of the Right Honourable John, Earl of Rochester, Written by his own Direction on his Death-bed," which enjoyed an almost fabulous success. It is still the most amusing, and perhaps the most curious, theologico-biographical production of the seventeenth century.

Rochester was an aristocratic Verlaine. The parallel was very close, closer than I choose to make it here. The French poet was ugly and poor and a pariah; the English poet was beautiful and the pet of great nobles, and, if not rich, in the constant neighbourhood of wealth. Yet, if these accidental circumstances are set aside, the resemblance is seen to be extraordinary. Each was the victim of instincts over which he had no control; each was as weak as a breaking wave in the presence of temptation; each alternated outbursts of rampant godlessness with equally passionate and sincere convulsions of piety. Verlaine, who was the author of " Parallèlement" as well as of " O mon Dieu, vous m'avez blessé d'amour," and whose gross invectives stand side by side with his loveliest lyrics, was the spiritual brother of the English poet who wrote " The History of Insipids," and yet could write " Absent from Thee I languish still." The soul of each, as Burnet stringently expressed it, is " disfigur'd with the marks of intemperance and lewdness," and yet each has something poignant and delicate in his genius that redeems the most prodigal excesses.

John Wilmot was the son of an Oxfordshire squire, who had been ennobled for hiding Charles II. in the oak and so saving his life. The first earl died in exile in 1657, when the poet was eleven years of age. He was brought up severely by his highly capable mother, always a stern figure in the background of the story, and he seemed a " hopeful youth, very virtuous and good-natured." Before he was thirteen he went to Oxford, to Wadham, having already adventured with the Muses. Two copies of verse, certainly written in 1660, survive and are more than promising. They are remarkable for the correctness of their versification and for the vigour of their rhetoric. Evidently a very precocious and gifted little boy ! But if he began brilliantly there was a worm in the bud. Although his tutor at Wadham " absolutely doted " upon him, and carefully instructed him, Rochester became idle. He was unwilling to steal for study sufficient leisure " from the Witty and the Fair." (One imagines that the Wadham dons may have been witty, but what " fair " ones did Oxford provide for frivolous undergraduates?) Still, his University career was successful, and the young earl became " thoroughly acquainted with the Classics, both Greek and Latin."

The Greek accomplishment has been questioned, but he was a sound Latinist to the end of his days.

He was sent on the Grand Tour in the usual way, and was conducted by " Dr. Balfour," in whom, I think, the biographers of Rochester have not recognised the distinguished botanist, Sir Andrew Balfour, who was the accredited bear-leader of young nobles at that time. The Grand Tour was considered to give a necessary polish, but it was a great snare, and I think it probably started the downfall of Rochester. It was perilous for susceptible Northern youths, especially with Wilmot's dark antelope eyes, to visit so early the

> Lands of singing or of dancing slaves,
> Love-whispering woods and lute-resounding waves,

and I am afraid he came back to Oxfordshire, although intoxicated with literature, much relaxed in morals.

He was called out of Italy to take his part in the Dutch War, where he showed courage in the great naval battle off the coast of Norway. On board ship he made friends with Henry Savile, a man some five years older than himself, with whom he remained in close relation until his death. He was perhaps more fond of Savile than of any other comrade, and to the influence of this diplomatist, who was witty, clever, and good-natured, but extremely debauched, may be traced the ruin of Rochester. It was through Savile that the younger man obtained his entry to Court and his introduction to the set of gay wits who circled round the King. Rochester was only nineteen when he tried to carry off " the rich fortune," Miss Elizabeth Malet, but the marriage was then prevented, and the heiress rescued. With ingenious persistence, however, Rochester pursued the chase, and two years afterwards he married the lady. It appears that the amount of her fortune had been greatly exaggerated, but Rochester was unupbraiding. The extraordinary inconsistency of his life, indeed, now began, since while indulging in every amatory excess, we find him indubitably in love with his wife all the time. We are faced with the extraordinary fact that, while making England reverberate with the scandal of his shameful adventures, Rochester was all the time, as his correspondence with his lady shows, " bonæ sub regno Cynaræ."

This double life was conducted partly at Whitehall, where Rochester, protected by Charles II., whom he amused, was indulging in every species of riotous licence, and partly in his wife's house in Somersetshire, where he calmed down into the affectionate and quiet country gentleman. But the roysterer gradually impinged upon the student, and more and more inevitably Rochester became the victim of " a violent love of pleasure." How he spent the years from 1668 to 1678 can now only be gathered from the anecdotes, mainly undated, which more or less scandalised memoir-writers have preserved. Mr. John Hayward, the best and, in fact, the only competent editor of Rochester (the Nonesuch Press), has carefully strung together what stories of his wild feats are extant. From the first, Rochester set no check upon his love of wine, which Henry Savile trained and encouraged. This grew upon him so steadily that he could tell Burnet a little before his death that for five years together he had been " continually drunk." This takes us back to 1675, about which time it is probable that the final degradation of his character set in, and doubtless the stories of his most disgraceful excesses belong to this late period, when, as Shelley said of Byron at Venice, he was associating with beings who had almost lost the semblance of humanity.

In the midst of these final extravagances, however, Rochester was partly retrieved by the latest emotion of his life, his attachment to Mrs. Barry, the celebrated actress, who was to Rochester what the Guiccioli was to

Byron, " a star on the stormy horizon of the poet's life."
She preserved his love-letters, which are brief, tender,
and sometimes incoherent, but full of passion. She seems
to have ruled his heart for a couple of years, and to have
resigned it only, at the last, to Lady Rochester. Whether
the beautiful songs which redeem the writer's fame and
alone place him among the poets of England were written
to his wife or to this charming and accomplished mistress,
who bore him a daughter, is uncertain. They could have
been written to none other of his myriad " loves." He
had grown to be a social pariah when he met Mrs. Barry;
he had presumed too far, and had lost the favour of the
King; he had quarrelled brutally with the Duchess of
Portsmouth. His own boon companions were disgusted
with him, and he had become " the irreconcilable aversion
of fine gentlemen." But in this social desert two fountains
were springing, not perhaps of the purest water, but very
different from the turbid pools out of which Rochester
had been drinking. To prove it there are the tender
letters to Mrs. Barry, there are the still more pathetic
epistles to " my most neglected wife," with whom, he
says, he could always be happy when " those rake-hells
are not near to disturb us." If we ask for further proof
that Rochester was not the mere monkey-devil of legend,
we have the beautiful letter of advice to his little son,
Charles, which Mr. Hayward prints.

Dr. Johnson, whose weakest point as a critic was his
insensibility to lyrical beauty, perversely stated that
Rochester's songs " have no particular character," and are
lacking in nature and sentiment. It is likely that this
censure accounts, in some measure, for the complete
neglect which they long endured. As a matter of fact,
they have the particular character of being by far the
best, the most natural, and the most emotional lyrics of
the Restoration period. No other poet of the age of

Charles II., not Sedley, not Dryden, approached the
unaffected sincerity of—

> When, wearied with a world of woe,
>     To thy safe bosom I retire,
> Where love and peace and truth do flow,
>     May I contented there expire.
>
> Lest, once more wandering from that heaven,
>     I fall on some base heart unblest;
> Faithless to thee, false, unforgiven,
>     And lose my everlasting rest.

Or the delicate humour of—

> My dear mistress has a heart
>     Soft as those kind looks she gave me
> When with love's resistless art,
>     And her eyes, she did enslave me;
> But her constancy's so weak,
>     She's so wild and apt to wander,
> That my jealous heart would break
>     Should we live one day asunder.

Unfortunately, these songs are very few, and they are
oases which almost disappear in the wilderness of Rochester's
writings. He was forgiven much on the ground of his
supposed wit, and the sparkle of his consummate genius.
That genius was mainly preserved in the form of satires
and lampoons, in which he set no bounds to the licence of
language. That his satires are gross is partly due to the
age in which he lived, and those of the puritan Andrew
Marvell are scarcely less obscene than Rochester's. But
there is this difference—that while Marvell is really angry,
Rochester seems more than half in love with the vices
which he flagellates. His voice is not the voice of Timon,
but an effeminate shriek, piercing and voluble, the falsetto
of which is very disagreeable. From a technical point of
view he deserves notice as the earliest of the new school
of satirists, preceding Oldham and Dryden by some years.
If the " Letter to Artemisia " was composed before 1670,

it justifies the high hopes which good judges expressed of
the young poet's future. But Rochester's verses were not
collected till after his death, and we are left to conjecture
and to internal evidence in any effort to arrange them.

We can best realise Rochester if we picture to ourselves
a weak, brilliant, and dangerously handsome English boy,
snatched from his studies and from his Oxfordshire home,
and projected into the midst of the exotic society in which
the Venus of Whitehall was worshipped after the ritual of
Versailles. All the extravagant acts of his career seem
imitative, not native. When he hires bravos to beat
Dryden in the street, we think of the Duke of La Feuillade
crushing the face of Molière against the steel buttons of
his doublet. When he hangs on the King's arm and
drops an impudent lampoon into the royal pocket, we
think of Lauzun. With women he had the misfortune to
be irresistible, and he flung them from him with insolent
disdain. There is a very curious letter of St. Evremond's
to the Duchess of Mazarine which illustrates that. In all
such matters, especially after his exile in 1669, he was
hopelessly Louis XIV.; he was like the detestable little
marquises who were the plague of Molière's life. But
there was always the other, the provincially English element
in him, and it is his contradictions, the incessant war in his
members, which make Rochester, with his insolence and
his tenderness, his malignity and his imagination, a unique
personage in the history of our literature.

# GENTLEST OTWAY

# GENTLEST OTWAY

THE Nonesuch Press confers a lasting benefit on students by its remarkable editions of the late seventeenth-century poets. We have welcomed the Congreve, the Wycherley, the Rochester, and now we receive an equally sumptuous Otway. It should emphatically be pointed out that these are not perfunctory reprints of existing texts, but are edited with minute care by the scrupulous and learned hand of Mr. Montague Summers. I hope that publisher and editor will not slacken in their zeal until they have added to their series a Southerne, who has never been edited, and, I think, since 1774 not even collected. It will then be invidious not to proceed to Nathaniel Lee, and there, perhaps, they may be allowed to pause from their labours.

Meanwhile, it would be difficult to praise editor and publisher too highly for removing a reproach from English scholarship. It is outrageous that all our handbooks should contain praise of English classics of whom no text is available. Otway, for example, though one of the most famous of our poets, has never before this been in any true sense edited. His plays were collected in 1691—Mr. Summers does not mention this publication, which was nothing but remainders of the quarto plays, re-issued in a thick volume as " The Works of Mr. Thomas Otway " —and frequently in the eighteenth century; but the only reprint which professed to be " edited " was that of Thornton in 1813, a well-meaning but valueless effort. Mr. Summers, with indefatigable industry, has had to till the field before he reaped the harvest.

For more than two hundred years the sorrows of "gentlest Otway" have been traditional, and there are hundreds of people who have heard of his piteous fate who never saw or even read his plays. He shares with Chatterton the legend of youthful genius, heartbroken by the caprice of the public, dying positively from lack of bread. His case is even more poignant than that of the marvellous Bristol boy, because Otway won success, and tasted happiness, only to lose them both. Among the hard-living, quarrelsome authors of his time, he is the one whose adventures appeal to our sensibility, the solitary figure to whom we can extend any affection. We may admire Wycherley and Etherege, but it would be ridiculous to love them; even Dryden, though he commands our deep respect, can hardly claim our affection. But for Otway, so feverish and frail, thrown so helpless on the thorns of life, so incapable of self-command, we feel as we might towards a beautiful fretful child, with its implicit claim on our forbearance. "A gentleman highly wronged and affronted," "Otway the hope, the sorrow of our stage," "the melancholy and incomparable Otway"— such are the terms in which this unfortunate young man of genius had always been celebrated. He was identified with the infatuated heroes and desolate heroines of his dramas, the Belvidera and Monimia over whom, as Sir Walter Scott put it, more tears have been shed than over Juliet and Desdemona. Such has been the popular image of this poet, whom the venom of envious rivals, the perfidy of a callous courtesan, the excess of his own nervous excitability, aided by the manners of a barbarous age, drove to despair, so that he died of want of food, "in an alehouse, unlamented," in his thirty-third year.

Such is the moving legend, and Mr. Summers, collecting every tradition and sifting every reference, is unable to do more than confirm it. "All this, I hope," wrote

Dr. Johnson, " is not true," but apparently it is, and no more distressing story darkens the chronicle of our literature. Thomas Otway belonged to the second flight of Restoration dramatists, the generation which stepped in between the age of Dryden and the age of Congreve. He was of a good north-country family, which had leanings toward Church preferment. One of the poet's cousins was an Irish bishop; another clerical cousin, I regret to say, was described in the unaffected language of the time as " a greasy blockhead fellow in a gown." The poet's father, the Reverend Humphrey, became rector of Woolbeding-cum-Trotton, in Sussex, where our " tender Otway " was born on March 3, 1652. Generations have wept for him by the banks of the Arun, but in error, since he saw the light, not near the banks of that melodious river, but by the West Rother. In his autobiographical ode Otway tells us :—

> I am a wretch of honest race :
> My parents not obscure, nor high in titles were ;
> They left me heir to no disgrace.
> My father was, a thing now rare,—
> Loyal and brave, my mother chaste and fair ;
> The pledge of marriage-vows was only I ;
> Alone I lived their much-loved, fondled boy.

This was written, or at least published, in 1680, when the prodigal was eating husks with the swine. He says that his—

> muse was crazy grown,
> Cloyed with the nauseous follies of the buzzing town.

and his memory, too, it would seem, for he had a sister, and his mother was still alive. But they seem to have long ceased to have any dealings with him.

Otway was educated at Winchester, and I am very glad that Mr. Summers has drawn attention to the beautiful

lines in which Lionel Johnson (a bard too little remembered)
has celebrated the author of " Venice Preserv'd." He
proceeded, in 1669, to Christ Church, Oxford, where he
must have winced under the stern eye of Dr. Fell, who,
however, can hardly have known that the handsome but
already tiresome undergraduate slipped up to London in
his nineteenth year to appear on the public stage as a
character in one of Mrs. Behn's plays. Mr. Summers, with
his extraordinary knowledge of the theatrical customs of
that age, builds up a shining picture of the scene, when
Otway, disguised with white hair and beard as a venerable
king, made his first and last appearance. " The full house
put him to such a sweat and tremendous agony " that he
could not utter one of the fifty-three verses he was bound
to speak. One wonders how the play proceeded. Mrs.
Behn, a good creature, if ever there was one, bore him no
spite, but it is evident that she was responsible for " infect-
ing " Otway " with the rhyming itch " and distracting him
from his studies. He stayed on at Oxford for two years
more, although, his father being now dead, Mr. Summers
pertinently asks who can have paid his college fees?
There seems, however, to have been a patron in the background, one " good Semander," of whom we know nothing
except that he also incontinently died. Meanwhile, Otway,
who had taken no degree, and had not applied himself to
learning—after several years in Oxford, he had still no
Greek—" strayed," as he puts it, to " Britain's great
Metropolis."

He must have had money from some source, for
he lived a life of complete indolence for two years, the
companion of—

> Gay coxcombs, cowards, knaves, and prating fools,
> Bullies of o'ergrown bulk and little souls,
> Gamesters, half-wits, and spendthrifts, such as think
> Mischievous midnight frolics bred by drink
> Are gallantry and wit.

From this idleness he was partly redeemed at the age
of twenty-three by having a tragedy accepted at Dorset
Garden theatre. It was named "Alcibiades," and Mr.
Summers, with fond indulgence, calls it a "spirited drama."
I rather find a miracle in the fact that the author of such
a mawkish piece of rhyming rant should afterwards write
well. Otway, at all events, immediately followed his first
play by a second, which is immeasurably superior to it.
"Don Carlos" is particularly interesting, because it proves
that Otway had become conscious of the genius of his
most eminent contemporary. He must, in fact, have been
the earliest English student of "Bajazet" and "Mithri-
date," and he still remains the most Racinian of all our
poets.

Otway's debt to the Elizabethans has been greatly
exaggerated. He was, on the other hand, a pioneer in
the new kind of elegiac tragedy which his London auditors
delighted in. Consider the effect in 1676 of such tirades
as this :—

> Oh ! matchless youth ! oh ! constancy divine !
> Sure there was never love that equall'd thine,
> Nor any so unfortunate as mine.
> Henceforth forsaken virgins shall, in songs,
> When they would ease their own, repeat thy wrongs;
> And in remembrance of thee, for my sake,
> A solemn annual procession make;
> In chaste devotion as fair pilgrims come,
> With hyacinths and lilies deck thy tomb.

Nothing could be less like Webster or Chapman than
this soft and yet nervous versification or this lucid rhetoric.
It seems a pity, save in the case of "Venice Preserv'd,"
that Otway presently left the heroic couplet for blank
verse. "The Orphan," less manageable perhaps as a
drama, might be a better poem if it were written in rhyme.

During the next seven years Otway, who had been
trained to no profession, and was totally lacking in worldly

H

wisdom, seems to have supported a precarious existence
by writing one play each year. Mr. Summers, whose
acquaintance with the pamphlets and lampoons of the
period is unapproached, has printed all that we are likely
to learn by hearsay. Otway, with his radical infirmity
of character, linked his fate with the caprice of two of the
most dangerous persons then living, the Earl of Rochester,
with whom it was a passion to flatter young men of talent
and then impishly to attack them, and with the first actress
of the age, whose perfidy was a byword. Mrs. Barry had
been to Otway what La Champmeslé was to the author of
" Bérénice," but this seductive woman had a heart on the
stage but a stone in place of it in real life. All the records
of the time paint her as detestable, and yet irresistible.
The tender, foolish Otway fell hopelessly in love with
this serpent, and his letters—which were preserved, it
appears, by her insolent protector, Rochester—are the
cry of a breaking heart. She was careful, however, never
to break off relations with so popular a playwright,
and on the boards she was not merely his Monimia and
his Belvidera, but Porcia in his latest play, " The
Atheist."

The excellence of Mr. Summers as a biographical expert
and a commentator is so great that I would gladly possess
equal confidence in him as a critic. But he is, to a remarkable extent, the willing victim of prejudice. It is hardly
a fault, it is almost a merit in an editor to take a slightly
exaggerated view of the subject-matter before him. It
is fatal to hate the author you are editing, as Elwin grew
to loathe the very name of Pope. But Mr. Summers,
from having lived closely with the playwrights of the
Restoration, has become oblivious of their faults and
obsessed by their " wit." He can hardly bear to think
that any drama published in quarto between 1670 and
1690 was not " spirited " and " effective " and " amusing,"

unless it came from the pen of a true-blue Protestant. So far as other authors are concerned, this does not, on the present occasion, matter very much. But to praise with uniform enthusiasm everything which so unequal a writer as Otway published defeats its own aim. The comedies of Otway are notoriously bad; even in that indelicate age it is difficult to point to another play so cold, virulent, and lewd as " Friendship in Fashion." In so saying, I lay myself open to Mr. Summers's vivacious reproof; to contend that " Friendship in Fashion " is a bad piece of dull and heartless work " merely shows a crass confusion of values and blurred outlook "! Well, well!

In political and social comment Mr. Summers is no less obstreperous. The " villain " Shaftesbury is a curious way of describing the greatest political figure of the reign of Charles II. Shaftesbury was a statesman whose conduct was often mysterious, and who was the victim of his own versatility, but whose general trend in public life was salutary to the nation. No one ought to forget that Shaftesbury was a fighter for political and religious liberty. But Mr. Summers really oversteps the border of what is permissible when he talks of " the foulness " of Shaftesbury's " private vices." The purity of Shaftesbury's private life has never been impugned, except at the time by one or two savage and reckless pamphleteers. Otway was no judge in such a matter, and as to the other backbiters, it sometimes looks as though Mr. Summers were ready to swallow any nonsense, however rank and poisonous, which a supporter of James II. took the liberty of printing. He sees blue as a bull sees red.

But I have been tempted aside into an expostulation with Mr. Summers, and I must come back to say again how much I admire his energy and erudition. His notes are astonishingly full of marrowy information, and, I should say, if I were not afraid again to incur his displeasure, are often more entertaining than the particular text they illustrate. Certainly, to read the twenty pages of Mr. Summers's notes on " The Soldier's Fortune " seems to me a more diverting exercise than to subject myself again to the scenes of that crackle of malignity.

# POPE AND MR. LYTTON
## STRACHEY

# POPE AND MR. LYTTON STRACHEY

Of the many points of view from which the character and genius of Pope can be observed, Mr. Lytton Strachey has chosen two for his survey of an hour. In the one case I find myself almost wholly in harmony with him, in the other I deprecate the impression which he passed on to his auditors, among whom it was my misfortune not to be included. A lecture is intended to be heard rather than read, and its appeal is both brief and summary. It cannot say everything, and what it does say is bound to miss the fine shades. The lecturer must be emphatic or else he will be dull. Now, it is impossible to imagine Mr. Lytton Strachey dull on any subject; he has a scintillating mind. I am told that when he assured his Cambridge hearers that the " Satires " and " Epistles " of Pope

" resembled nothing so much as spoonfuls of boiling oil, ladled out by a fiendish monkey at an upstairs window upon such of the passers-by whom the wretch had a grudge against,"

they broke out into laughter and applause. If it had been my privilege to be present, I must have buried my face in my hands, and when Mr. Lytton Strachey went on to say that if Pope had been a Frenchman and had written as he wrote in English, he would never have been tolerated, " the monkey would have been whipped into silence and good manners in double quick time," I should have been lost in astonishment at Mr. Strachey's momentary forgetfulness. Was Boileau " whipped into silence "?    Had Régnier been exiled for his malevolence?

No doubt it is a matter of temperament to like Pope or to dislike him.   Mr. Lytton Strachey says that " the fate of Pope's soul leaves us cold."   He must speak for himself; there are some of us who always keep a warm place in their hearts for Pope.   But Mr. Lytton Strachey strikes, at the outset of his lecture, a note which jars upon my ear.   He says that we can congratulate ourselves that we run no danger of waking up one morning to find that we are " hanging by the neck and kicking our legs on the elegant gibbet that has been put up for us by the little monster of Twit'nam."   The picture is vivaciously designed, but labours under the disadvantage that it is radically false. The idea of " a fiendish monkey " flinging boiling oil at everybody, without a purpose, without responsibility, without selection, is highly amusing, but perfectly unjust. If Mr. Lytton Strachey had been living in 1725, he would not have run the slightest danger of being scalded by Pope. The oil was reserved for persons whose faults demanded it. That the attacks of the poet were too virulent, and were pitched in too shrill a key is not to be denied, but that they were flung about insanely, as a maniac pours revolver-bullets into a crowd, is to perpetuate an absurd injustice. With a few exceptions, the people attacked by Pope deserved the punishment they got, however much we may be conscious of want of dignity and loss of temper on the part of the chastiser.   Mr. Lytton Strachey congratulates himself on not having lived in the age of Anne.   Does he imagine that he would have shared the fate of Oldmixon and Arnall?   By no means: he would have been with Swift, with Gay, with Arbuthnot, " friend of my life," with all those

whose fires
True Genius kindles and fair Fame inspires.

I do not share Mr. Lytton Strachey's pity for the poetasters whom the Mud-nymphs sucked down, and I hold that the very invective upon Atticus, if it is carefully analysed, shows the genuine value Pope set upon genius and virtue.

Hatred of incompetence and dullness, impatience with presumption, scorn of ignorant conventionality, these were qualities which animated Pope throughout his painful and frustrated career. He early realised, with that amazing courage to which his detractors are so strangely unwilling to do justice, that an author who should, in so tumultuous a generation, attempt to serve the intelligence of his race must, as he said in 1716, " have the constancy of a martyr and a resolution to suffer for the sake " of literature. He demands respect for his loyalty to the cause of intellectual honesty, and he should not be treated as a monkey flinging hot oil at random because an anger, which, of course, was not entirely disinterested, betrayed him into thinking that all blockheads must be scoundrels. His resolution to clear out the Augean stable was a noble one, if sometimes rather ignobly executed, and we owe him an immortal debt of gratitude for the zeal with which he fought for the status of literature. Even Mr. Lytton Strachey admits that the society of the beginning of the eighteenth century " was perhaps the most civilised that our history has known." But who did more than Pope to civilise it—who so much? If a monkey inspired the " Third Epistle," it is a pity that we have not all got tails.

If Mr. Lytton Strachey does not seem to me to be as clairvoyant as I should wish in his estimate of Pope's moral character, which is clouded for him by certain dust-storms in the " Dunciad," I cordially approve of his remarks about the technique of the poems. He exposes Macaulay's mischievous fallacies on the subject of " correctness," and he quotes the argument of a modern French poet, who is the darling of the moment. It was hardly necessary that the lecturer should go so far afield as M. Paul Valéry, since the case of Macaulay was confuted nearly a hundred years ago, in better terms, by De Quincey. Pope is not " correct " in the maturing and connecting of his thoughts, but in strict obedience to prosodic rules. Walsh reminded him in his early youth that " we have had great poets, but never one great poet that was correct." Pope took the advice, and became beyond all precedent correct. But what is, or was, " correctness "? The nineteenth century, from Keats and Wordsworth down to Matthew Arnold, deemed it equivalent to stiffness and dullness, and therefore persuaded itself that Pope was dull and stiff. But if we recognise that " correctness " is nothing more nor less than the extremity of artistic selection, moving along a particular line, by making the very best possible use of words, of rhyme, of metre, of virtuosity in general, leaving nothing rough and discordant for want of taking time and pains in polishing, we shall begin to understand why Pope, in becoming the most correct of the poets of his time, became also the most amusing, various, and inevitable of them. This is what Mr. Lytton Strachey sees, and his advocacy is valuable.

Still more valuable is the further step he takes in analysing the principal element in Pope's correctness. Here he deals with Matthew Arnold's famous definition, which has done more than anything else to obscure the genius of Pope during the last forty years. Arnold, in his most pontifical manner, decreed that Pope was without " high seriousness " and lacked an " adequate poetic criticism of life." He also decided that Pope was " the high priest of an age of prose and reason," thus, although he wrote in verse, continuing outside the precincts of Apollo, and never " a classic of our poetry." This dictum, uttered when Arnold was at the height of his authority, was widely read and generally accepted. It has never been completely refuted, and could not be so long as the romantic theory of

what constitutes poetry was accepted without demur.
There was one aspect in which it could not be repudiated.
The singing element, the lyric, was conspicuously lacking
in Pope. We are told that when Porson had drunk more
brandy than usual, he would chant the whole of " Eloisa
to Abelard," an effort which must have tried the endurance
of the company. But I know of no other instance of Pope's
verses being sung, except, of course, in the extremely unfortunate experiment of " Amphion thus bade wild discussion cease."

But Mr. Lytton Strachey has made a brilliant discovery,
which condemns Arnold's pinched restriction altogether.
He boldly asserts that Pope's " poetic criticism of life was,
simply and solely, the heroic couplet." Mr. Strachey's
words in expansion of this idea are among the best which
he has written, and will mark a turning-point in the criticism
of what is called "classical" poetry. He traces, very
rapidly, the development of the couplet from the rude and
accidental practice of it by the Elizabethans, delightfully
including, what I think is an actual discovery, a passage
of six lines which ought to come from one of the " Imita-
tions of Horace," and are as a fact to be found in " Othello."
The summary he gives is not less excellent than rapid :—

" Though Waller was its creator, the heroic couplet
remained with him, in an embryonic state. Its evolution
was slow ; even Dryden did not quite bring it to perfection.
That great genius, with all his strength and all his brilliance,
lacked one quality, without which no mastery of the couplet
could be complete—the eloquence of perfect finish. This
was possessed by Pope."

We are apt to lose sight of the fact that finish is one
expression of high intellectual energy. In the career of
Pope, by far the most finished of all English writers, we see

one refinement after another added to build up an unsur-
passed poetical magic.

His first aim, Mr. Lytton Strachey says his great achieve-
ment, was the triumph of simplification.  In his " Pastorals "
we see little else, and not much in " Windsor Forest " and
" The Temple of Fame."   Gradually, while he pursued the
art with unwearying ardour, he gained other qualities,
richness, melody, passion of the intellectual order, and
finally the limpid ease and fluidity of " The Epistle to Dr.
Arbuthnot."   Even to these were added, when he came to
close " The Dunciad," weight and sonority.   But all these
performances, all this sumptuous embroidery of poetic
beauty, was woven upon a single basis, since, whatever
we reveal in dissecting the verse of Pope, we come down at
last in every instance to the heroic couplet.   Mr. Lytton
Strachey is as correct as he is courageous when he turns
upon Matthew Arnold and says that Pope had " a high
seriousness," and that it was—not that it was supported by
or attached to, but that it *was*—the heroic couplet.

Certainly Pope's poetic criticism of life will appear to us
" adequate " to an extraordinary degree if we approach it
by accepting this view.   In the case of this poet, the
technical instrument was itself so delicately precious, so
elaborately perfected, that it involved that serious inspiration, that intensity of life which Arnold hastily denied to
it.   There is nothing in the rest of English literature comparable with the colour, variety, and effectiveness of the
couplet as Pope used it.   It was his lyre, and the brain
which struck the chords.   We may take examples anywhere, and here is a passage less hackneyed than most.   It
is from the satire on Timon's pompous hospitality :—

> But hark !  the chiming clocks to dinner call !
> A hundred footsteps scrape the marble hall ;
> The rich buffet well-coloured serpents grace,
> And gaping Tritons spew to wash your face.

Is this a dinner? This a genial room?
No, 'tis a temple and a hecatomb,
A solemn sacrifice performed in state,
You drink by measure, and to minuets eat.
So quick retires each flying course, you'd swear
Sancho's dread Doctor and his wand were there.
Between each act the trembling salvers ring
From soup to sweet-wine, and God bless the King.
In plenty starving, tantalised in state,
And complaisantly helped to all I hate;
Treated, caressed, and tired, I take my leave,
Sick of his civil pride from morn to eve;
I curse such lavish cost, and little skill,
And swear no day was ever passed so ill.

That seems easy, but for two hundred years since it was written very clever people have been trying to equal it, in vain.

# NOTRE DAME DES AMOURS

# NOTRE DAME DES AMOURS

IT was inevitable that M. Emile Magne, who has illuminated the history of the seventeenth century by so many monographs of extraordinary penetration and research, should at last be arrested by the temperament which pervades the whole epoch like a perfume, and should produce, for the first time, a trustworthy portrait of that queen of fabulous romance whom Horace Walpole called " Notre Dame des Amours."

In 1913, M. Magne, as the result of his investigations, gave the world a sketch of the life of Ninon de Lanclos. Since then, in the inexhaustible treasuries of French manuscript memoirs, he has discovered so much that is new, and is able to expose so many errors in accepted legend, that he has completely rewritten his book, and gives us a biography of genuine historic importance. I might hesitate to call attention to a life essentially so far from what Victorian ladies called " nice," if it were not that it is impossible, in studying the greatest epoch of French civilisation, to avoid Ninon de Lanclos. There she is, in every memoir, in every correspondence, and we can no more escape from her than we can from Louis XIV. or from Molière. M. Magne does not attempt to " whitewash " her reputation, but he reduces it from fable to fact. When all is done, she remains a figure of extraordinary originality and significance.

The national archives of France are rich in documents beyond all probability of exhaustion. M. Magne, who is always dipping his bucket and bringing up new treasures,

has found in the *dossiers* of the Criminal Parliament all the
history of Ninon's parents.    She belonged authentically to
the *petite noblesse*, and her father, Henry du Lanclos, was
an officer in the armies of Henri IV.    He was a musician,
a voluptuary, and a sceptic.    He married a Mlle. de La
Marche, who, after a youth which was scarcely dubious,
adopted religion in its most acrid form.

In 1620 to this disparate couple was born their only child,
Anne, afterwards and always known as Ninon.    At the
babe's baptism someone said that her lips seemed to be
modelled by Venus herself, and, if this was a prophecy,
none was ever more completely fulfilled.    Meanwhile, there
raged battle royal between the libertine father and the
fanatical mother, struggling for the soul of Ninon.    Henry
de Lanclos, whose adventures would have enchanted the
Elder Dumas, murdered a rival when Ninon was thirteen,
and vanished into thin air.    He had, however, already
begun to instruct his daughter in the ways of the world,
and had instilled into her what remained in her to the end
of her days, a passion for the spirit of Montaigne.

Even M. Magne has not discovered much that happened
to Ninon for the next nine years, except that she and her
mother kept up a struggle of opinions until the latter died
in 1642.    Ninon, now twenty-two years of age, was left
alone, armed with a competence and entirely mistress of
her own person.    In those days everybody of the least
consequence married, if only as a step to something better.
Ninon, already a honey-pot, found herself surrounded by
suitors, but came to the settled conclusion that marriage
was a slavery.    In spite of an unrivalled experience, she
was to die a demoiselle.    She thought for a moment of
becoming a Carmelite nun, but this was a whimsical reaction.    She read the historians of antiquity, and she was
fascinated by the example of Aspasia, who secured the
devotion of Pericles, not more by her beauty than by her

high mental accomplishments. She became, deliberately
and simply, the first courtesan of that age of passion and
adventure. " Loin d'elle des lors la pruderie et les airs
chattemittes." The first half of M. Magne's biography
recounts what was palpably unedifying, but in terms exempt from reproach. All I will venture to say of the early
adventures of this type of *l'inconstante* is that Ninon chose
her lovers and was not willing to be chosen. Men were like
marionettes in her hands.

From the first, the breadth and daring of her mind produced even more scandal than the effrontery of her conduct.
She was practised in all the intellectual ingenuities of the
age, and she was only saved by her humour and her good
sense from becoming a typical pedant in that age of
*précieuses*. The poets adored her, and a murmur of verses
made the door of her house like the entrance to a hive.
She held her own with all kinds of men, and did not scruple
to tell the philosophers that she preferred their metaphysic
to their caresses. A prince of the blood was told to wait
and see; "attends mon. caprice," Ninon remarked, as she
looked him up and down. Dukes and marquesses trembled
and wheedled, but were ruthlessly judged in body and
mind, and were only too often found wanting.

Meanwhile Ninon de Lanclos became as eminent in
friendship as in love. The personage who asserted the
dominating force over her moral life was no lover, but a
great philosopher and diplomat—Saint-Evremont, whose
acquaintance she made as early as 1639. It was said of
him that he lived in a perpetual paradox, the slave alike of
Epicurus and of Pyrrho, abandoned by turns to pleasure
and to ascetic doubt. Ninon seems to have shared this
double character of the *libertinage* of the time. She
studied the sceptical writers of Italy and Spain; she dipped
more deeply than ever into Montaigne, and she hardened
herself in her revolt against religion.

The cynosure of all hearts, Ninon's remained uncaptured until, when she was about thirty-four, and in the heyday of her singular popularity, Louis de Mornay, Marquis de Villarceaux, swooped down upon her like an eagle, and carried her away to his eyrie in the Vexin. Ninon, who had always been the despot, found her master in this eccentric, unscrupulous, and passionate adventurer. For three years, from 1652 to 1655, she was his slave, until Saint-Evremont warned her that this exile was becoming ridiculous, and that her place was in Paris. With docility Ninon obeyed his counsels, abandoned Villarceaux, and once more made her house in the capital a centre of gallant intrigues, the echo of which rang from one end of France to the other. They roused the indignation of the devout, and that very powerful body, the Company of the Holy Sacrament, determined to ruin her. Queen Anne of Austria supported her enemies, and Ninon formed the momentary idea of escaping to America.

But her friends were more powerful than she knew, and they rallied round her. Another queen, Christina of Sweden, consoled her with gifts and caresses, offering Ninon an asylum in Rome. This she declined, but she withdrew to a quieter part of Paris, and furnished the little house in the Rue des Tournelles, which still exists but slightly changed. Here she resided for the rest of her long life, and here she received all celebrated men and some reputable women. Among the latter was Madame Scarron, presently to become Madame de Maintenon, and herself a secret queen. Ninon was still a honey-pot, and serious suitors, several of them of high degree, buzzed anxiously round her. If Le Sage is to be believed, she made curl-papers of their offers of marriage. She desired to enjoy a full independence, and she amply achieved it. For thirty years Ninon du Lanclos ruled a certain section of the world from her modest throne in the Rue des Tournelles.

One of the romantic calumnies which has pursued her has presented her to us as immortal in her pursuit of love, and chained to the chariot of Venus long after her eightieth year. One legend pretends that at the very close of her life she attempted to seduce the youthful but already saintly Bourdaloue. Voltaire, who was admitted to her company in his boyhood, lent himself to these tales. M. Magne has proved them to be false. Charles de Sevigné was her latest lover, and that intrigue closed in 1659, in Ninon's fiftieth year.

Having dismissed Sevigné, she told her faithful mentor, Saint-Evremont, that her caprices would for the future give place to " solid and severe qualities." She kept her word, as far as conduct was concerned; the long evening of her life was pagan, as the morning of it had been, but it was stoical and serious. She devoted herself to conversation and to her friends, and she gathered around her the most eminent personages of France. Even those who, from the height of their virtue, had reproved the open scandal of her behaviour came under the charm of her intelligence. Even Madame de la Fayette and Madame de Sevigné forgave her. The circle of her acquaintance widened so far that it touched no less exalted a soul than Pascal. With her eminent good sense, she said that, after the age of fifty, a life of gallantry was ridiculous, and she completely abandoned it. None the less, she preserved to the full that intellectual and spiritual *libertinage* which she had imbibed from Montaigne and Saint-Evremont, and when the Court began to sink into a formal piety which impressed itself upon every stratum of social life, Ninon remained true to her old liberal convictions.

She lived so completely in the company of men of letters that she, too, became an author. In 1659 she had published a little volume, " La Coquette Vengée," which seems to have been a series of satirical portraits of living persons, in

the taste of that day.  This book has become excessively
rare, but M. Magne, who has read it, discovers in it a curious
resemblance to " Les Précieuses Ridicules," which was, at
that very moment, being played at the Petit Bourbon.
Her friendship with Molière certainly dates from this time,
and was continued until his death.  A character in " Tar-
tufe " resembles the hero of that play, and M. Magne
ingeniously suggests, as, indeed, Tallemant recorded, that
Ninon proposed to Molière the celebrated type of the
arch-hypocrite.  The splendid wits of the age now began
to make her house their rendezvous, and the woman, however morality may deplore the scandal of her youth, could not
be despicable who enjoyed the friendship of Boileau, of La
Fontaine, of Madame de la Sablière, of Racine.  Saint-
Simon records with emphasis that—

" Mlle. de Lanclos was surrounded by all the respect and
outward decency which the most virtuous princesses cannot
always command.  She enjoyed the friendship of those who
were most refined and punctilious at Court, until to be
received in her house became not merely the fashion but
an honour that was ardently competed for.  There was no
gambling there, no romping, no disputes, no wrangling about
religion or government—nothing but wit elegantly expressed
and conversation sustained on a high level of delicacy and
harmonious propriety."

This is not the Ninon de Lanclos of loose eighteenth-
century gossip.
The taste of the age was for maxims, and many of those
fashioned by Ninon have been preserved.  They have not
a little of the point of La Rochefoucauld, and a good deal
more benevolence.  That acidulated moralist is one of the
few masters of wit in her time whose name does not seem to
occur in her history : Madame de la Fayette perhaps con-

sidered that it was needless that her best friend should cultivate the society of so dangerous a personage. He might have appreciated too well the axiom of Ninon : " It is odd that modesty should be enforced on women who esteem nothing so much in men as impudence "; and " You must choose whether you will know a woman or love her." I should like to read more of the maxims of Ninon than M. Magne quotes, but he does not say where they are preserved.

Her flashes of improvised verbal wit were even more celebrated than her polished epigrams. She said that the jokes of the Duc de Lesdignières set her teeth on edge like the scraping of a knife on a plate. She did not spare the Great Monarch himself; when Louis XIV. gave some appointment to M. de Louvois, Ninon remarked that the King was like Caligula, " who made his horse a consul." Louis XIV. himself dreaded the tongue of this formidable observer, and when he took any step of importance could not avoid asking : " What will Ninon say ? " Arsène Houssaye has gone so far as to declare that, towards the end of her life, Ninon became " the conscience of the King and of public opinion." Perhaps this is going too far, although a sarcasm of hers, repeated at Court, is known to have prevented Dom Pelot from becoming Bishop of Sisteron. She died, calm and impenitent to the last, on October 17, 1705, having reached her eighty-sixth year.

A portrait of Ninon de Lanclos, in the Marseilles Museum, betrays that persistent juvenility which was the wonder of her time. The hair, doubtless with the aid of artifice, is worn in the curious mode familiar to us in the best-known painting of Mme. de Sevigné; it has become blonde, whereas in the portrait Mignard painted of Ninon in her youth it was as black as a raven's wing. The eyes, however, have retained their extraordinary charm, and the little pouting mouth, with its full, small lower lip, has all the appearance of girlhood. She was never, it would seem, a beauty in the same sense as was her great rival, Marion de Lorme, but she excelled in a voluptuous sweetness wedded to an enchanting brightness and freshness of expression. The moralist may contemplate her features with indulgence, since no figure of the same triumphant type will ever trouble the sensibilities of mankind again.

# CIBBER'S APOLOGY

# CIBBER'S APOLOGY

WHETHER the books which are loosely called " English classics " should be reprinted with notes and prefatory matter, or should be reproduced in the naked majesty of their original, is a question which has been hotly contested. It must be decided, if at all, in accordance with the taste of the reader. There are those who, like the late Austin Dobson, confess that in many books they like the notes much better than the text, while there are others who prefer that their " Paradise Lost " or their " Rape of the Lock " should reach them exactly as the writer left it.

There is no arguing about such matters, but I think it must be admitted that certain works can hardly be trusted out of the book-shop without some aid from the costumier. Cibber's famous " Apology " is one of them. A completely un-edited reprint of it, such as the handsomely printed one before me, cannot be called satisfactory, because it is incomplete and misleading on a multitude of points where the nature of the subject demands exactitude. Besides, although Cibber wrote very pleasantly, his text is hardly one of those sacred arks of style which the profane commentator may not so much as touch. Cibber really calls out for an editor, and I must not praise the Golden Cockerell Press for having sent him into the wold with no shadow of guidance.

Although the " Apology " has been frequently reprinted, and is a very accessible book, so far as I am aware it has only once received the editorial care which it demands. The late Robert W. Lowe, whose early death deprived us of

a most painstaking scholar, issued in 1889 a reprint which
was a miracle of patient research and accurate interpretation.   This edition, which seems to have become rare, has
not been superseded.   The " Apology " is a delightful work,
but it is one which cannot be accepted as a flawless com-
pendium of facts.   It was composed during the last retirement of the author, who signed it on his sixty-eighth birthday.   He prepared it at Bath, probably with few documents
at hand, depending largely on his memory, which was
powerful but treacherous.   The character of the book
suggests to me that it was dictated, not written, since it is
masked by a curious indolent volubility, as of an extremely
lively old gentleman, leaning back in a padded chair and
talking to a secretary.

The " Apology " is always quoted among famous auto-
biographies, but that term hardly describes it with accuracy.
It is not a Life in the strict sense, since it passes rapidly, or
even in complete silence, over many of the principal events
of the author's career.   Looking back into what he calls
" this chiaroscuro of my mind," Colley Cibber saw little
or nothing outside the walls of the theatre.   It was the
stage and nothing but the stage, with his own figure strutting about in front of the footlights.   The reader, less interested in the theatrical intrigues of past times than the
author, wishes that the latter could have been persuaded
to dwell on his general adventures.   Some of the slight
occurrences of his childhood are delightfully told, and then
he disappears into the green-room for good and all.   We
must, however, accept his " Apology " for what it really
is, a short history of the English stage from 1660 to 1730,
with particular reference to the vivacious author of " The
Careless Husband."

One of the most vivid and amusing objects exhibited in
the National Portrait Gallery is the bust of Colley Cibber in
plaster, coloured to imitate life, which was given by Cibber

himself to Mrs. Clive, and by her (I think) to Horace Walpole. This bust is not signed, but who can have modelled it if not Roubillac, for it is a masterpiece? On this question I should like to have the opinion of Mrs. Esdaile, who is the best living authority on Roubillac. Colley was accustomed to the air of a studio, since his father was the famous Caius Gabriel Cibber, the Danish statuary, who carved the maniacs over the gates of Bedlam, and those four statues on the façade of Trinity College Library, whch are familiar to all Cambridge men; he married a Rutlandshire heiress, Jane Colley. The future dramatist was born in London on November 6, 1671. We should be glad to know some particulars of his early life, but he is in too great a hurry to be off strutting on the stage. He went to school near the home of his mother, whose family seem by this time to have lost their money. Charles II. died when Colley was a schoolboy, but he remembered seeing that affable monarch playing with his dogs and feeding his ducks in St. James's Park, and he celebrated his decease in an Oration. This and an Ode composed in praise of the new King have fortunately perished.

Rude wits, when the " Apology " was being widely discussed, called it " Colley upon Cibber." But what else should an autobiography be? Our complaint to-day may rather claim that we ask for more of Cibber from Colley. The author introduces himself in a clever but uneasy dedication " to a certain gentleman," who has been identified as " that wise and honest Minister," Henry Pelham. This is a long and very self-conscious document, dealing with what Cibber garrulously analyses as " my vanity." For some reason or another, he seems to have been always docketed as the typical frivolous egotist, and he suffered from the sneers of men who, he was convinced, were quite as vain as he was. Probably he exasperated his contemporaries by his flightiness, his bursts of high and low

spirits, his incessant reference of all subjects to their bearing
on his own career.   When he retired into private life, and
looked back over his adventures, he was conscious that his
levity had done his credit wrong; he was anxious to prove
that he was not such a fool as he had looked.   This showed
a wise discrimination, but did not enhance the merit of his
performance as an autobiography.

We have to bear in mind that this long book does not
cover nearly the whole of Cibber's life, which was extended
to the verge of ninety years.   The personal part of it begins
with his début on the stage in 1689, and ends with his
first leaving it in 1697.   But although he continues to make
copious references to his own more or less successful appear-
ances, he ceases to be a very prominent figure in his own
book, which aims in reality at offering an exhaustive
commentary on the inner history of the stage from the
reopening of the theatres at the accession of Charles II. to
the far-reaching result of the attacks on the immorality of
the stage made by Jeremy Collier.

This summary covers the whole of one of the most
rounded and detachable periods in all our literary history
—namely, our drama from the Resoration to the Revolution.   Cibber is the latest, as Davenant was the earliest,
of our Restoration dramatists, and he was well fitted
by his position to review the whole theatrical scene.   The
drama, in a literary form, came almost suddenly to an
end with the seventeenth century.   One or two survivors,
in particular Farquhar and Southerne, with Cibber himself,
may be quoted, but on broad lines the death of Dryden and
the production of " The Way of the World " closed in 1700
what had started in 1660.

To this body of drama Colley Cibber himself contributed
so abundantly that the bibliographers mention nearly
thirty of his compositions.   But most of them were poor
affairs, the best being " Love's Last Shift " (incautiously

translated by a Frenchman as "La Dernière Chemise de l'Amour ") and " The Careless Husband." These are comedies in the Congreve-Vanbrugh tradition, and are not without a sprightly grace. I wonder that in these days of revival no one has retrieved " The Careless Husband," which was described long after the author's death as containing " perhaps the most elegant dialogue extant in any dramatic piece that has yet appeared in any language whatever." I am afraid that my colleague, Mr. Agate, would not endorse this eulogy, though I feel sure that he would have applauded Mrs. Oldfield in the part of Lady Betty Modish. Mr. Agate would agree with Congreve, who said that the play was nothing but a set of fine gentlemen and ladies talking together to dazzle the ridiculous town. But most Restoration comedy is little more than that, and I fancy that a performance or two of " The Careless Husband " might be found endurable to-day. Cibber's farces and tragedies and adaptations from Shakespeare are terribly flat and empty, but the comedies of his early youth are not dull.

The most amusing episode in Cibber's life, so far at least as modern readers are concerned, is his quarrel with Pope. Everybody knows that, in revising " The Dunciad," Pope removed Theobald, that worthy Shakespearian pedant, from the lap of the goddess of Dullness, and let Cibber sprawl there instead. This has been regarded by successive critics as " a lasting injury " to the poem and an instance of injudicious spite, Cibber, though a fribble, or, as we should say, a light-weight, being anything but dull. Even Leslie Stephen thinks that Cibber cuts a thoroughly incongruous figure among the dullards. In fact, it has come to be a commonplace that this was the one great tactical blunder in Pope's satiric career. But I think something must be said in defence of this piece of savage pleasantry.

It was not the Colley Cibber of the comedies and the

farces of whom Pope was speaking.   We must bear in mind
the date and the occasion of the first attacks.   I discount
the old story that Pope was infuriated by some gag introduced by Cibber into a revival of " The Rehearsal."   I
do not find that the hits at the comedian began to be at all
severe until, in 1731, Cibber contrived to be appointed Poet
Laureate.   This really was a scandal, although no better
writer was at the moment his competitor.   But he outdid
Eusden, his immediate predecessor, in pompous mediocrity
and proved himself, indeed, as a serious versifier, the worst
who ever wore the laurel in England.

Now, it is too often forgotten—it was forgotten the other
day even by so penetrating a critic as Mr. Lytton Strachey
—that Pope's leading characteristic was loyalty to the
dignity of literature.   It animated alike his loves and his
hatreds, his irony on Atticus no less than his scorn of
Oldmixon.   His gibes at Colley Cibber have seemed to be
the one exception, but let us examine them.   We must put
out of mind the comedies of more than thirty years before;
we must think of what Cibber was when he chose to present
himself as a Laureate.   The fulsome compliments of " dukes
and butchers " which welcomed the Odes :

> then swells the Chapel Royal throat—
> " God save King Cibber! " mounts in every note.
> Familar White's, " God save King Colley ! " cries;
> " God save King Colley ! " Drury Lane replies :
> Back to the Devil the last echoes roll,
> And " Coll " each butcher roars at Hockley Hole.

The fulsome praise of thoroughly bad verse by incom-
petent and venal critics—this was what always infuriated
Pope.   Nor could there be a graver instance of dullness than
was exemplified by Colley Cibber as a Pindaric Laureate :

> While o'er our vanquished hearts alone
>   Dullness, great queen ! would greatly reign;
> She binds old Colley to her throne,
>   And Colley hugs the leaden chain.

He continued to hug it till he died, and each successive year he justified the scorn of Pope.

It was a very different Colley who wrote those invaluable portraits of the great actors of the Restoration which form the best pages of the " Apology." His talent lay, certainly not in writing horrible odes, describing how

> George, our Faith and Rights defending,
> Gives to god-like glory grace,

nor even in turning out neat feathery dialogue between fine gentlemen and smart ladies, but in analysing with keen discrimination the qualities of the principal ornaments of the English stage before its decline and fall. Were it not for Cibber's description of the appearance, manners and peculiarities of the most eminent performers, our conception of the Restoration stage would be almost blank. In his pages, the majesty of Betterton, the grace of Kynaston, the merriment of Nokes, the sullen force of Sandford live again for us, as though Holbein had survived to paint them. We see once more the shining dignity of Mrs. Oldfield and the blooming passion of Mrs. Bracegirdle, for whom it was ever a whim among the youthful and the gay to have " a taste or *tendre*." The impressions of Hamlet have been myriad, but there is room among them for

" the light into which Betterton threw the scene [with the Ghost], which he opened with a pause of mute amazement. Rising slowly to a solemn trembling voice, he made the Ghost equally terrible to the spectator as to himself. In the descriptive part of the natural emotions which the ghastly vision gave him, the boldness of his expostulation was still governed by decency, manly but not braving, his voice never rising into a seeming outrage or wild defiance of what he naturally revered. To preserve this medium between mouthing and meaning too little, to keep the

K

attention pleasingly awake more by a tempered spirit than by mere vehemence of voice, is of all the master-strokes of an actor the most difficult to reach.   In this none yet have equalled Betterton."

Cibber has much that is interesting to say about the relation of the theatre to dramatic literature.   The attempts which have been made in our own time to revive Restoration tragedy on the stage have failed because of our modern repugnance to rant.   The comedies, though what is styled "artificial," please us much better.   We are inclined to regard Dryden, and more particularly such writers as Otway and Nat Lee, as charlatans of passion, because of the windy violence of their tirades.   Cibber shows that it was the taste of the pit which forced this kind of writing on the poets, and insisted that the actors should mouth and roar their lines.

By far the most popular of Revolution tragedies was Lee's "Rival Queens," in which ridiculous bombast is veiled, or as it were varnished, with a coat of language often considerably beautiful.   The part of Alexander the Great in this piece was the very acme of rant, and Cibber shows what danger Betterton and even Kynaston ran in attempting to moderate the fustian by delicate acting.   It was the fustian which the public wanted, not the charms of Betterton's elocution, and they no more desired sense in Lee's grandiloquence " than connoisseurs think it essential in the celebrated airs of an Italian opera."

The opera is a cloud on the horizon of all Cibber's narrative.   He regarded it as the enemy which would ultimately destroy the theatre.   Operas were forbidden until the Lord Chamberlain released them in 1708.   Cibber says : " After this new Regulation, the first opera that appear'd was ' Pyrrhus.' "   R. W. Lowe has no note on this statement, but I think this must have been the version of

Scarlatti's Italian made by MacSwiney and performed at the Haymarket in 1709. The incursion of the opera was something like that made by the cinema at the present time, and filled old playgoers with indignant alarm. It enjoyed what Cibber sympathetically calls a " disagreeable prosperity," and synchronising, as it did, with an almost abrupt collapse of talent in the dramatists, it was indeed alarming. But hope springs eternal behind the illusion of the footlights.

# A  SENTIMENTAL  SHEPHERD

# A SENTIMENTAL SHEPHERD

A HUNDRED and fifty years ago the little estate called The Leasowes, in Shropshire, was commonly admitted to be " amongst the principal of those delightful scenes which persons of taste are desirous to see." It lay, and in sadly diminished glory still lies, about half a mile short of Halesowen, on the way from Birmingham to Bewdley. So early as 1763 a fear was expressed by those who " trod with awe those favour'd bowers " that time or a change of taste might destroy its peculiar beauties, since these were elaborately artificial. The fear was not unfounded. What the present condition of The Leasowes may be I do not know, but when I visited it many years ago—an excursion neither difficult nor attractive—it had sunken to a state so squalid and ruinous that it was hardly possible to believe that it had once been the cynosure of landscape gardening and the theme of a choir of poets. When it was at the height of its elegant redundancy, The Leasowes was a little paradise in an agricultural wilderness, and ravished the imagination with its gloomy groves, its easy swells, its aquatic rock-work, and its sublime cascades. All this was the work of a fat bachelor bard to whom posterity has not been kind, and of whose celebrity several of his most powerful contemporaries were jealous. William Shenstone, the typical figure of mid-eighteenth-century sensibility, deserves to be reviewed without prejudice.

His father was a " plain, uneducated " local yeoman ; his mother, of slightly higher rank, had some landed property. William went to Pembroke College, Oxford, where, although

135

his dress was negligent even to a fault, he was accounted a beau.   He wore his own hair, which had early turned grey, " in a particular manner "—that is to say, to judge by the portraits, smooth at the top, but curled and very much fluffed at the sides.   During ten sleepy years at the University he did nothing except write verses; his parents being dead, trustees looked after his business so carefully that in middle life he was able to abandon himself to the beautifying of his little estate in Shropshire.   He was about thirty-five years of age when, having been crossed in love, he settled at The Leasowes, and devoted himself to landscape gardening.   Nothing can improve Dr. Johnson's account of what happened :—

" He began from this time to point his prospects, to diversify his surface, to entangle his walks, and to wind his waters; which he did with such judgment and such fancy as made his little domain the envy of the great, and the admiration of the skilful; a place to be visited by travellers and copied by designers."

For fifteen years he lived a hermit's life among his grottoes and his shrubberies, seldom leaving home, but eager to receive at The Leasowes, not merely a group of poetical friends, but distinguished strangers and sprigs of exotic nobility.   There is evidence that he became eccentric and peevish from battling with an army of domestic, agricultural, and social difficulties, since the whole adventure at The Leasowes was a struggle between art and nature. A forgotten novel by Richard Graves, author of " The Spiritual Quixote," should be examined by those who are interested in Shenstone.   In this work, called " Columella: or the Distressed Anchoret," Graves, who had been one of Shenstone's most intimate friends, makes not unkindly fun of his final troubles at The Leasowes.

These troubles culminated in financial disaster, or rather in the fear of it, for Shenstone died just solvent, although gravely embarrassed. All his little fortune had been dissipated on his woods and his waters. His death, which was " hastened by his anxieties," occurred in his fiftieth year, but we are told that he seemed much older, for " he was a lamp that spent its oil in blazing." But " blazing " seems to be too strong a word for Shenstone, who glimmered rather than flared; he was more a glow-worm than a torch. Dr. Johnson, who was so near-sighted that he could see nothing six yards in front of him, mocked at Shenstone's embellishments, but to more normal eyes they seemed beautiful and praiseworthy. They responded, with curious exactitude, to his verses, which enjoyed great popularity and exercised remarkable influence for half a century. No doubt there were always readers who said :—

> I sits with my feet in a brook,
>     And if anyone axes me why,
> I hits him a crack with my crook,
>     For sentiment kills me, says I !

But they were the exception. Most persons of culture liked to indulge their sensibilities, and honoured those who sacrificed everything to the pursuit of Elegance. Among such prophets, no one had been more devoted, more plaintive or more truly rural than the impassioned Shepherd of The Leasowes.

The extensive popularity of Shenstone's poetry is rather difficult to account for, since he does not seem to have done anything to foster it. He printed for his friends an anonymous pamphlet in 1737, including in it the first draft of " The School-Mistress," of the revised form of which the Clarendon Press now issues a very pretty facsimile. This was a mild burlesque piece in Spenserian stanza, and remains to-day the most durable work of Shenstone, but it produced no effect in 1737. Later, Shenstone attracted the admiring friendship of Robert Dodsley, who was the most influential publisher of the day, and who was untiring in the collection and dissemination of Shenstone's scattered writings. But the real reason of the success was, doubtless, the exactitude with which the bard of The Leasowes responded to the taste of the age. No one could be more middle-eighteenth-century than he was. "The School-Mistress" is doubtless Shenstone's cleverest poem, but it is the least characteristic. To see him in his essence, we must brace ourselves to read the "Elegies," and then the "Songs" and "Ballads." It has been the habit of critics, who find eighteenth-century lyric tiresome, to complain of its "insincerity." No doubt a good deal of what once was read, and is read no more, deserves this blame. It is written about nothing in particular by people who felt themselves called upon to write. But this was not always the case of those who cultivated the Elegy, by which they did not mean to invoke the genius of the tomb, but to produce a kind of verse which, being "treated in such a manner as to diffuse a pleasing melancholy," should express the genuine sentiments and experiences of the singer.

If we examine, with a genuine desire to apprehend, the twenty-six long "elegies" which form the body of Shenstone's poetry, we may be baffled at first by the apparent conventionality of the style. Reading more carefully, we find that each poem is an exact transcript of the situation of his own mind. The language is simple and diffuse, and as flowing as a mourner's veil, but underneath the dimness we detect the features of a real man. Shenstone was tenderness itself, tenderness which he knew bordered on weakness, and which his friends lamented as rendering him unfit to battle with the world. Very little ever happened to him outside the hedge which ran round The Leasowes, and his idea of subjects fit for artistic treatment was limited.

The modern reader is alarmed at being told that " the

most important end of all poetry is to encourage virtue."
Nowadays, our young bloods seem to think that its most
important end is to illuminate vice. But if we contemplate the eighteenth century, we must try to grasp
the eighteenth-century meaning of language. "Virtue"
is not used by Shenstone and his disciples in the Victorian
sense. In a very different part of his essays he defines it
himself; "virtue," he says, "is the motion consonant to the
system of things." It meant harmony, delicacy, decorum;
it involved the rejection of what was shapeless and violent
and ugly. As an example, we may look at the "Elegy on
the Folly of Superciliousness," in which he describes how
he met, on Salisbury Plain, one Ianthe, a female nobly
born, with whom he dared to attempt a flirtation. Ianthe
was extremely indignant, and quitted him with the pretext
that it was going to rain :—

> Scornful she spoke, and heedless of reply
> The lovely maniac bounded o'er the plain;
> The piteous victim of an angry sky !
> Ah me, the victim of her proud disdain !

This is an incident treated in the eighteenth-century spirit
of virtue. It is also, notwithstanding its ludicrous expression, the record of an obviously real event.

After Shenstone's death, Dodsley collected his prose
writings under the title of "Essays on Men and Manners."
This work is a sort of commonplace book, doubtless filled
during lonely evenings at The Leasowes, and destined to be
read to indulgent friends on their next visit. The contents
are highly miscellaneous, passing from long essays in the
style of "The Rambler" to brief apophthegms and even to
"levities," which last, however, are not very funny. The
whole suggests good prolonged conversation on a bench
in the Lovers' Walk or under the cupola of that "slight
and inexpensive edifice," the Temple of Pan. Shenstone
kept up a stately correspondence with an accomplished

(but very plain) blue-stocking, Lady Luxborough, who was Bolingbroke's half-sister. Their letters are said to be in the British Museum, and to defy perusal. The Essays, on the other hand, are sentimental, but not dull at all, and the Maxims, though they would not awaken jealousy in the breast of La Rochefoucauld, are often neat and shrewd. There is observation of country life, as Shenstone saw it, in the following :—

"A person's manner is never easy, whilst he feels a consciousness that he is fine. The country fellow, considered in some lights, appears genteel; but it is not when he is drest on Sundays, with a large nosegay in his bosom. It is when he is reaping, making hay, or when he is hedging in his hurden frock. It is then he acts with ease, and thinks himself equal to his apparel."

Shenstone has contributed a few quotations to the permanent store of English literature. Everybody knows the epigram written in an inn at Henley, ending

> Whoe'er has travell'd life's dull round,
> Where'er his stages may have been,
> May sigh to think he still has found
> His warmest welcome at an inn !

and each generation, in spite of the crook and the pipe and the sheep, is pleased with the " Pastoral Ballad " :—

> She gaz'd, as I slowly withdrew;
> My path I could hardly discern;
> So sweetly she bade me adieu,
> I thought that she bade me return.

But " The Dying Kid," which was long regarded as the utmost triumph of sensibility, is a dead kid now; while a touch of the hurdy-gurdy spoils the anapæsts of " Yes, these are the scenes where with Iris I strayed." Even Mr. Iolo Williams, who is the main champion of eighteenth-

century lyric, moderates his transports when he deals with
the Shepherd of Halesowen.

When Shenstone passed away, on February 11, 1763,
the cleverest of his disciples, John Cunningham, brought to
the funeral a pastoral elegy, in which he summed up the
character of the deceased bard.   As this neat elegy seems
to be little known, I will quote the opening stanzas :—

> Come, Shepherds, we'll follow the hearse
>   And see our lov'd Corydon laid :
> Tho' sorrow may blemish the verse,
>   Yet let the sad tribute be paid.
> They call'd him the pride of the plain :
>   In sooth, he was gentle and kind;
> He mark'd, in his elegant strain,
>   The Graces that glow'd in his mind.
>
> On purpose he planted yon trees,
>   That birds in the covert might dwell;
> He cultur'd his thyme for the bees,
>   But never would rifle the cell.
> Ye lambkins that play'd at his feet,
>   Go, bleat—and your Master bemoan :
> His music was artless and sweet,
>   His manners as mild as your own.

With regard to rifling the cell, I think Cunningham must
have made a mistake.   Shenstone was not the man to keep
bees and not eat the honey.

# HANNAH MORE

# HANNAH MORE

On the first page of Mr. Brimley Johnson's pleasant selection from the " Letters of Hannah More," the Editor abruptly states that " her one novel is deservedly unread." Just that! I do not raise my feeble voice against so stringent a verdict, although I think that " deservedly " is rather harsh, but when Mr. Johnson does not proceed to give even the title of this " one novel," I feel hurt, because " Cœlebs in Search of a Wife " took a considerable place in my own youthful economy. Novels were excluded from my Plymouth Brother home, as being essentially " worldly " in their tendency, and that " Cœlebs " lurked in my father's swept and garnished library I can only account for by presuming that it was looked upon as a work of pure edification. It was a story, it is true, but devoted to reflections on religion and morals, while its author was a tried Evangelical. But the moralising part of the book made no impression on my infant mind, which was fascinated by the pictures of frivolous society and even perilous intrigue which were introduced (I feel sure) to indicate what should be avoided. These I revelled in, at that tender age, as being essentially " worldly," but I will not disturb the ancient illusion that " Cœlebs in Search of a Wife " was rather naughty. I shall never read it again. If I were alone with " Cœlebs " on a desert island I would not read it. I deliver it over to the scorn of Mr. Brimley Johnson, but again I ask, Why " deservedly " ?

Hannah More is a curious instance of an author whose works were immensely read in her own time, and were sold to a degree then almost unparalleled, yet have now become unreadable. Her Letters are the best of them, and that is because these are really conversation and illustrate her character. That is all that we can say survives of Hannah More; character and conversation, herself and her friends. The mass of her writings, of which no bibliographer has yet dared to give a complete list, is quite alarming, and she poured it out in an unbroken stream of strictures on Female Education and Practical Piety, and Reflections on Prayer, and Moral Sketches for more than fifty years.

She fought with " Jacobins and Levellers," and with every sort of profligate and idler, as with beasts at Ephesus. She was the perfect Evangelical warrior, " clad in shining biblical armour," dauntless in resisting every inroad of Satan into society. She was particularly fierce after 1795 in resisting the French variety of Satan. She did it because she zealously believed her message and thought it was her duty to distribute it, but she was amply and uniformly rewarded. It is said that of her " Shepherd of Salisbury Plain " more than a million copies were sold. Hannah More, in an age when women had little chance of success, rose from nothing at all to wealth. In spite of her hospitality and her lavish benevolence, she was worth £30,000 when she died, and she had made it all by her pen. Mr. Brimley Johnson rather severely calls her " scribbling Hannah," but she scribbled to some tune.

She did not, however, scribble for the twentieth century. It is difficult to suppose that one human being breathes who has read " The Influence of Religion on the Conduct of Life," which made a sensation, in two volumes, in 1811. Even to think of it now induces a faintness at the heart. Nor is there any hope of popular revival for an " Estimate of the Religion of the Fashionable World," issued anonymously in 1791. Yet when these and a multitude of similar works were published they were snapped up like hot cakes. Of " Cœlebs " itself, the " deservedly unreadable," ten editions were sold in the year of publication. (This was 1809. In his introduction Mr. Brimley Johnson gives no dates, not even the date of Miss More's death, 1833. I like an introduction to be informative.)

With this complete disappearance of her published writings, it might seem that the writer, too, would disappear, but this is not the case. Miss Hannah More lives, and will always live, in the gossiping annals of her age, as a bluestocking, as the friend of great wits, and as an educational reformer. We no longer regard her as a great author, but we shall always think of her as a personage.

The Letters which Mr. Brimley Johnson has deftly boiled down from some eight unwieldy volumes of correspondence begin in 1773, when, at the age of twenty-eight, Hannah More proceeded to London. Her career before that time had been very quiet. She was the fourth of the five daughters of a Gloucestershire schoolmaster; all the girls were active and clever, but Hannah surpassed the rest in precocity. They all had to work for their living.

From early childhood it was Hannah's ambition " to go to London and see the bishops." In the fullness of time this wish was gratified to the full, for she was received in town with open arms, and she saw Dr. Samuel Johnson, who was better than many bishops. If we may believe some of her biographers, she had published a pastoral drama at the age of seventeen. But has anyone seen an edition of " The Search after Happiness " earlier than 1773, when Hannah was twenty-eight? My own belief is that this little drama was printed under the auspices of Garrick, and was an early result of the young lady's surprisingly triumphant entry into the Metropolis.

Oddly enough, the date of this entry, the most important event in Hannah More's life, is doubtful, but it probably occurred early in 1773. She had just gone through an embarrassing but lucrative amatory experience, on which Mr. Brimley Johnson lightly touches. No doubt a change of scene was called for, and with a sister she sallied forth to conquer London. She formed " the resolution to avoid a similar entanglement," and accepted with cheerfulness the prospect of a long single life. She would exist solely for literature and religion and friendship.

Her introduction into the most select intellectual society was instant; her naïveté, her enthusiasm and her vivacity prevailed. All the pride of London—" every wit and every wit-ess "—was at her feet, and that in spite of a tactful modesty which declared that she " felt a worm in such society." An impromptu on her first sight of Garrick in " King Lear " captivated the famous actor and his wife, and she passed at once into their intimacy. He introduced her everywhere, and we find her staying for months at a time in the house of the Garricks, by whom she was presented to Johnson and his circle of celebrated literary ladies.

The fact about Hannah More which is most widely known is that Dr. Johnson snubbed her with extreme severity on a famous occasion. According to Mrs. Thrale, Miss More began " singing his praise in the warmest manner," and the sage received it all with complacency, until suddenly she went too far in her " peppering," as Goldsmith called it, and the terrible old lion " turned suddenly to her, with a stern and angry countenance, and said, ' Madam, before you flatter a man so grossly to his face, you should consider whether or not your flattery is worth his having.' "

That Dr. Johnson said something of this kind is confirmed by Boswell, but there are comments to be made upon it. The most complete version is given by Fanny Burney, in 1778, on the authority of the Sewards, who were the most spiteful of backbiters. But Hannah More had known Dr. Johnson intimately since at least 1774. They were the closest friends in 1776, when Mrs. Montagu merrily, but " publicly," declared that she did not think it prudent to trust Dr. Johnson and Miss Hannah alone together, " with such a declared affection on both sides." It was " duck " and " deary " and " little fool " and every sort of familiar pleasantry between them, and so it continued to be until long after the terrific snub which is so often quoted.

It is absurd in treating Dr. Johnson's vagaries of speech to accept them at their present face-value. The reproof administered, according to the gossips, to poor Hannah More would have put an end to all friendship and, indeed, all communication, if it had been seriously administered. But we may well believe that the " stern and angry coun-tenance " is an invention of the Seward and the Thrale, and that Johnson merely snapped at Hannah, as he so often snapped at his oldest and most faithful friends, with terrific reverberation at the moment, but with no further result. The curious may note his not dissimilar reply, also to Hannah More, about the armchair, where Johnson instantly undid the effect of the blow by turning it against himself.

It is plain that Hannah More, in this early stage of her career, earned a reputation for flattery. She found herself in the midst of the famous club of " The Blues," learned ladies who had gathered round the blue worsted stockings of that redoubtable philanderer, Dr. Benjamin Stillingfleet, and who, now that he was dead, continued to outdo one another in azure feats. Among these eminent literary gentlewomen, Mrs. Elizabeth Montagu, the Shakespearian critic, and Mrs. Chapone, famous for a work on the " Im-provement of the Mind," were predominant, but there were many others whose names are still familiar to students of the Johnson period.

They were accustomed to high praise from accepted authorities—" I have known several ladies eminent in literature, but Mrs. Montagu excels them all "—and the young enthusiast from Bristol had to earn her place in the warm circle. She did so with a flow of compliments which was perhaps overpowering.

She published, after a few years' experience, a poem which is doubtless the most agreeable of her works, though no critic to-day would echo Dr. Johnson's outburst that " no name in English poetry might not be glad to own ' Bas Bleu.' " This was a glorification of the female members of the " Blue Stocking Club," written in easy verse which emboldened the infatuated sage to declare that Miss Hannah More was " the most powerful versificatrix " of the age. Flattery, it is plain, was not the monopoly of the lady, who in " Bas Bleu " does go very far in eulogy. Fanny Burney, who never appreciated Hannah More very much, declared that the lines addressed to herself :

> Mute Angel, yes ! Thy looks dispense
> The silence of intelligence ;
> Thy graceful form I well discern
> In act to listen and to learn ;
> Thy wondrous power, thy secret charm
> Shall Envy of her sting disarm,

and so on, were " preposterous," although she liked them. But it was not easy for any Blue to regard with complacency any other lady whom Johnson called " ducky."

When she was approaching her forty-third year, Hannah More, who had always been serious, took up religion very earnestly. The death of Garrick was a great shock to her, and the ministrations of that terrible evangelist, John Newton, completely weaned her from the world. But not from literature, since her great activity as a writer begins with her conversion. Mr. Brimley Johnson gives an excellent account of the work she did, in education and religious politics, through the second half of her life, which, as he justly says, was sharply divided into two parts. The institution of Sunday-schools in the wild parishes of the

Cheddar Hills was a famous example of her zeal and intrepidity in the face of almost insuperable prejudice.

In her advanced age, her views drew her into sympathetic intimacy with the family of Zachary Macaulay. It was here that the future historian, then four years of age, politely asked leave to bring her a glass of old spirits, startling the excellent lady, who had never aspired beyond cowslip wine. When Hannah More asked Thomas Babington what he knew about old spirits, he could only reply that Robinson Crusoe always took them. Mr. Brimley Johnson does not tell this story, but he gives some pleasant letters to Zachary Macaulay, in which there are impressions of " Tom." Macaulay said of her, after her death, " Hannah More was a very kind friend to me from childhood. Her notice first called out my literary tastes. Her presents laid the foundation of my library. She was to me what Ninon was to Voltaire."

The literary value of Miss Hannah More's writings has ceased to exist. At the best, they were what is called " occasional," and responded with unconscious adroitness to the immediate instincts of her own generation. Her disquisitions on morals and piety were edifying in the highest degree, and not oily or priggish, yet of a kind no longer capable of stirring the pulse or the conscience. Even in her own day there were those who resented her cascade of lukewarm eloquence. Fanny Burney, always inclined to the sub-acid, remarked that in her hortatory pamphlets Miss More " points out imperfections almost unavoidable, with amendments almost impracticable." The ungrateful Mrs. Anne Yearsley, the milk-seller poetess, was extremely rude, and there was a clerical enemy, calling himself the Rev. Archibald Macsarcasm, who pursued her with the venom of a gadfly. But, on the whole, the long life of Hannah More was as happy and successful as it was innocent and useful.

When I came up to London as a youth, I lodged in the house of a charming old lady, who, when she was a very little girl, had imbibed the elements of knowledge under the care of the Misses More at their famous female academy in Park Street, Bristol. This school was given up in 1789, and Hannah More had taken no part in its administration. However, she visited her sisters on occasion, and my aged friend remembered the sweet dignity of her movements and the almost excessive attention which everybody paid to her. This is a trifling reminiscence, no doubt, but when I recall that the nurse who tended Hannah through her infancy had waited upon Dryden in his last illness, I feel the recollection to be thrilling. And, indeed, it is surely a remarkable link to-day between 1699 and 1927.

# THE PHYSIOLOGY OF TASTE

# THE PHYSIOLOGY OF TASTE

GASTRONOMY, or the ritual of the worship of Belly-God, has been much neglected in England, where it is contemned by two great classes—the Puritans, who think it wrong to enjoy food, and the Barbarians, who do not notice what they eat. Under the shadow of this Gog and Magog, the English, although they have eaten abundantly, have shown an awkward prudery, a sort of stomachic false modesty, in discussing the arts of the table. They are afraid to approach the subject with elegance. There has been no lack of technical cookery-books, the number of which since the sixteenth century has been surprising. In 1903 Mrs. Elizabeth Robins Pennell published in America an illustrated bibliography of her remarkable collection of cookery-books. This is a very handsome quarto, which will stand on our bookshelf by the side of Mr. Peter Davies' translation. By the light of the former I peep into an absolute swarm of " closets open'd," " rich cabinets " and " complete housewives," crammed with receipts and curious directions for the kitchen. The " Bibliographie Gastronomique " of Georges Vicaire describes no fewer than 2,500 works on cookery, and he, it appears, was sadly ignorant of English enterprise in this direction.

This myriad of cookery-books, however, in whatever country it was produced, was not of an intellectual character. An enthusiast once stated that " a cookery-book has every good quality that a book can have." I think this excessive when we apply it to the ordinary companion of the housekeeper. A book should have, among other good qualities, style and originality, and these are wanting in the treatises on cooking which have pullulated in England. Hannah Glasse, who published her famous " Art of Cookery " in 1747, a folio for which extravagant prices are now given, was no philosopher, although to her is attributed the maxim " First catch your hare." If this be hers, it constitutes her sole claim to be thought an amusing writer. For the rest, she merely explains, in a perfectly humdrum way, how hogs' puddings should be made, and how cherries should be jarred, and how to arrange " a number of pretty little dishes fit for a supper." The French have always excelled us in this department, and I suppose that " Le Vrai Cuisinier François " of La Varenne (which I have not seen) is greatly superior to Gervase Markham's " English Housewife " (which I possess and delight in). These are both of the early seventeenth century. But I do not believe that there was one gastronomical literary artist in Europe until the beginning of the nineteenth century, although cookery-books swarmed in all languages.

This is why I insist on comparing Mrs. Pennell's ingenious work with the outwardly similar volume before me. The latter supplements the former, and takes up the subject where that left it. It is notable that the American lady, whose erudition is manifest, makes but one reference, and that a casual one, to the greatest of all gastronomes—our illustrious Brillat-Savarin. The reason is that she breaks off at the end of the eighteenth century. The old school of cookery-book, brought down in long descent from the ancient classic Apicius, came to an end about the time of the French Revolution. Out of its ruins arose Grimod de la Reynière, who wrote an Almanac of Gourmands, in eight volumes, which approached the subject from an entirely fresh point of view, and so led the way for Brillat-Savarin, who produced in the fulness of time what is by far the most eloquent and distinguished work on gastronomy which the world has seen. This book, " La Physiologie du Goût," was issued in 1825, and the present volume is a celebration of its centenary. During the last hundred years Brillat-Savarin has had a host of imitators but no rival. His book remains the one masterpiece of its order.

The old cookery-books had been compiled by professional cooks, such as the once-celebrated Will Rabisha, or Sarah Martin, who was " many years housekeeper to the late Freeman Bower, Esq., of Bawtry." When the closet of the eminently learned Sir Kenelm Digby was opened, and excellent recipes for conserving and candying were revealed, it was doubtless in the kitchen, not the library, of the knight that they were recorded. Even the stately La Varenne was the servant of the Marquis d'Uxelles. But Brillat-Savarin was not a cook, nor even a *maître d'hotel*. He had never had to dress roasts and boileds for his living, nor to tremble for the fate of his kickshaws and his poignant sauces. He was an artist and a gentleman; to be more particular, he was a lawyer in active practice.

Mr. Davies gives a life of Brillat-Savarin, succinct but sufficient, and it is odd to discover that this unruffled philosopher of the appetite, whose temper suggests the quietude of a Leyden jar, actually lived through and in the midst of the wildest social turmoil in history. Jean Anthelme Brillat-Savarin, afterwards Chevalier of the Empire, was born at Bellay in the Ain on April 2, 1772. The thoughtful reader will note the propinquity to the Bresse, a district unrivalled to the present day for succulent poultry and other delicious meats. He was well connected —the beautiful Madame de Récamier was his cousin—and he rose rapidly in the law. Accepting the Revolution, he held important legal posts in the Parisian Government, but was denounced during the Terror, and fled to America. In 1796 he was allowed to return to France, and he lived in Paris, wealthy and respected, to the age of seventy. He

had only just finished his famous book when he caught cold
in church and died on February 2, 1826. Brillat-Savarin
was a learned and affluent gentleman, who chose for his
pleasure to become the hero of gastronomy.

Brillat-Savarin was determined to give dignity to a
subject which had been treated with sufferance, if not even
with contumely. His work opens with a series of aphorisms
which he designed to be the foundations of a science of
gastronomy. " Beasts feed : man eats : the man of
intellect alone knows how to eat." Would that it were so !
" The discovery of a new dish does more for the happiness
of mankind than the discovery of a new star." What an
uplifting thought ! " Tell me what you eat : I will tell
you what you are." Listen to that, ye High Brows, and
be wise ! Brillat-Savarin is alive to the necessity of charming
and even amusing his reader, and he is not averse from a
certain exaggeration, which, however, we shall greatly
misjudge if we think it either satirical or frivolous. The
author, a man of wide social experience, is acquainted with
many things, but dwells specially on food. He regards it
quite seriously as the most important thing in existence :
" The fate of nations hangs upon their choice of food," and
the happiness of individuals is bound up in it. He is
intensely desirous to make converts to what is his religion ;
he admits no trifling with the sacred theme. Those who
decline to admit the merit of a roast turkey, varnished in
golden gravy, emit a paradox which demands, and obtains,
a double refutation. He is anxious not to be thought a
compiler. His notes represent the entirely original observation of many years. He had watched the effects of diet on
the human body through a whole lifetime, and so vast
was the subject that he constantly postponed his manual,
for the sake of greater completeness. At last his physician,
Dr. Richaud, obliged him to release his MS. to the printing
press, only just in time, as we saw just now.

The old cookery-books had been pedestrian affairs, indifferent to form and grace. Brillat-Savarin was the first, and continues to be the best of gastronomic artists with the pen. He was an excellent writer in the mode of the end of the eighteenth century, nourished on a study of Voltaire and Buffon, but enlivened by little eccentricities of his own, He rather whimsically considered that the French language, as spoken in polite circles, was not rich enough. Like Malherbe in an earlier age, he descended to the quays to catch the colloquialisms of the porters and carters. He introduced the local names of foods and methods into his style. For instance, he thought to use the English *sip* instead of the awkward phrase *boire à petites reprises*, when, just in time, he discovered the old French word *siroter*. He is academic, and yet at the same time an innovator. For some odd reason he thought that French was dying as a pure language—" in the year 2825 I shall only be read with the help of a dictionary." We cannot guess what will be read after a thousand years, but certainly Brillat-Savarin can at present be read with perfect satisfaction, even by dyspeptics.

When the effect of his measured enthusiasm has begun to wear off, the reader watches for his anecdotes as for purple patches. Brillat-Savarin is a perfect narrator, and he tells his stories with incredible gusto. I do not think that he mentions Dom Jean de Watteville, a learned Carthusian about whom Saint Simon has something to say in an early volume of his Memoirs, and I may therefore remind the reader that the Dom slew, in a country tavern, a gentleman whose only fault was that he proposed to share a capon, which was the sole substantial food in the inn. This gentleman wanted a wing and a slice of the breast, and therefore the monk, who meant to eat the whole bird, ran him through the body. Brillat-Savarin would not have commended this act, but I do not think that he would have blamed it very severely. He would have considered that Dom Jean's gastronomic enthusiasm partly condoned his rash act. He himself proposed the foundation of an Academy of Gastronomy, and believed that if he had the good fortune to accomplish this feat, his name would go down " from age to age, linked with the names of Noah and Bacchus, Triptolemus, and all the benefactors of humanity." The genuineness of his zeal was patent beyond all cavil.

From Brillat-Savarin's notes and conclusions we easily gather that the art of dining rose to its height of excellence towards the end of the eighteenth century, and was rudely shaken by the Revolution. This is what we should expect. No gourmand would go to-day to Soviet Russia for a Lucullus feast. Some of the stories in the " Physiology of Taste " betray the devotion of the clergy to the table. I like the case of Father Fabi, who, in Brillat-Savarin's youth, always appeared at Bellay when the beccafico season began, and remained there until those delicate birds withdrew. Beccaficos were to him what golf is to the well-to-do clergy of the present day. The appetites of the *ancien régime* were amazing, and where all were on a grand scale, those of the clergy continued to predominate. Among these soutaned athletes the Curé of Bregnier stood eminent. The youthful Brillat-Savarin saw him steadily devour a leg of mutton to the ivory, a capon to the bone, and a salad to the bottom of the dish. He then did justice to a large white cheese, and " during the whole operation, which occupied three-quarters of an hour, the venerable priest was perfectly at his ease." Such were the men of old, but Brillat-Savarin lived to see a different race, and it is only just to say that he himself was always on the side of quality as against quantity.

This book is full of information on curious points which lie outside the range of ordinary knowledge. It is surely not generally recognised that sugar, which has become an essential part of our life, was introduced in comparatively recent times. Brillat-Savarin, who has a long and interesting chapter on the use of sugar, states that the very name of this now universal condiment was almost unknown in France in the reign of Louis XIII. By the close of the eighteenth century not a woman in Paris, who had any money, but spent more of it on sugar than on bread. Brillat-Savarin describes the foundation of the beet-sugar factories in France, and their success when the Napoleonic wars made the use of cane-sugar almost impossible. He was in favour of a great extension of this industry, and he is scornful of the narrow-mindedness of Great Britain, where, he says, " not ten persons will be found in a hundred to believe in the possibility of making sugar out of beetroot." His remarks about coffee are not less interesting. It appears that towards the year 1770 " all minds in France were simultaneously bent on discovering the best way of making coffee." Brillat-Savarin himself was among these explorers, but he has sufficient candour to confess that in his case the result was a mixture of residue and bitterness, " only fit to rasp the throat of a Cossack."

The reader will browse for hours in the pasture of this delightful book, from whose pages I must now tear myself away. The translation before me is made, I understand, by Mr. Peter Davies, who is also announced as the latest-comer among publishers. He is warmly to be welcomed in the latter as well as the former capacity. His edition is a very handsome quarto, adorned by appropriate and amusing designs, and it is prefixed by a brief essay by Mr. Machin, who always writes well, but in the present instance has hardly been inspired by the amenity and old-world charm of Brillat-Savarin. The smiling French gourmand seems on good terms with everyone, but the prose of Mr. Machin, in this particular instance, too much resembles the coffee that rasped the Cossack's throat.

M

# TOM MOORE IN WILTSHIRE

# TOM MOORE IN WILTSHIRE

In the Wiltshire church of Bromham, the tall west window, a tulip-bed of florid colour, is dedicated to the memory of a writer who is now more often derided than admired. The visitor to that remote and beautiful structure reads that " This window is placed in this church by the combined subscriptions of 200 persons who honour the memory of the poet of all circles, and the idol of his own, Thomas Moore." Out-of-doors, by the side of the plain slab which covers not merely Thomas, but Bessy and the boys, a tall Celtic cross repeats the sentiment, which it attributes to " byron " (with a little " b "). It is not easy for us to reconstruct the edifice of Moore's fame, which in the course of less than a hundred years has crumbled into dust, nor to recover the magic of the music which " floated," as Haydon said, " out of his sparkling anacreontic mouth." Nothing exemplifies the instability of taste better than the famous *dictum* of Jeffrey, stated with all the authority at his command, that of the poets of the first half of the century—who included Wordsworth, Byron, Shelley, and Keats—only two would be read by posterity, Rogers and Moore. Alas, for the foolishness of prophesying—Rogers is no longer read at all and Moore survives in a very slender sheaf of songs and a few pages of metrical satire, while " Adonais " and " Hyperion " enjoy an aftermath of universal admiration.

The fame of Thomas Moore rose to its height some ninety years ago, when, in default of professional competition, he became the most adulated man of letters in the country.

165

The decline of Scott, the death of Byron, Shelley, and Keats, the retirement of Coleridge, left the little Irish bard without a rival, and his successes were wonderful. Crabbe occasionally approached, and Tennyson was presently to exceed them, but in 1835, after the conclusion of the "Melodies," no one was so obstreperously or so amiably applauded as the poet who entered Wexford under nine triumphal arches, conducted by Nine Muses ("some of them remarkably pretty girls") to the tune of "There's a health to thee, Tom Moore!" If it was more emotional than critical, the enthusiasm was at least widespread; it embraced the humblest of the land (or of the two lands) and did not exclude Cabinet Ministers. Owing to an unfortunate circumstance, the robbery by his representative in Bermuda, the financial aspect of Moore's life was tantalising : he made, for an author of a hundred years ago, unprecedented sums of money; if he lost them, that was by a legal accident. The golden water of Pactolus dropped into a sieve, but it might have been caught in a pitcher, and then Moore would have been very rich. As it was, he enjoyed boundless notoriety and public congratulation; he lived in the company of the highest in the land. The critics agreed that he was "surely the greatest of English lyrical poets"; Irishmen revered him as their leading patriot; and when he died, a Prime Minister paused in his imperial duties to publish, in eight solid volumes, the "Memoirs, Journals, and Correspondence" of his illustrious friend.

The young gentlemen who confidently predict an immortality of fame for themselves and their friends might well reflect on the fate which has befallen Tom Moore. It would probably be difficult to find to-day a score of persons who have read the eight volumes which Lord John Russell piously put forth between 1853 and 1856. Fortunately, however, Mr. Priestley, who has a fine taste in literature, has done so, and has perceived that they can be judiciously dealt with. Here, if ever, a part is better than the whole, and it is not unreasonable to expect that this excellent selection from the too-garrulous and too-comprehensive " Memoirs " may pleasantly revive the memory of a good little man whom it was the foible of his age to treat as a great one. Moore began to keep a Diary in 1818, and he continued it until 1847, when his memory was no longer under his control. From the record of thirty years, Mr. Priestley has gathered a posy of two hundred pages which contain really everything which a reader of to-day can possibly be curious about. Here is Tom Moore, long concealed by his own verbosity, made visible again, and nothing can be more just than Mr. Priestley's attitude towards him :—

" Moore's chief faults [as a diarist] are, first, that he is apt to concentrate his and our attention upon the wrong people; in short, that many of his·swans are now geese, and little geese at that; and, secondly, that he is far too prolix, burying his good things under loads of chit-chat. For this reason there is probably no diary that gains more from a fairly drastic but judicious process of cutting and selecting than this of Moore's."

I would suggest that Evelyn is a parallel case, while, on the other hand, to cut down Pepys would be a crime. Moore's Diary, at all events, gains greatly by being compressed.

We open with the year 1818, when Moore was approaching his fortieth year. His reputation was firmly established by eight folio numbers of " Irish Melodies " and by the voluptuous romance of " Lalla Rookh." He had offended nobody, and was the friend of everybody, even of the Prince of Wales. That he had been the intimate companion of Byron did not prevent him from supporting the grim conversation

of Wordsworth with respect and sympathy. He was
at the height of his popularity, and then the clouds began
to gather. His eldest child died, his wife grew melancholy,
and the gay life in the Whig mansions of London palled
upon the poet. When it was known that the Moores were
willing to reside in the country, noblemen competed for the
honour of entertaining them. The most splendid of these
would-be hosts, the enlightened and erudite Marquess of
Lansdowne, bore off the prize, and in the autumn of 1817,
for an almost nominal rent, the poet was settled in a cottage
close, but not too close, to the magnificence of Bowood.
Through a great variety of vicissitudes, this remained
Moore's home for the rest of his life, and the cottage is the
background of the whole volume of selections before me.
Perhaps Mr. Priestley might have made this more clear, for
his volume would almost be described if we called it " Tom
Moore at Sloperton."

The opening entry is " August 24 (1818). Arrived at my
cottage." Mr. Priestley amusingly and justly says that
throughout the diary Moore " starves our visual sense."
Perhaps in sympathy with his author, who was curiously
indifferent to external objects, Mr. Priestley continues that
starvation. The only fault I can find with the mode in
which this book is prepared is that it gives the reader no
more sense than the diarist gave of the actual scene in which
the events took place. That Mr. Priestley is not hunting
for local colour is apparent from his casual use of names.
On the very first page, Bowles' parsonage at Bremhill is
called " Brenhill," and Sloperton throughout is " Slopper-
ton," in defiance of local pronunciation.

I will not emulate Mr. Priestley's austerity, for I think
that some brightness may be added to Moore's record by
a few words on the setting of the story. Sloperton lies far
outside the track of the ordinary traveller. It is a sequestered hamlet, reached by winding lanes, and after being

long sought, is hardly recognised when found. Between the two great rolling uplands into which Wiltshire is divided there lies in the very centre of the county a region of deep woodlands and winding streams, a land of elms and corn. In the heart of this sylvan haunt of silence the lovely village of Bromham sleeps in a slumber that nothing disturbs. You reach it from Devizes, turning out of the main road into a labyrinth of lanes, and from its noble church a path over the meadows brings you in a mile to Sloperton Cottage.

The Cottage is exactly what Moore would like; it is what Coleridge called " a cottage of gentility." It deprecates all comparison with grandeur, and bids you forget Longleat and Bowood, and even the vicarages of the other poets, Bowles and Crabbe. But it is commodious and almost elegant, with its three gables modestly projecting in the Wiltshire style, now denuded of the ivy that disguised them. There is nothing ancient about it, except the old red-brick wall, dividing the garden, on the further side, from the vast cornfield which Moore must often have crossed when he strolled to see Lord Lansdowne. There is still current in Devizes a legend that when the poet took his walks abroad the farmers would stop him and ask him what the weather was going to be, persuaded that he was the mystery-man of " Moore's Almanack." Mostly, however, it is held that he kept to an avenue of elms within his little domain, which he paced, rehearsing his facile and patriotic melodies. Nothing more exclusively English than Sloperton can be conceived, and it is whimsical to remember that this was the spot where the Minstrel of Erin struck the dear Harp of his country and gave all its chords to light, freedom, and song. Among the perfumes of the clover and the beans, with the tufted woods of Wiltshire blowing around him, and the bells of Bromham faintly ringing far away, Moore seems remote indeed from the land where his Young

Hero slept. Perhaps this incongruity had something to do with the fact that Ireland so soon began to look askance at her darling Bard.

Persons who have not visited Sloperton Cottage give a wrong impression when they describe it as a sort of lodge or appendage to Bowood. As a matter of fact, it is more than three miles from that hospitable pile. Bremhill, where Bowles amused himself with his grottos and his fountains, is almost as far on the other side. Trowbridge, where Crabbe wrote the "Tales of the Hall," lies further still to the west. It puzzles me to guess how the three poets met so frequently at Bowood, since no one of them could afford to keep a carriage, nor, whatever the robust Crabbe might do, can we imagine Moore or Bowles on the back of a horse. Probably the Moores walked, or, when Bessy also dined at Bowood, they would hire Phipps's gig in Bromham. No doubt, on fixed occasions, Lord Lansdowne would send a carriage; and Moore's stout little legs would carry him far. At Sloperton Cottage his walking-stick is preserved; it is strangely diminutive. In trying to reconstruct the life in 1818 and onward, a memory of "Emma" is helpful; a coach ran from Devizes to Calne, but that would not lessen the distance by more than a mile. Later on, the Moores set up a little carriage of their own, but with disastrous results, for Bessy was immediately upset in driving it and knocked it and herself "almost to pieces." Her unlucky nose kissed the ground, but, though much swollen, was not broken. After this we hear no more of this carriage: "it was a great effort for me to compass the expense of this little luxury; and such is the end of it." We still do not know how he contrived to dine so often, and sometimes to sleep, at Bowood.

But I give a false impression. The basis of the "Diary" is at Sloperton throughout, but the bright bird is far from being inside that green cage all the time. His restlessness was extraordinary, and we find him everywhere—in London, in Paris, in Dublin, flitting hither and thither, preening his plumage in the sun, and ceaselessly warbling his harmless amatory songs. The poetry of Tom Moore is so innocuous that we are amazed to find him weighed down by a reputation for licentious writing, founded on the indiscretions of the juvenile " Little " volume. When he published that very mild tale, " The Loves of the Angels," in 1823, his dearest friend, Lady Donegal, would not allow her daughter Barbara to read it. Moore was wild with fright, and talked of withdrawing the book, till that master of the proprieties, Lord Lansdowne, comfortably reassured him by pronouncing the poem " not only beautiful, but perfectly unexceptional and pure." This may have been the occasion on which an Irish gentleman, indignant at hearing Moore censured, shouted out, " Me friend Mr. Moore is an infant sporting on the bosom of Venus ! " This is not in the " Diary." The modern reader will agree with a Mr. Byng, who declared that " The Loves of the Angels " might " safely be trusted in the nursery," where indeed at the present day not even the most high-browed nursery-maid is likely to disturb it.

In his brief introduction, which gives an excellent précis of the " Diary," Mr. Priestley defines the character of the book. It is not kind of him, but it was doubtless irresistible, to quote Hazlitt's witty fling : " Mr. Moore converts the wild harp of Erin into a musical snuff-box." His ideal of life was not sublime, yet it is only justice—and a justice which has commonly been refused—to admit that Moore accepted his preposterous popularity with modesty and common sense, and was by no means the dupe of his flatterers. Even he was not always flattered, and I will tell a little story, never, I think, hitherto published, which was told me fifty years ago by the old " Orion " Horne. Horne met Moore one evening at the Leigh Hunts', Wordsworth being also present. Moore sang some of his own songs at Mrs. Hunt's piano, and was much complimented. Wordsworth was asked if he also did not admire these songs, and he replied : " Oh ! yes, my friend Mr. Moore has written a great deal of agreeable verse, although we should hardly call it *poetry*, should we, Mr. Moore ? " To which the bard of Erin, sparkling with good nature, answered, " No ! indeed, Mr. Wordsworth, of course not ! " without exhibiting the slightest resentment. I think this little anecdote is characteristic of both poets, and therefore worth preservation.

Moore's " Diary " largely consists of repartees, stories, and traits of character picked up at the tables where his merry face and delicate, polite vivacity were always welcome. This is the sort of thing :—

" Breakfasted at [Sir Walter] Scott's : Rogers there, and another person whose name I did not make out. Talking of practical jokes, Rogers' story of somebody who, when tipsy, was first rolled in currant jelly, and then covered with feathers; his exclaiming, when he looked at himself in a glass, ' A bird, by Jove ! ' Scott's story of the man whom they persuaded that the place he was walking in was full of adders; he fancying he felt an adder in his foot, and striking his foot violently with his stick, in order to kill it; hearing a hiss from out the boot, and then (as Scott said) ' pelting away ' at it again with his stick. ' Ah, now he is silent, I think I have done with him,' then taking off his boot, and finding that it was his watch which had slipped down there, and which he had been thus hammering away at, the hiss having been the sound of the spring breaking. Scott's acting of this story admirable."

So doubtless was Moore's when he repeated this harmless tale to Bessy among the roses at Sloperton Cottage in the evening.

# LA NOUVELLE HÉLOÏSE

# LA NOUVELLE HÉLOÏSE

WE may do worse in holiday times than turn to some famous book that all the world knows, at least by name, and read it, as though for the first time, so as to gauge what impression it really leaves upon the mind. Doubtless the novel, in the literature of the world, which has been more talked about than any other, and in its day had more influence, is the " Nouvelle Héloïse."

Anyone who doubts that statement, or who puts forward the claim of " Pickwick " or of " Don Quixote," has only to read the amazingly full and exhaustive prefatory essays which M. Mornet has issued as prolegomena to the edition, to be completed in four volumes, which has just been started by Professor Lanson. He will discover that " La Nouvelle Héloïse " was reprinted seventy-eight times (if not more) between 1761, the year of its publication, and 1800; and nobody knows how often since then.

Nor is the mere distribution of millions of copies by any means the end of its activity; it has been denounced, exposed, defended, explained, and repudiated more often, and more vigorously, and by more distinguished persons than any other modern book. But does anyone read it now, and is it anything but a worm-eaten relic of the past, resonant and dignified, but empty? Well, let us try to read it for ourselves and see.

Rousseau was a great reader of novels, and yet a great scorner of those of his own day, which indeed appear, from the summary of M. Mornet, to have been in the main very poor affairs. From this contempt of fiction Rousseau

175

excluded the new English novels, and particularly those of Richardson, whose "Pamela," but still more whose "Clarissa," he admired to distraction. He was bewitched by the long-drawn analysis of female virtue struggling against fate. He himself was in revolt against the dryness of the philosophers, and he had become more and more the denizen of an imaginary world, when, in the winter of 1756, he started on a mental journey of which he did not for a long time see the goal.

In the Ninth Book of the " Confessions " we may read that he began to be haunted by two imaginary women, and slowly determined that he would invent around about their contrasted beauty such a story as had never before been told in French. It was to be a fountain of fresh water springing in the desert of Philosophedom. At first, he tells us, he walked without a purpose through a land of phantoms, where all was loveliness and sensibility; gradually, against this vague background, " une espèce de roman," a sort of novel, began to evolve in his mind, and he created an image of himself, which he called Saint-Preux, to act in relation with the two perfect creatures, to be named Julie and Claire. Gradually the outline of a story defined itself, and in the autumn of 1757 Rousseau seized a quire of the finest gilt-edged paper, blue tape to bind the sheets together, and sand of mingled azure and silver to sprinkle over the burning ink. He started the work of creation, like a new Pygmalion, in an ecstasy, " avec une plaisir inexprimable."

Thus the " Nouvelle Héloïse " was begun, but it proceeded slowly. Rousseau had no experience in this kind of writing, and his pen constantly fell from his dreaming fingers. He was distracted by the composition of the " Vicaire Savoyard." There was a scheme in his mind, although at first it did not come to much, and it is a distinct misfortune that we are obliged to read the two opening books before we reach the real kernel of the story. But the essence of the novel, its entire and surprising originality, is clear from the first, although the unpractised author seems long in getting into his stride.

What we ought to note first of all is the realism of the scene. French fiction hitherto had been abundant, but vague, and all for entertainment; Rousseau is photographically Swiss, and in deadly moral earnest. His original idea was to place his story on the delicious Borromean Islands, in the Lago Maggiore, but he decided that they had " too much ornament and art for the simplicity " of his characters. It would be an entirely new thing to read a tale placed in actual landscape, with real features which everyone could recognise, genuine names and familiar incidents. The action takes place in the Pays de Vaud, at Vevey, at Lausanne, at other romantic spots on the shores of the lake. The mountains are round us, the woods, the waterfalls, the materials of the newly discovered romantic aspect. Much is effected by insisting on the innocence and gaiety of the pastoral life of Switzerland, hitherto little known in France.

Rousseau in his preface very artfully points out the novelty of his scheme by pretending to think that no philosophers, or pious people, or debauchees, or honest women, or abandoned women would read his novel; they will hate its " Gothic tone," he says. That was all non-sense; he knew perfectly well that this new manner, with its Vaudois scenery, its passion, its obstreperous virtue, its frenzied clash of emotions, would captivate a world of readers; and so it did.

The reader of to-day, accustomed to ingenuity of plot and extravagance of action, may find the opening chapters of the " Nouvelle Héloïse " tedious. Let us, however, hasten through them. A Swiss nobleman, the Baron d'Etange, has a beautiful daughter, Julie. She cannot marry below her rank, and at the dictation of her family she

N

is engaged to a virtuous neighbour, young M. de Wolmar.
But at the age of eighteen she falls in love with her tutor,
M. de Saint-Preux, who is poor and of lowly birth. The
novel, which, in imitation of Richardson, is written entirely
in letters, opens with startling abruptness, for Saint-
Preux writes to Julie, " I ought to fly from you, Made-
moiselle, I am well aware of that." He is no less infatuated
with her than she with him; after a long resistance she
yields to his passion. There is no open scandal; Saint-
Preux retires, and sails round the world with Admiral
Anson; Julie, after desolating paroxysms of remorse,
consents to marry Wolmar, and does so, swearing at the
altar fidelity to her husband. This oath is sincere, and the
remainder of the novel proceeds to describe the battle between love and loyalty which rages through the remainder of
her virtuous life. This is the point at which the " Nouvelle
Héloïse " becomes really interesting. The reader should
study with attention the silent vow which Julie makes in
church on her wedding day, for this is the key to the
story.

Six years roll by and Julie has almost forgotten Saint-
Preux, when Wolmar, ignorant of the past, invites him to
re-enter the family. Meanwhile, though he has been round
the world, he has not lost his faith in Julie. They meet;
and immediately realise that children, husband, friends,
God himself are insufficient to fill a heart which is invaded
by a permanent passion.

The modern reader must be prepared to find the
" Nouvelle Héloïse " a very long novel full of nothing but
love. It is the record of an implacable duel, not, like
" Clarissa," between virtue and a persistent seducer, but
between chastity and passion. Julie, a gentle, languid
blonde, is ever on the brink of a second fall, and is perhaps
only saved from it by the irresolution of her lover. M. Lanson has excellently said that the " Nouvelle Héloïse " is

" a voluptuous dream turned to suit a moral purpose," and this is the exact truth. There is no display of wit in it, no social subtlety, but it translates, as was never before translated, what Rousseau called—thus inventing a phrase— " the language of the heart."

The book is full of palpitations and ecstasies, revulsions and adorations, full, too, of theories and opinions. It is full of the peculiar genius of Rousseau himself, who, not easily moved to respond to love, was yet always devoured by the need of being loved. He thought of the girls in the cherry orchard at Thônes, " the idols of my heart " of twenty years before. But there was another and a later inspiration.

Rousseau had arrived at the close of the first part of his novel, and was doubting how to proceed, when his whole being was transfixed by a passion doubtless the most real that he ever experienced. He met Mme. d'Houdetot, and was like a man felled to the ground. For the first time, and for the last time, Rousseau was overwhelmed with genuine passion. The lady bore little physical resemblance to the tall blonde Julie of his dreams, for she was swarthy, marked by the smallpox, and almost a dwarf, but youth seemed to radiate from her, and in her presence Rousseau became like a man bewitched. Her character was gentle and " angelical," but her heart was given to a soldier, the Marquis de Saint-Lambert, for whom she had left her husband. She broke off, however, a fragment of her heart and gave it to Rousseau, who dreamed of such a triple relation as animates the " Nouvelle Héloïse." There was an incident, without consequences, which recalls, in a comic vein, the spiritual tragedy of the Rocks of Meillerie. The behaviour of everyone concerned would be inconceivable if we were not dealing with the end of the eighteenth century and with Rousseau. It would also be uninteresting if it were not for the effect the episode had on the composition of the famous novel.

The work now proceeded apace, and the relation between
Rousseau and Saint-Lambert was brilliantly reflected, with
quite new eloquence and ardour, in that of Saint-Preux to
M. de Wolmar.  The latter, however, is more philosophical
and complaisant than was the sarcastic lover of Mme.
d'Houdetot.  But the wild hope of Rousseau to win the
affections of that lady, and the mode in which his passion
resolved itself into virtuous friendship, are accurately
reproduced in the second half of the novel.  The careful
reader must not fail to note how the vague sentimentality of
the early books changes to substantial passion as soon as
Saint-Preux returns from the South Seas, and that is
because in the meantime a real Mme. d'Houdetot has
flashed across the life of the novelist.  If we study the
famous, and most beautifully conceived and executed,
" promenade sur le lac," we realise the new force which the
imagination of the author had gained by being founded on
experience.  The cry of Julie, " Let us go back !  The air
of this place is not good for me ! " is a prominent example
of what Rousseau had gained as an artist by being wakened
for a moment out of his sensuous melancholy, away from
the sickly world of what he called his " oneiromancy," into
an observation of real life.

The subsidiary characters in the " Nouvelle Héloïse " are
drawn with remarkable assurance.  It is true that the
patience and tact of M. de Wolmar are almost absurd, but
his position is a very difficult one, and in Saint-Preux he is
confronted by no fiery Don Juan, but by a being docile and
discreet, whom he may well judge to be without guile.
The weakness of Saint-Preux is not attractive to a modern
reader, but it endeared him to the sentimental women of
that age.  When he described his tears falling melodiously
into the Lake of Geneva, a thousand feminine bosoms beat
in dreamy delirium.  He was looked upon as a model of
virtue in distress, and lest his hero and heroine should seem

too lachrymose, Rousseau invented Claire d'Orbe, a small, vivacious brunette, all laughter and good sense, who is Julie's confidant.

The English reader will notice that as Julie is to Clarissa, so is Claire to Miss Howe in Richardson's novel. She has lived in Paris, and though Genevese, has a lively wit. The intervention of Lord Bomston (Milord Edouard) is another relief, artfully contrived. He invites the lovers to fly to his own hospitable mansion in Yorkshire, but Virtue lifts her warning finger, and they refrain from so fatal a step. The eccentric English peer, all magnanimity and independence, lightens the strain and pleasantly distracts attention. These figures animate a pastoral landscape, a Swiss Arcadia, a world of meadows flushed with flowers, runlets hurrying through the tall grass, rustic grottos, vineyards, the lake beyond, and the chill mountain theatre behind it all.

The style of " La Nouvelle Héloïse " must always preserve it for a few readers, although the immense audience it once commanded has disappeared and can never return. There is too much declamation in the letters, especially when Saint-Preux holds the pen; the book is often verbose and almost always diffuse. It is disordered, full of repetitions; it was the exact opposite of the neat style of Marivaux, then the model for novelists. But it was written with the extreme of care and diligence, since Rousseau was no improvisatore, and revised his writings with the utmost labour. M. Mornet gives the proof of this by describing the four or five versions of the text which still remain in manuscript. But this assiduity was not thrown away. The novel, remote as is its tone from what the twentieth century admires, fatiguing as we must all find its loquacity, still holds a select company by its fire, its melody, its delicious ease, its seductive sweetness. It still carries the charm of Rousseau's unsophisticated ideal, " in an orchard by the lake, with one loyal friend, one tender woman, one cow, and one small boat." Few men, and fewer women, may have the patience to read " La Nouvelle Héloïse " to-day, but for those of us who do, it

> will keep
> A bower quiet for us, and a sleep
> Full of sweet dreams.

# " ORIGINAL  POEMS "

# " ORIGINAL POEMS "

MISS BARRY has introduced the Prose and Poetry of a
charming old writer. But Mr. E. V. Lucas will, I think,
be as painfully shocked as I am by her opening sentence.
She says of Jane Taylor that "her name is almost forgotten."
The author of

> Twinkle, twinkle, little star,
> How I wonder what you are !
> Up above the world so high,
> Like a diamond in the sky

" forgotten " !   What, then, will be remembered ?   " The
Green Hat," I suppose, or " If Winter Comes " !   Has a
course of psycho-analysis for nursery use or a dialogue for
infant Communists destroyed all appetite for " My prayers
I said, I went to bed " or " In an elegant frock, trimmed
with beautiful lace " ?   Has the gloomy sophisticated child
of 1927 an undeveloped " complex " which forbids it to
enjoy " Young Jem at noon returned from school " and
" One ugly trick has often spoiled " ?   I do not believe a
word of it.   Jane Taylor is not forgotten," nor shall be,
so long as the English language is in use.

But when I say " Jane Taylor," I understand the expression to include Ann, and even Adelaide O'Keefe, though she
was only a Taylor by adoption.   The three wonderful
girls cannot be separated.   We may distinguish one Brontë
from another, but the Taylors are inseparable.   There
has been some injustice done; for Adelaide has never
received her due.   She has always been less known than
her companions, and, indeed, if Miss Barry had said that

Adelaide was "almost forgotten," I could have found no fault. Yet it was she who wrote " His petticoats now George cast off, For he was four years old," and " As William and Thomas were walking one day," that grisly monument to the barbarity of our ancestors. Indeed, the only fault I can bring against the charming little book before me is that it dislocates and therefore impoverishes the sisterhood. We have never thought before whether Ann or Adelaide or Jane wrote this or that enchanting lyric, and now the isolation of Jane distresses the memory. Our pleasure continues to exist, but it is divided by three. I ask to have back my trinity of Taylors.

In the year 1804 there slipped unobtrusively from the press an anonymous volume entitled " Original Poems for Infant Minds, by Several Young Persons," with a motto from Dr. Isaac Watts :—

> In books, or works, or healthful play
> Let my first years be past,
> That I may give for ev'ry day
> Some good account at last.

The " Young Persons " (I include Adelaide) were the daughters of an engraver, Isaac Taylor (the Second). They were brought up at Ongar in an atmosphere of literature and art, as those subjects were innocently conceived a hundred and fifty years ago. Their brother, Isaac (the Third), became the author of a famous book, " The Natural History of Enthusiasm." They were part of a happy busy family, all the members of which spent life dancing like so many fays in a moonshine of innocent enthusiasm. When the sisters published their " Original Poems," they were not old ladies, nor related to Lady Rigid of Austere Hall; Ann was twenty-two and Jane not yet twenty-one. Their youth gave their morality an attractive force, and Mr. Lucas has observed very acutely that their supreme success in

catering for little people was due in large measure to the
fact of their own childishness.

The vogue of " Original Poems " has been prolonged
beyond parallel; no " hungry generations " have trodden it
down, and the secret of its perennial effectiveness is the
direct appeal which it makes to children. In almost all
nursery literature there is a suspicion of patronage, or
at least a tendency to talk to the grown-ups over the heads
of the young audience. Even the masters of such writing
have not escaped this insidious snare. When I was a very
young man, in Copenhagen, I was once at a party where
Hans Christian Andersen told one of his famous stories to
a group of children. The occasion was perfectly charming,
but I could not help feeling that the illustrious and then
aged fabulist kept half an eye all the time on the adults.
This tendency often shows itself in an exaggerated simplicity, or even in a silliness, which is supposed to be
necessary for very young people. But children are really
serious, even savage, often remarkably didactic. Nonsense
appeals to them less readily than it does to their parents.
Hence, when they read " The Little Fisherman " (which
Miss Barry omits, I suppose because of its savagery), they
took a stern pleasure in it, as in a dreadful tale told them
by another, and older, child. No grown-up person, thinking
of other grown-ups, would have written

> Poor Harry kicked, and called aloud,
> And screamed, and cried, and roared,
> While from his wound the crimson blood
> In dreadful torrents poured,

but Jane knew by instinct how directly this false realism
would appeal to the imperfect imagination of the nursery.

That " Original Poems," like all the Taylors' writing, is
rigidly, even violently moral, has never interfered with its
success. Little children, however naughty and wilful,
enjoy hearing plain fables directed against gluttony,

selfishness, and love of dress.   With a cheerful complacency
they have listened to the depravity of " Young Thomas " :—

> In vain his mother's watchful eye,
> In vain his master's care;
> He followed vice and vanity,—
> And even learned to swear.

For generations they have been moderately moved by—

> And has my darling told a lie ?
> Did she forget that God was by ?

and interested, without special conviction, in

> 'Tis better to have a sweet smile on one's face,
> Than to wear a fine frock with an elegant lace;
> For the good-natured girl is loved best in the main,
> If her dress is but decent, though ever so plain.

" In the *main*," yes !   But there is always the underlying
sense that when you ride in a party " to see an air-balloon,"
it is best to have on your plumes and ribbons and your
India frock.   They will not make you less beloved, if only
you refrain from bragging about them.

The urgent and even rude morality of the literature of
that first Georgian age is curious and rather difficult to
account for.   It reached its apex, its sharp and shining
crest, in the prose of Maria Edgeworth and the verse of the
Taylors, and that is all, perhaps, that we remember now,
or need to remember, although there must still be readers
who recall the charm of Mrs. Brunton's two stern novels.
It is perhaps worth noticing that the " Moral Tales " were
published two years earlier than " Original Poems," while
" Self-Control " was actually being written in 1804, though
not immediately published.   This was an hour of gross
decline in the novel proper, which had sunken into what
Jeffrey called " the jargon of fashionable life " in a ridiculous riot of romance, presently to be swept away by Scott

and Miss Austen.   The field was free for the moralists with
their severe utilitarianism and their humorous censure of
sentimentality.   The output of strictly " moral " prose
and verse was enormous.   It is all turned to dust now,
except in parts of great Maria and the shining Taylors, but
there we are still made indignant by Rosalind's Purple
Jar and still smile indulgently at poor Sophia and her
Fool's Cap.

This ardour for plain domestic morality is so simple that
it does not produce the irritation which is sometimes caused
by the strenuousness of early Victorian ethics.   It has no
wide horizon, no touch of ideality, no tincture of romance or
even of religion.   The God to whom appeal is sometimes
made in it is no more than a shadow of Mamma cast vaguely
on a cloud.   About Mamma herself there is no vagueness at
all ; she is the centre of the visible universe, the final judge
beyond whose fiat there is no appeal.   The maternal
austerity is tempered by no interference from Papa, who is
rarely mentioned and is invariably ineffective.   Mamma is
the sole arbiter of conduct :—

> A lady, fashionably gay,
> Did to Mamma a visit pay;
> Sophia stared;  then whisp'ring said,
> " Why, dear Mamma, look at her head !
> To be so tall, and wicked too !
> The strangest thing I ever knew."

This office of the matriarch is universal in the moral
literature of the time, and may, I suppose, be traced to a
simplification and purification of the educational theories
of Rousseau.   The severity of domestic discipline was,
doubtless, a reaction from the licence of the French Revolution, then still regarded with extreme horror in pious
English households.   The clean didactic cut hewn between
right and wrong affects all the authorship of that first
decade of the century.   We see it in Wordsworth, in

Crabbe, in Godwin, but it yawns most uncompromisingly in Miss Edgeworth and the Taylors.

The gifted girls did not quite fulfil the brilliancy of their promise. Adelaide wrote so poorly after she left the Taylor family that it has been suggested that the poems she had signed were really the work of Ann or Jane. I do not think so, for there is an individual character in Adelaide's admirable contributions to the "Original Poems" of 1804. Probably her early talent just faded away. Ann wrote other books, married a Mr. Gilbert, and, before she died in 1866, composed an autobiography which was published in 1874. But Jane Taylor survives more actively, and this, no doubt, is why Miss Barry has severed her work and life from those of the other two. Jane was an invalid, and she died at the age of forty-one, but not until she had written the "Contributions of Q.Q.," prose essays which Mr. Lucas assures us " are often witty and always shrewd." She also wrote the novel called "Display," from which Miss Barry gives copious and amusing excerpts, and, what is more important, she published "Essays in Rhyme" which are models of their class. As a neat, graceful satire, the poem called "Recreation" deserves high praise; it occupies pages 97 to 101 in Miss Barry's selection. It recounts the visit of a young and an elder lady to a neighbour, who fed them with tea and scandal. Its humour is inimitable.

The affiliation of Jane Taylor to Pope (which I cannot discover) and to Cowper (which is obvious) has often been affirmed by her critics, but I do not think that her still closer relation to another, and contemporary, poet has ever been noticed. Yet, consider this passage :—

> That long, low shop, where still the name appears,
> Some doors below, they kept for forty years;
> And there, with various fortunes, smooth and rough,
> They sold tobacco, coffee, tea, and snuff.
> There labell'd drawers display their spicy row—
> Clove, mace, and nutmeg : from the ceiling low

Dangle long *twelves* and *eights*, and slender rush,
Mix'd with the varied forms of *genus* brush,
Cask, firkin, bag and barrel, crowd the floor,
And piles of country cheeses guard the door.

This is pure Crabbe, and not a line or an image in the piece but might come straight out " The Borough." It is a belated specimen of that utilitarian poetry which was at the height of its popularity when the tide of romanticism suddenly swept it away. The simplest, but perhaps the most durable, relics of this period of strenuous morality are " Harriet and Lucy " in prose, and " Original Poems " in verse.

# SIDONIA THE SORCERESS

# SIDONIA THE SORCERESS

WHAT a pity that no parcel-post from earth can be delivered in the Elysian Fields ! If it were, the admirers of Dante Gabriel Rossetti might club together to buy a copy of this superb edition of his favourite romance and send it to him on his hundredth birthday. He had a positive passion for " Sidonia the Sorceress," referring to and quoting from it incessantly, until he inoculated the whole Preraphaelite circle with something of his own enthusiasm. Even William Morris succumbed to the charm of the Pomeranian romance, and several minor members of the coterie made drawings and painted pictures the subjects of which were taken from its pages.

This limited but intense appreciation gives an odd value to the book, which, without it, might continue to be unknown here, as it is in its native Germany, where it was never well recognised and now is completely forgotten. It was translated by " Speranza," Lady Wilde, the mother of Oscar, and came into Rossetti's hands from some Irish acquaintance, probably William Allingham. As an example of the obscurity of the book, it is notable that the " Dictionary of National Biography," in the memoir of Lady Wilde, does not so much as mention " Sidonia," although it obviously retains far more vitality than any other work of that fervid authoress. In German literature it takes no place, but in its English garb it enjoys a curious little continuity of fame, due to the zeal of Rossetti and his friends.

The present edition, which is produced with great

magnificence of paper, print, ingenious illustration, and vellum cover, offers no explanation of the history of the book or of its author. It is, indeed, by no means easy to obtain any information on this subject, since Wilhelm Meinhold's name is unknown to the current encyclopædias and dictionaries. Even König, who includes a multitude of names in his German " History of Literature," is silent about Meinhold. But from obscurer German biographical sources I have found out certain facts which were, until now, quite unknown to me, and are probably not familiar to my readers, or to purchasers of this stately quarto of " Sidonia." It appears that Wilhelm Meinhold, in whom I had begun to see a mystification, was a real person. He was born in 1797 on the island of Usedom, in the Baltic, and, living there most of his life, remained always a typical and local Pomeranian. This is important, because, in both his books, what gives animation to the scenes is their minute reproduction of Pomeranian conditions. Moreover, although his two principal romances are so worded as to suggest that the author was not the dupe of superstition, there is yet a gusto about his descriptions of sorcery which points to his early familiarity with a peasantry that, quite late in the eighteenth century, still believed to the full in the malignant power of witches.

Meinhold was a Lutheran clergyman in his native island, and steeped himself in the legends of his credulous parish-ioners. He early began to write verses, and he was encouraged by Jean Paul Richter, to whom he sent them. Goethe took notice of him, and published the singularly unlucky advice that he should confine himself to pastoral and pensive themes. This Meinhold, who sneered at the German sentimentality of his day, was determined not to do. In fact it was the terrifying, the horrible, the atrocious which alone appealed to Meinhold, who had a tincture in his veins of the Mrs. Radcliffe sensationalism.

Like our English purveyors of this class of writing, Meinhold liked to cultivate mystery. His first romance, " Bernsteinhexe," published in 1843, but known to English readers in Lady Duff Gordon's translation as " The Amber Witch," professed to be a report of a State trial which Meinhold had discovered in the Pomeranian archives. This book achieved a considerable success in Germany, and Meinhold was commanded by the King of Prussia to produce the original documents for his Majesty's inspection. This was highly embarrassing, and Meinhold had to confess that there were no such documents. He was graciously forgiven, but interest in " The Amber Witch " began to flag, since it is wonderful how people delight in being deceived. Who reads " Cleone Knox " now that the fiction is confessed?

Meinhold published a great many insignificant works, and then, towards the end of his life, a second witch-romance, " Sidonia the Sorceress," which appeared, however, for the first time in three volumes of his collected works in 1747. It never attracted much notice in Germany, although it is far superior in vigour and variety to " The Amber Witch." How the attention of Speranza, Lady Wilde, was directed to it I am quite unable to report, but it is hardly a paradox to say that this German romance did not begin to exist until an Irishwoman revealed it to a select English circle.

The objects which Meinhold held before him in composing his curious books are not very easy to define, and not perhaps worthy of close attention. But his purpose was certainly not merely to amuse the reader, nor to make his flesh creep. He was oddly involved in theological controversy, and while he attacked the doctrines of the Rationalists, he was a rationalist himself in his own way. He argued that if he could take people in with faked documents of the Seven Years' War, Biblical scholars might be deceived about the canon of Holy Scripture. He boldly says that anyone who doubts the genuineness of "Sidonia" may refer to the authorities which he names, but he appears to have invented the authorities. This is an old trick; and Meinhold finally shelters himself behind a learned anti-quary of the eighteenth century, Heinrich Gustavus Schwalenberg; but he also is a Mrs. Harris. Sidonia, when put to the torture, confessed that she had caused the death of a Dr. Schwalenberg. But I am afraid that this was the fabulous ancestor of a fictitious historian.

Rossetti had the courage to assert that "Sidonia the Sorceress" was the best novel "as regards power and sound style for two ages." Without accepting so loose and so excessive a judgment, it must be admitted that, in spite of the awkward form and tone of its composition, "Sidonia" is a very remarkable work. We see how mysterious is the way in which literary Providence moves, when we consider the contrast between the other tame and poor writings of Meinhold and this sinewy and ferocious narrative. The lamb does not here so much lie down with the leopard as become a leopard himself. In Great Britain the heroines of witch-tragedies were mainly persons of humble birth and education, often besotted with their own ignorance, and always incapable of resisting the attacks of society. But in Meinhold's romance the heroine belongs to the highest local nobility, and is protected by the privileges of her rank and station. She makes a splendid fight for life and power.

This Lady Canoness of Pomerania, who was burned at the stake for witchcraft on August 19, 1620, was born in 1539 into one of the most powerful families of the Duchy. She was in her youth "the most beautiful and the wealthiest of the maidens of Pomerania." Ambition was her bane from a child. Wooed by the first gentlemen of the duchy, she refused them all, stating her intention of marrying, if she married at all, none but the Duke of Pomerania. She was told that she was like a silly infant clamouring for a glittering knife, but this did not divert her from her purpose.

When at last, almost in sight of the altar, she was torn from the arms of the young Duke Ernst Ludwig von Pommern-Wolgast, she became like the hero of " The Cask of Amontillado," of whom we are told that he had long borne injury in silence, but that when his enemy ventured upon insult, he determined on revenge. Sidonia, aided by infernal powers, ran amok among the nobility and gentry of Pomerania. Her crimes " caused such a panic of horror that contemporary authors scarcely dared to mention her name, and even then by merely giving the initials." However, we know all about them now, thanks to Meinhold and Lady Wilde.

The main accusation brought against Sidonia was that by means of her vengeful charms and incantations she had so bewitched the princely house that every branch of it became sterile. There were six promising scions, each wedded to a young wife, but all, through the machinations of Sidonia, died childless. The last Duke, finding himself without an heir, charged the witch with being the cause, and she admitted that an old woman had taught her the secrets which she practised.

"The Duke promised her life and pardon if she would free the other princes from the ban, but her answer was that she had enclosed the spell in a padlock, and flung it into the sea; and having asked the devil if he could restore the padlock again to her, he replied, ' No ! that was forbidden to him,' by which everyone can perceive that the destiny of God was in the matter. And so it was that, notwithstanding the intercession of all the neighbouring Courts, Sidonia was brought to the scaffold at Stettin."

One neighbouring potentate, who we may be sure would warmly approve of the execution, was King James I. and VI.,

who had very decided views about sorceresses. But it
is not likely that Meinhold ever heard of that monarch's
zeal against those detestable slaves of Satan whom he had
so rigorously exposed in the " Dæmonologie."

The fascination which " Sidonia the Sorceress " exercised
over Rossetti and the painters of his school is easily accounted
for. The method of the romance lends itself in an extraordinary degree to the practice of the Preraphaelites.
There are pictures everywhere in the conduct of the story;
every page suggests a brilliantly, rather crudely, coloured
vignette. The violence of the action lends itself to this
pictorial result; we seem less to be listening to a narrative
than to be looking on at a series of *poses plastiques*. Where
Sidonia faints under the excitement of the Lapland drum;
where the Prince bursts into the little chamber in the tower
and finds Sidonia on the bed weeping, " in a green velvet
robe, laced with gold and embroidered with other golden
ornaments, and her head crowned with pearls and
diamonds "; where Sidonia is caught with the groom;
where she sits spinning, like a Lady of Shalott, at the
window of her prison in Saatzig Castle, and sees, far below,
the life of the town and the motion of the boats on the
lake—all these episodes, and a hundred more, seem ready
for the pencil of Millais or Frederick Sandys. The spectre
of the Serpent Knight, the changing of the calves into
hares, the apparition of the evil spirit called Chinn, Dr.
Martin Luther letting the Duchess's ring fall on the floor
at her wedding, Sidonia repulsing the advance of her lovers
with her hands and her feet, these belong to a somewhat
different category, but these, too, are pictorial in their
essence.

Moreover, the constant and abrupt introduction of the
supernatural, which is a preposterous feature of " Sidonia,"
but without which the story could never have been written,
was calculated to attract the senses of a group of artists

whose minds were in an equal degree mystical and plastic. Something of the direct influence of " Sidonia the Sorceress " may be traced in several of Rossetti's important poems, and especially in " Sister Helen." His was an illustrious example of that class of mind which rejects the supernatural in its direct theological sense, but delights to conjure up picturesque disturbances of the course of nature, and will pore over the legends of a Thessalian witch while it treats the accredited miracles of an apostle with indifference.

# WALT WHITMAN

# WALT WHITMAN

MANY authors of the past make a strong appeal to some persons while they repel the attentions of others. But there is one author who has the peculiarity of being attractive or repulsive to the same persons at different periods of life, or condition, or even weather. There can be no consistency in the attitude to Walt Whitman; those who approach his work are thrilled by him to-day and disgusted by him to-morrow. It depends not so much on him as on themselves; on whether they are young and eager or weary of life; on whether they are passing through certain moods or have ceased to have a particular experience; on whether the sun is shining and they are out of doors or whether they sit in an armchair before the fire. Whitman is himself so various within definitely recurrent outlines, so uncompromisingly violent, that, as he stands before the reader in his blank nudity, it depends not on him so much as on the reader whether the aspect of him pleases or annoys, and in consequence we have the phenomenon of careful judges inspecting Whitman to-day and giving him the first prize, when to-morrow they will indignantly eject him from the category of competitors. It all depends on the reader himself—on his mood, on his physical state, on his accidental attitude to life. I know of no other writer who depends so much on our nerves and our digestion for the mode in which we welcome or repulse him.

Whitman's "Songs of the Body Electric" have lent themselves to so much critical commentary that it might seem unlikely that a fresh examination of them could yield much profit, and yet Mr. John Bailey, in the English Men of Letters series, has contrived to give remarkable freshness to the well-worn theme. Mr. Squire deserves commendation for his courage in inviting this particular critic to assume the task of writing about Whitman. It was an experiment, since Mr. Bailey is a mandarin of matured and traditional taste, to whom, it might be supposed, the extraordinary qualities of Whitman would be unintelligible. But the selection is justified by complete success. This is perhaps the best book Mr. Bailey has written, and it is marked by a sympathy which supports the writer over very grave difficulties, and yet never stoops to indulgence. It approaches Whitman in Whitman's own spirit—with audacity and caution.

We run great danger if we read " Leaves of Grass " carelessly or blindly. The discreet companion of Whitman's extraordinary mind has to fix his attention and to reserve his judgment. He must be prepared to accept the almost delirious self-revelation of " Translucent mould of me " with intelligent comprehension ; and then the terrible " I dote on myself, there is that lot of me, and all so luscious ! " with the reserve of a cultivated man. He must let Whitman conduct him, and yet must remain his own master. Whitman's amazing inequalities, which are not merely inconsistencies of style, but are inherent in his barbarous originality, set traps for the infatuated reader at every turn, and yet the reader must be infatuated or Whitman has nothing to say to him. Mr. Bailey is infatuated, and perfectly calm and clear-sighted at the same time.

The early career of the author of " Leaves of Grass " is of significant interest, and it is curious to notice how two features of it moulded his temperament and future work. On the one hand, there was the serene and dreamy childhood in Long Island, where he loafed on the hot sand with

limitless ocean " madly pushing " on the shores beside
him, where he grew " enamoured of living outdoors,"
where he conceived his passion for the harmony and
loveliness of " voluptuous and cool-breathed earth." It
was from these memories of a sweet-scented and untrammelled infancy that all the beautiful freshness of his
happiest poetry sprang. Here he gained the serenity of
soul which inspired the descriptive and yet emotional
vignettes which are so attractive in what Mr. Bailey aptly
calls his Wordsworthian manner.

But there was another side to the medal. From his
twenty-second to his thirtieth year Whitman was immersed
in the journalism of New York, which at that time was
perhaps the worst in the world. Mr. Bailey skims lightly
over an experience which, I believe, was responsible for
the main offences of Whitman against language. What
sub-editing the " Brooklyn Daily Eagle " must have been
in 1845 may be gathered from the somewhat jaundiced and
exaggerated reports of Dickens. When the innocent
Whitman arrived at the office of his newspaper, would he
not find Mr. Jefferson Brick " at his usual post in the van
of human civilisation and moral purity " ? Would he not
be taught to admire and to emulate the rhetoric of Mr.
Zephaniah Scadder ? Would not the English of the Water-
toast Association be the model of his prose ? Was all this
not responsible for the hideous crudity of phrase which
seems to be always lurking to leap out upon Whitman's
most ambitious periods ?

In this connection, it is useful to distinguish the first
edition of " Leaves of Grass " (1855) from the numerous
reprints and enlargements which Whitman published almost
to the year of his death. My own copy, which belonged to
the late Lord Carlisle, happens to be the earliest which
reached this country. It is a very odd-looking book, a
thin folio the poetical text of which is printed in large

and almost handsome type, but is prefixed by a long essay in prose in small and shabby print. This preface Mr. Bailey does not discuss, indeed it has never been part of the Whitman canon, and was immediately suppressed, although I believe that it was once reprinted, in " Specimen Days " (1882). It is, however, historically interesting because it displays the poet still shackled by the chains of New York journalism. The amusing thing is that this preface reads like a flattering review of " Leaves of Grass " written by Mr. La Fayette Kettle for the " Rowdy-Dowdy Journal." What is prodigious in the poetry becomes mean and bumptious in this dreadful prose, which repeats in poorer phrase the principles of the poetry. Here we have interminable lists of nouns, an uncertain use of showy foreign words, self-praise of the author's " gigantic and generous treatment " of the colossal theme, a local and purely American scorn of tradition, of " the gaggery and gilt of a million years." These things are occasional defects in the tissue of the poems, but they do not ruin it; in the Preface of 1855 they run rampant, and are sufficient to explain, though not perhaps to excuse, the resistance made by the sensitive New England culture of the hour to a form of art so recklessly hung about with the worst tinsel of a bunkum style.

The one exception to this New England repulse was the famous letter of Emerson. I do not think that full justice has ever been done to the courage and foresight of the Concord philosopher. In 1855 Emerson was still the centre of the transcendentalist movement, and looked up to by a rapidly widening circle as a guide in morals, ethical and intellectual. He had a great sense of what is called responsibility. But a recent visit to Europe had widened his views, and he showed a tendency to react against the prejudices of the American hour. Consequently, " Leaves of Grass," containing so much that was terrifying to the average New England intelligence, might come into Emerson's range at a moment when he was asking Evil to become his good—admitting, as we must admit, that to a sheltered nature like that of Emerson the immodesty, the self-consciousness, the "barbaric yawp" of "Leaves of Grass" would appear definitely "evil"—and yet that he might welcome it as an element in that stimulus to emotion which he was always trying to introduce into the sluggishness of the American conscience. To this must, of course, be added the response that Emerson's catholic taste in style could but make to the extraordinary lyrical beauties scattered through the strange, wild book. But when we have thought of all this, there remains a justified surprise at the courage of Emerson—"I give you joy of your free and brave thought," "I find incomparable things said incomparably well." The letter was magnificent in its generous perspicacity, and the more admirable because it was for many long years practically the only recognition which any American critic gave to Whitman's genius.

We have been told that Emerson was afterwards vexed with himself for having welcomed "Leaves of Grass" so impetuously. If it were so, it would but be another example of the way in which the writings of Whitman affect the nerves of the reader. Evidently the strange dark green folio, with the haunting frontispiece of the author "stout as a horse, affectionate, haughty, electrical," would reach Emerson at a moment when his own moral and physical condition prepared him to receive its message. A year or two later he would open the book in another mood, and find it utterly distasteful. This is not how we take up other writers. It is not necessary to be well or ill, to have received an appointment, or to be crossed in love, to recognise the qualities of Milton or of Keats. You may be the luckiest of men, and yet enjoy the verses of Leopardi. But Whitman, in a very curious way, makes himself part of the

P

element which surrounds each of us, and our response to his blunt and direct challenge is likely to be disturbed by any accidental sensation. "Stranger, if you passing meet me, and desire to speak to me, why should you not speak to me?" he asks, and the reader replies, "I desired with something like ecstasy to speak to you yesterday, but to-day I can't bear the sight of you!"

The reputation of Whitman is lowered by the excess of what he published, and of what his disciples have collected. I do not undervalue the interesting revelations in many of the "Carols" and "Calls" and "So Longs!" of the poet's later years, but they do not mark any particular advance in his thought. It would be unfortunate to miss the beautiful and mysterious "Calamus," which no one has been daring enough to fathom, or a few of the "Drum-Taps," but on the whole the volume of 1855 gives us all in Whitman which is essential. It contains the novel and transcendent view of modern life, especially of masculine life, the incomparably daring physical suggestions, the profound sincerity, the confusion of things adorably with things hideously stated. It contains some of the very best of those sudden vignettes, "snap-shots" of nature, and of the adult man in nature, which form the principal ornament of Whitman's poetry—the trapper's wedding, the jolting hay-cart, the bathers, and others still more audacious than these.

The intense personal vitality of Walt Whitman, the emphasis he lays on the physical condition of the typical athlete, in whom he pre-eminently sees himself, is fully indicated in his first collection of what it is convenient to call "lyrics." But most of his readers, even Mr. Bailey among them, are distracted by the capricious way in which, after 1855, he broke up his text into fragments to which he gave fortuitous titles. In the original edition, now a very rare book, his first intention is betrayed by "Leaves of

Grass " appearing as a single poem, in sections, but without
sub-titles. The unity of purpose of the author is thus displayed less attractively, perhaps, but more consistently
than it is now, when we skip over a foreground of " Inscrip-
tions " to " Pent-up Aching Rivers " and " I Sing the
Body Electric." But the essence of the " message " is
exactly the same; it is the disgusted son of Tammany
throwing off the horrible atmosphere of the " Daily Eagle "
and descending to the " far-swooping elbow'd earth, rich
apple-blossom'd earth " of Long Island. And there, in
sound of the sea, lying at ease, through the transparent
summer morning, on the soft pure grass, which is like the
handkerchief of the Lord, the exile from Manhattan medi-
tates on his own bodily condition, and on that of millions
of his fellow-males.

For that is really the one subject of Walt Whitman, the
masculinity of other men, illustrated by the phenomena of
his own body, while his peculiarity is the fact that he is
without sentimentality in the directions in which most
other persons are, or think they are, sentimental. His
interest is centred in the male, the youthful but mature
man, in the open air, untroubled by self-analysis; and all
his study is of the instincts, habits, sensations of this
type. He has no real interest in any other. His references
to women are perfunctory; he is occasionally occupied
with matrons, but only, or almost only, as the mothers of
future American heroes. When Whitman seemed to be
most audacious, he was often most secretive, and those who
study him closely will not be the dupe of " Children of
Adam," nor of the subterfuges of his alarmed correspondence
with John Addington Symonds. It is best not to inquire
too closely about all this, but to accept Walt Whitman for
what he gives, for his prodigious candour, his zest in life,
his " sweet aromatic presence," the undeniable beauty and
originality of his strange unshackled rhapsody.

# THE SQUIRE OF BLANKNEY

# THE SQUIRE OF BLANKNEY

AFTER so many records of stately, responsible, and fussy persons, after so many squalid and dowdy pictures of existence " as it really is," the refreshment which such a fairy-tale as Lord Chaplin's biography brings with it is almost startling in its sharpness. We learn, without dismay, that the Squire of Blankney " throughout his life had a profound zest for the simple material pleasures of existence." Certainly he had; perhaps his zest was more acute and was prolonged further than that of any other recent personage known to fame. His daughter admits that he grasped with both hands the enjoyments and adventures that life brings to a handsome and flamboyant young man. He would have been out of his element at Rosmersholm; he is inconceivable in a Gorki setting. If the severe reader, fresh from an earnest contemplation of our social misfortunes, should ask whether all this hedonism and frivolity, this passion for eating and drinking, and for horses and hounds, this spreading of a satin sail upon a halcyon sea, is really the best way in which an earnest Christian can spend his life, we have to shirk the irritating question.

Of course, a nation of Harry Chaplins would be bankrupt in a fortnight, but an exception can do our consciences no harm. Lord Chaplin was the type of a race that has disappeared, dragged down by circumstances. There will never be another specimen of this particular species of popular hero. His magnificent physical abundance, his lavish hospitality, his reckless outlay on sport, combined with beautiful manners, and a sort of charming innocency, lifted him into legend, and we are justified in observing him in his splendour, as though he were a meteor slowly passing across the sky, particularly interesting because it can never return.   Lady Londonderry has realised that this is the mode in which her father ought to be inspected, and she does not dwell unduly, as a less skilful or more timid biographer would do, on his political adventures, respectable as they were.   She tells us that Lord Chaplin admitted, at the close of his life, that Providence intended him to be a huntsman rather than a statesman.   Of course, It did, and she was wise to let this side of his nature take the foremost place.   He was a sort of Chiron, until he let the poisoned arrow wound his foot; he resigned his immortality, but continued to shine.   Lady Londonderry has preserved, with great justice and vivacity, the outline of the fairy-tale.

Everything combined to produce and to foster this unique specimen of a race which could exist only in England and be perfected only under the early sway of Queen Victoria.   The old jingle of resisting all temptations to belong to other nations was never more appropriate to anyone than it was to Henry Chaplin.   Not merely was there nothing exotic about his character or condition, but he lifted to a pitch of eminence the most picturesque and insular of our national habits and modes of thought.   The environment was absolutely in keeping with the man. We seem to see him on horseback, in the foreground of some Georgian painting, with conventional woodlands and a spread of rich turf behind him around an ample Adams mansion.   The rider is solid, bluff, infinitely courtly, in a world where opposition is unknown and the authority of the squire unquestioned.   If a shade of vexation crosses that large, comely face it is due to no personal or political annoyance, but to the fact that his huntsman has just told him that he is rather short of foxes. English it all is, incredibly English, in a landscape that breathes of sport and contented feudal peasantry, a good corn country, where security reigns and whatever is, is right. We are presented with the portrait of a man of ability and character, not without some of the gifts of statesmanship, yet pre-eminently the final avatar of that singular deity, the English County Gentleman. The type is amusing, yet it also demands sympathy and respect. The ichthyosaurus may be dead, but before its decease it was a portent in the primeval waters.

Henry Chaplin was born in 1841 (unless he was born in 1840, about which an odd doubt persists) at Ryhall Hall, near Stamford, which is close to the Lincolnshire with which he was identified. His father was a fox-hunting parson and lord of the manor, a glorified example of that peculiarly English institution, the Squarson. Henry was his third son; the father died early, and the children went to live with their uncle, Mr. Charles Chaplin of Blankney, " a survivor of a most ancient order of squires." Of this gentleman, her grand-uncle, Lady Londonderry gives an entertaining account. He was a complete autocrat, returned seven members to the House of Commons, and exercised over parts of three counties a beneficent but unquestioned sway. To a lawyer from London who criticised as illegal one of his pronouncements from the Bench, Mr. Charles Chaplin thundered, " Young man, you are evidently a stranger in these parts or you would know that my word *is* law." Apparently his authority was unresisted; he was a sort of rustic Miltiades, " a tyrant, but our tyrants then were still at least our countrymen." The effect of all this on the temperament of Henry Chaplin was formative in the highest degree. He grew up in a pastoral environment, and at Blankney, even in childhood, he had " an opportunity of acquiring that intimate and affectionate

knowledge of the land and the farmers which was to serve
him so well in later life."

His father had died when the boy was eight, and at
seventeen he lost his mother, described to us as a woman of
remarkable gifts. One of these, her financial ability, she
did not bequeath to her third son. The old Squire died
when his nephew was eighteen, and by this time, I presume
(though Lady Londonderry does not say so) that the two
elder brothers were also dead. Henry, at all events,
appears, when he comes of age, as the owner of an immense
fortune and master of his own affairs. The only guiding
influence appears to have been that of a most remarkable
man, Lord Henry Bentinck, familiar to students of Disraeli.
Towards the close of his own life, Lord Chaplin wrote down
his recollections of Lord Henry, to whose guidance, particularly in hunting and racing, he owed a great deal. He
himself, at Oxford, led the sort of life which a centaur
might be expected to live, and Lady Londonderry gives a
merry instance. Harry Chaplin, convicted of wearing
hunting kit under his surplice in Cathedral, and of other
ritual delinquencies, is called into the awful presence of
Dean Liddell, who begins austerely :—

"As far as I can gather, you seem to regard Christ
Church as a hunting-box. You are hardly ever in college,
and I must request you, unless you change your habits. to
vacate your rooms and make way for someone who will
benefit from his studies during his residence at the University." "But, Mr. Dean, what do you expect me to
do?" "Do?" replied the Dean, "you must go in for an
examination." "My dear Mr. Dean, if you had only told
me before, I should have taken the necessary steps; but
when is there one?" "In three weeks," was the curt reply.

Always capable, if he chose, of concentration, the youth
positively passed Mods. with distinction, but when the

Dean congratulated him on his "excellent performance," and entreated him to go in for Honours, Chaplin blandly replied :—

"Mr. Dean, if only you had told me before, I would have done so, but after my last interview with you, in which you intimated that I should have to vacate my rooms, I am very sorry to inform you that I have arranged to go for a trip to the Rocky Mountains."

In 1864 an event occurred which had all the appearance of an irreparable social misfortune, but which proved in the long run to be not merely a master-stroke of good luck, but a basis of permanent public sympathy. Extremely good-looking and good-tempered, quick in intelligence, overflowing with health and (perhaps above all) with money, the young man of fashion, just back from shooting bears in the Rockies, seemed predisposed to grow idle and indifferent, perhaps also to be dangerously envied. Suddenly, on the eve of his much-advertised marriage, there befell him the ignominy of being publicly jilted by his betrothed, Lady Florence Paget. The circumstances were without parallel in those days, and the sensation was universal. I was a schoolboy in a remote Devonshire village, without fashionable connections, but I heard of it; all the world heard of it; from Shetland to Land's End the news of it rang and rang. To this day, after more than sixty years, it is a legend that Lady Florence left Mr. Chaplin in the carriage outside Marshall and Snelgrove's, dashed through the shop and out at the back entrance, immediately becoming the wife of Lord Hastings, a notorious rip who was "already in bad health and threatened with financial catastrophe." Public sympathy was universally diverted from the volatile bride to her humiliated suitor. Lady Londonderry deals frankly with this very curious episode.

As opinions may differ as to the propriety of her treatment
of it, I will say that in my judgment she was not merely
justified, but obliged, to throw a clear light on what has
been the subject of generations of tittle-tattle, and that if
she has shown some severity in her narrative, she has gone
no further than justice to her father demanded.

Henry Chaplin felt the blow severely, and for a time
withdrew from society altogether. But a healthier mood
prevailed, and, assured of the sympathy of a world of
friends, he reappeared, to their general satisfaction. They
learned with surprise that the young Squire of Blankney
had embraced a new enthusiasm, and had started a career
on the Turf with the purchase of two colts for what was
looked upon as a monstrous sum. His successes in the
racing world are matters of history, and are described in
the volume before me by an old friend of Lord Chaplin,
whose " desire for anonymity " Lady Londonderry is
" bound to respect." I respect it with the greater ease
because I have not the faintest inkling of the name of this
able disciple of Surtees. If Breadalbane was a giant,
Hermit was a god, and all the sporting public bowed down
in adoration when the latter won the Derby in 1867. The
tactics of Lord Hastings, who behaved like an inebriated
monkey, magnified Henry Chaplin's triumph, but all this,
and much more, must be read in the breathless narrative
of the Anonymous. The Squire preserved his passionate
interest in the Turf to the last hours of his life. If he shared
it with any other pursuit, it was with hunting, for he was a
devout follower of the fox. On this subject, his daughter
asks no help from the Unnamed, and her section on it
is brilliant and amusing in a high degree.

In 1868, at the age of twenty-seven, Chaplin entered
Parliament as Tory member for the Sleaford Division of
Lincolnshire, and he was prominent in successive Houses
for over a quarter of a century. We are reminded here that

he " was a sincere and straightforward politician," and this
is no more than the truth. That he was a great statesman
will hardly be maintained. He befriended the cause of
the farmers, he opposed Home Rule, he defended the Irish
Church. Mr. Gladstone thanked him "for having so
sharply challenged us " in his maiden speech, and Mr.
Disraeli shook him by the hand. It was impossible for a
beginning to be more auspicious, but it was Chaplin's luck
always to start brilliantly in everything. He was staunch,
very consistent, and much better prepared for political
contest than his opponents realised. He made no incom-
petent Cabinet Minister. His political career was honourable and continuous, but Lady Londonderry does not
conceal its limitations. He was engaged on other things.
He married, with exquisite success; he flourished in every
field in which the Country Gentleman invites a generous
rivalry; his hospitality was ostentatious; his daughter is
able to say that he achieved " the complete sum of happiness." And then the poisoned arrow fell upon Chiron's
foot.

Henry Chaplin had never realised that such a fortune as he
had inherited could possibly be exhausted, and his indifference to economy was proverbial. The amusements which he
affected—racing, deer-stalking, hunting, hospitality—were
expensive in the last degree. His friends saw the coming
crash, but failed to make him credit its immanence. In
vain did the Duke of Westminster tell him that if the
crowned heads of Europe combined to give him £100,000 a
year, he would spend every penny of it. The crisis came
rather suddenly in 1870, and Blankney saw its princely
Squire no more. His friends rallied round him, and he
bore his reverses with intrepidity and dignity. He did not
allow his altered position to check his appetite or interfere
with his Parliamentary activities, which latter, indeed,
from this time forward were more than ever before con-

centrated upon public service. It is unnecessary to dwell
on his last years, which are excellently described by his
daughter. Although his means of displaying it were
removed, the legend of his magnificence remained, and he
lost, with a wide and sympathetic public, none of the glory
which made him a legendary figure. With all his faults—
and his biographer does not refrain from a gentle recapitula-
tion of them—Henry Chaplin was a man worthy of that
general admiration which he continued to enjoy until his
death on May 29, 1923. He was courteous and kind,
intelligent in the bluff old English way, a god among
hounds and horses, and a faithful public servant according
to his lights and aptitudes.

# THE MATRIARCH

# THE MATRIARCH

WHEN Jeremy Taylor was called upon to preach the funeral sermon for that noble hostess of Golden Grove whose wings had so long been spread to shelter him from the tempest, he defined in his own matchless language the virtues of her moderation.   He said :—

" I have seen a female religion that wholly dwelt upon the face and tongue; that, like a wanton and an undressed tree, spent all its juice in suckers and irregular branches, in leaves and gum, and after all such goodly outsides you should never eat an apple, or be delighted with the beauties or the perfumes of a hopeful blossom.   But the religion of this excellent lady was of another constitution.   It took root downward in humility, and brought forth fruit upward in the substantial graces of a Christian, in charity and justice, in chastity and modesty, in fair friendships and sweetness of society.   She had not very much of the forms and outsides of godliness, but she was hugely careful for the power of it."

These words might be applied, with close accuracy, to the venerable lady of whose span of a century modest report is given, by several responsible hands, in the very charming little volume which her daughter, Miss Elizabeth Haldane, has compiled.

The day has passed when the mere extension of life over a hundred years could awaken astonishment and even scepticism.   It is not half a century since a careful anti-quary, W. J. Thoms, caused a certain sensation by denying

Q                          225

that human life was ever so extended, and by plausibly
suggesting that in every case the plea of the centenarian
was founded either on fraud or, more frequently, on confusion of documents and memories.   Whether conditions
are much more favourable to life than they were, or whether
much more care is taken nowadays to register the date of
birth, genealogists must decide.   From whatever cause,
the instances of people living to be over a hundred are too
numerous to awaken more than a local curiosity.   But

> It is not growing like a tree
> In bulk, doth make man better be,
> Or standing long an oak, one hundred year,
> To fall at last, dry, bald and sear,

as a rule, there is nothing about the existence of a
centenarian to attract notice except his vegetable longevity.
The earliest, and, until recently, perhaps the only instance
of a life continued over a hundred years in brilliant activity,
is that of the illustrious French chemist, Michel Eugène
Chevreul, who died in 1889, having unquestionably been
born in 1785.   Chevreul was isolating his stearin and his
olein to the close of his wonderful career, calm and clear
and studious in his hundred and third summer.   The only
other case of prolonged and unimpaired mental activity on
a high grade which is known to me is that of the illustrious
lady whose death early in 1925 attracted such general
attention.

The little monument to Mrs. Haldane of Cloan which the
piety of her family and friends has erected in the volume
before me is original in form and marked by a graceful
reticence.   It opens with a short essay by the Archbishop
of York, at whose instance the work was undertaken.
This is followed by " Recollections " of her youthful days
written by Mrs. Haldane at the age of ninety-nine, and
showing in its texture how completely the aged lady
remained mistress of her memory and her judgment.   As

usual, however, in cases of this kind, her interest seems to have flagged with the record of middle life, and at her marriage the story is skilfully taken up by her daughter and constant companion, Miss Elizabeth Haldane, who completes it. Then follows a " Note " by her eldest son, Lord Haldane, adding a close observation of character, and then impressions by several persons who knew Mrs. Haldane well in her last years. Among these are Mrs. Carruthers (" Violet Markham "), Sir James Barrie, and the Archbishop of Canterbury. Although Mrs. Haldane lived and died a Presbyterian, the two leaders of the Anglican Church were among the most intimate and the most devoted of her friends. She called the Archbishops her two Golden Candlesticks, and feigned that she herself was the unseen pipe which fed them both with the oil of intercession. In the very last letter she wrote, being already in her second century, she told her " dear Golden Candlestick," the Archbishop of York, that she was " praying without ceasing for you and the Archbishop of Canterbury."

Mary Elizabeth Burdon Sanderson was born on April 9, 1825, at Rotherfield, in Kent. She belonged to a wealthy and influential family of County Durham, and her father, Richard Burdon, was the youngest son of Sir Thomas Burdon, of Jesmond, where her early years were passed. Her grandmother, Jane Scott, Lady Burdon, introduced the legal element which has been so prominent in later generations, for her brothers were those eminent judges Lord Eldon and Lord Stowell. Of these grand-uncles Mrs. Haldane says little in the present sketch, but her friends will recall that she had of them both picturesque memories which she was ready to produce in conversation. Nothing, indeed, gave so vivid a sense of the vast extension of her intelligent life as her personal recollections of these two great lawyers, of whom one was born in 1745 and the other in 1751. Eldon was actually Lord Chancellor when Mrs.

Haldane was born, although shortly to be succeeded by
Lyndhurst.  He was not, in her memory, the figure of
Fraud in an ermine gown, dropping big tears that turned to
millstones as they fell, in Shelley's angry vision, but an
apparition of almost unearthly magnificence as he stepped
from his state-carriage at the door of his house.

Of her other grand-uncle, Lord Stowell, she remembered
less, although he lived, over ninety, until she was eleven.
Mrs. Haldane refrains from reminding us that this once-
celebrated maritime and international lawyer is now
mainly recalled by his phrase, " The elegant simplicity of
the Three per cents."   Mrs. Haldane's childhood was spent
in an atmosphere of Catholic Emancipation, and in the
sound of a general vague cry for Reform.   The long-later
efforts of her son to promote universal education were
being foreshadowed by Lord Brougham's Society for the
Diffusion of Useful Knowledge.   It was the hour of the
revelation of Cuvier and Malibran, of Goethe and Guizot,
of Greek independence and of Anglican High Churchman-
ship.   The highly intelligent but somewhat eccentric
society into which Mary Burdon was introduced neglected
none of these interests, but it was the religious crisis which
most affected them, and her.   Her maternal grandmother
was greatly moved by the temper of the age as it became
diverted from indifference into an evangelical channel.
She was subjected, like so many others of her generation,
to the Biblical tyranny of the Rev. John Newton, of Olney.
She was occupied in putting religious pressure on her
daughter, who, however, an heiress in her own right, " very
attractive, besides having a clear intellect and power of
influencing others," took her life into her own hands and
married a staunch adherent of the Church of England,
friend of Keble and Whately.   Unfortunately, she leaped
out of the frying-pan into the fire, for Mr. Burdon Sanderson
rapidly developed into a typical 1830 Puritan.

Some diversion from the growing obsession of the young
husband's religiousness was caused by his becoming the
owner of Jesmond. But his rigour was reflected in the
severity with which he thought it proper to educate his
children. Mary Elizabeth and her sister were given over
to a bitter and fanatical governess, whose system of
education was " to administer corporal punishment." The
sinfulness of the child's nature was incessantly impressed
upon her; she was taught to regard herself as a great sinner,
whom God, as a just judge, was bound to condemn and
chastise. Miss Taylor, the preposterous governess, seems
never to have been checked in the slightest degree by the
parents, who were themselves no doubt afraid of her. My
own recollection supplies me with memories of acidulated
women, doubtless what is vaguely called " sincere," who
would plant themselves in a family and exercise a fantastic
tyranny over every member of it by dint of a constantly
recurring reference to their own perception of the Divine
Will. They intimidated everyone by their assumption of
direct communication with God. Apparently, the sway of
this baleful governess ceased before the future Mrs. Haldane
was seven years of age, but the effect of her discipline was
indelible, and minute instances of it were present in the
mind of her unfortunate pupil to the last. The child's
next governess, a product of Jane Eyre's Carus Wilson
school, was a more normal human being.

But the gloom of religious frenzy had stamped itself
deeply on the child's mind. She would have been happy,
she says, had it not been for " the thought of my own sinfulness, which never left me." This was when she was nine
years old, when the fresh joy of a liberal life on the Northum-
berland moors was ruined for her by the poison of an
incessant " introspective religion." Nothing in Mrs. Haldane's recollections is more interesting than the mode in
which she deals with this dismal spectre, which was not

peculiar to her experience, although perhaps more intensely present there than in most evangelical homes of the hour. She has been expressing her satisfaction at the way in which at present the full light of thought is permitted to stream upon childish conduct, and, looking back over ninety years, she continues : " My own life was saddened by this Jesuitical system. . . . We were watched continually, and our actions and words and thoughts construed into meanings of which we never dreamt. Prayers were directed *at* us by our governess." It is a proof of the wholesome vigour of her own nature that she was not ultimately warped in either direction, towards a more gloomy pietism or towards a complete revolt. She achieved the perfect balance of the Lady whom Jeremy Taylor described.

This book is not in any sense a biography, and perhaps the ordinary reader would find a page or two of quite definite information helpful. But the life of Mrs. Haldane, though spent in the midst of manifold intellectual movement, was in itself very quiet. As the Archbishop of York admits, " her powers were not shown in the activities of public life," but in the remarkable influence which she exercised over everyone who came within her range. She lay in her bed at Cloan, sequestered from the world, and yet burning there, like a lamp, with sympathy and intelligence. It was the attractiveness of her moral nature which induced so many of the leaders of thought and action to turn to her in moments of difficulty. It was this which impelled Lord Ypres in the dark hour of 1915 to confide in her his sense of the " terribly arduous task " before him, and the " terrible doubt " which had assailed him, while taking his aged friend to witness that he was " absolutely confident as to final and ultimate success."

If there is any feature of Mrs. Haldane's character which the piety of her family has concealed in the volume before me, it is her force. Hence, the recollections of Miss Violet Markham, who did not know her till late, are of value as noting what those who had spent their life in her company no longer observed. Miss Markham dwells upon the impression of strength which Mrs. Haldane gave in extreme old age. Beneficent and calm, in the mellowness of a sheltered antiquity, the extreme moderation with which she spoke and acted started rather from a determination of the reason than from any weakening of the will. She ruled her family and the circle around her with undiminished firmness to the end, with a calm resolution which would have been almost droll if it had not been so dignified. She was a Mother in Israel, a Matriarch in unquestioned authority.

From the pages of reserved and exquisite piety with which her eldest son has enriched this volume, I cannot resist the pleasure of quoting a passage. Lord Haldane, who has been defining his mother's private creed, continues :—

" Thus she was intensely religious, with expressions for her religion which were characteristic of her mind. Of what these expressions meant the children were keenly conscious. But her views were never thrust on them. She claimed liberty of thought, and she accorded it equally freely. No apparent aberrations in her children surprised or distressed her, for from the highest point of view she saw the truth present, notwithstanding the form of its expression."

A succession of portraits will be examined with curiosity by all readers of this little book, who will observe with interest that Mrs. Haldane advanced in physical beauty with her years. Mr. James Paterson's study, drawn in 1914, has a quality of aquiline strength and regulated

comeliness superior in every way to the conventionality
of the portrait of 1882, yet is itself greatly surpassed in
diaphanous beauty and spirituality by the very fine photo-
graph taken in her hundredth year. Here she lies, as
Wordsworth might have seen her, " a resplendent stranger,"
just starting for her home in Heaven.

# RENÉ  BOYLESVE

# RENÉ BOYLESVE

AT no previous point of its history has French imaginative literature suffered such cumulated losses as it has during the last three years. The successive deaths of Pierre Loti, Maurice Barrès, Marcel Proust, Anatole France, and Elimir Bourges have deprived France of the most noted ornaments of her contemporary fiction. Of the elder school, M. Paul Bourget alone is left. We have now to mourn the death of the leading French novelist of the middle generation, whose loss makes the gap between the old and the new more obvious than ever.

René Boylesve, after a short but extremely painful illness, died in a hospital in Paris on the 14th of January, 1926, a calm and prosperous career of unbroken domestic happiness thus tragically and abruptly closing. He will be remembered by the serenity and delicacy of his genius, in which the classic elements of the French temperament were preserved through a time of strain and revolt. No writer of our time has been more intrinsically and traditionally French.

The real name of René Boylesve, it now appears, was Tardivaux. The French have a passion for pseudonyms; Anatole France was actually Jacques Anatole Thibaut and André Thuriet was Adhémar They, and Pierre Loti was Lieutenant Viaud. René Boylesve, as he called himself in later years, was born on April 14, 1867, at Haye-Descartes, a little town in the Indre-et-Loire, distinguished as the birthplace of the philosopher whose name it has adopted.

When René was a child, by leaning out of window he could see the house in which Descartes was born.

His father, M. Tardivaux, was a successful notary, and all the child's training was in the pleasant " tourangelle " tradition, cosy and old-fashioned, as one sees it depicted in all the best of his novels.   He is identified with Touraine as closely as Mr. Thomas Hardy is with Wessex.  If a reader turns to " L'Enfant à la Balustrade "—and however often he has read that enchanting tale he will enjoy reading it again—he will breathe the very atmosphere of Haye-Descartes half a century ago.   The books of René Boylesve in a very particular manner reflect his early memories.  They are not autobiographic, but he revolves in their pages the kaleidoscope of his transposed impressions.

He seldom cared to speak about himself, but in one of his rare moments of confidence René Boylesve gave the following account of his initiation into literature :—

" My taste for writing came to me quite suddenly one winter's evening, in the country, in the house which I have described in ' La Becquée,' while the others were playing loto in front of a great blazing fireplace.  I was seven years old; I had no more love of games then than I have now, and I was in a corner, by myself, reading the ' Magazin Pittoresque.'  I was reading a short account of the death of Lamartine, and, suddenly, I cannot tell why, nothing that had ever happened made such an effect upon me as this vision of a great poet whose name I had never heard before, who lived in a villa at Passy, surrounded by greyhounds, and who took snuff !  I sat hypnotised by this half-column of the ' Magazin Pittoresque.'  I medi-tated deeply upon it, and I asked my parents to let me have, for my birthday-present, some sheets of white paper. When I got them, I wrote nothing on them, but I walked for hours in the garden making up stories that I would later on write down on my sheets of paper. That was my earliest literary adventure."

His education was conducted on the usual lines, first in the Jesuit college of Poitiers and then at the lycée of Tours. So far as has been revealed, nothing in the boy, who was docile and rather reserved, pointed to any special aptitude, so that his father, after trying to start him as a lawyer and then as a diplomatist and then as an antiquary, could not tell what to do with him. He was allowed to go to Paris, with a small allowance, and look around. When he looked around he saw nothing but books, and behind them visions of the old life in Touraine.

It was characteristic that when he devoted himself, as he soon did, entirely to literature, he did not join any of the *cénacles* which were about 1890 almost imperative on an ambitious youth in Paris. He was never seen at clubs or cafés, and throughout his life René Boylesve, though in later years markedly hospitable, was always an isolated figure, not identified with any set or clique. Doubtless for this reason his rise into fame was very slow, since it owed nothing to friendship. He began to publish little stories as early as 1888, but these attracted no attention, and it was not until nine years later that René Boylesve became a figure.

What it was that unfastened the floodgates I do not know, but in 1897 Boylesve began to publish a series of novels which must have been written, in part at least, long before. " Le Médecin des Dames de Néans " and " Les Bains de Bade " were the earliest. These I have never seen, but " Sainte-Marie des-Fleurs " came to me when it was published. I have just read it again, after nearly thirty years, and I find it still fresh and bright, though more juvenile than I remembered. This was one

of the books in which René Boylesve used his impressions
of a lengthy visit to Italy; afterwards he returned, for
good, to Paris and his native Touraine.

" Sainte-Marie des-Fleurs " is a very simple tale of
tender passion frustrated. A young man sees a girl with
her family in Venice, and they fall impetuously in love
with one another. She is the daughter of a rich Parisian
banker, and he is a poor student; moreover, she is engaged
to a large middle-aged gentleman from Chicago, a " strong
silent man." The lovers meet in Paris, again in Florence,
fly together to Ferrara, where Sainte-Marie is captured and
carried off by her parents to Venice. Finally, she has to
marry her Chicago *prétendant*, to whom, by the way, she
has been rather attracted all along. And so " all is gas
and gaiters."

Hardly had these volumes left the press when another
novel appeared, and this time the young gentleman
achieved a splendid success. " Le Parfum des Iles Borromées " was the book of the winter season of 1898, and
the position of René Boylesve was secured. The scene of
" Le Parfum " is the lovely Lake Maggiore, of which the
novelist gives charming impressions. The novel is long,
sentimental, and sarcastic; it is pervaded by a comic
enthusiast, the English poet, Dante Leonard William Lee,
and by a tragic Norwegian maiden, Solweg, since was it
not the epoch of Ibsen and Oscar Wilde?

" Le Parfum des Îles Borromées " is beautifully written,
and it has continued to be a favourite with the female
audience of Boylesve. But I cannot think it very characteristic of him. It was time to return to the more
nipping air of Touraine, and opposite the title-page of the
first edition of " Le Parfum " was advertised, as about to
appear, a novel called " Les Bonnets de Dentelle." As a
matter of fact, unless I am much mistaken, these lace
bonnets never did make their appearance, but it is evident

that they were to have flapped through a tale reminiscent
of Haye-Descartes.

Such a tale was, or may have been, the book which he
published next, " Mlle. Cloque." The heroine is an old
maid who, when she was a girl, saw and was spoken to by
Chateaubriand, then at the height of his magnificence,
author of " René," peer of France and champion of the
monarchical and Christian world. She is hypnotised by
the great man, and for the rest of her long life she has
but one aim—to live up to the ideals of her hero. We see
her settled in Tours, wealthy and influential, the mainstay
of conservatism, but gradually the pressure of modern
thought invades all her surroundings. She alone will not
budge an inch from the principles of 1825, and from being
a support she becomes a stumbling-block to the devout.
She refuses all concession, and the Bishop himself deserts
her.

How she is ridiculed and robbed and persecuted, and
how firm she remains to the last, is told with inimitable
humour and pathos. The conflict of opinions, the rich
variety of manners, the intrigues which surround and
destroy poor Mlle. Cloque are vividly depicted. The next
novel of René Boylesve, " La Becquée," contains a somewhat parallel figure in Aunt Félicie Planté. There is a
little of the spirit of Balzac in these careful provincial
studies.

In 1902, René Boylesve turned rather surprisingly from
these pictures of " tourangelle " manners, and published a
fantastic book, " La Leçon d'Amour dans un Parc," which
has been a great favourite with his public. He called it a
" conte," not a " roman "; but it is quite as long as a
novel. It is a work of pure fantasy, like a boudoir romance
of the eighteenth century, avowedly " libertine," but of
a very innocent libertinage. There is a marquis, who
has a château by the banks of the Loire, and there is

a park, and in the park a lake, and in the lake an
island, and on the island a statue of Cupid, the adolescent Eros.   There are shepherds and nymphs, or naiads,
and they swim out to the island, and there are " goings
on."   It might be rather offensive, but it is not;   the
French tread these dangerous dances so gracefully.   The
author asserted his right for once to write entirely to
please himself, and to fill a little world of fantasy with
fairy people.   He wished to tell a delicate story, set in a
time when a certain licence was permitted.   " Comme c'est
charmant à écrire librement," he said; and then he came
back to his sober Touraine once more.

It would be tedious to mention all his writings here, and,
besides, I have not read them all.   With the passage of
years there has been an increasing sobriety in his work,
which has gradually lost something of the gaiety and
buoyancy with which it charmed us at the outset.   What
has not been lost is the constructive gift, the fine sense of
proportion and symmetry.   Probably one of the best of
Boylesve's later novels will be judged to be " Elise," which
appeared in 1921.

This book has the curious feature that it opens with the
suicide of the heroine, and then goes back to recount the
succession of incidents which led to this catastrophe.   Elise
is the daughter of an old maniac of nobility who cares for
nothing but genealogies, while her mother is a pronounced
though belated flirt.   Much left to her own devices in the
Norman port of Granville, which is described with Boylesve's
customary minuteness, poor Elise takes one false step after
another, and finds herself unable to withstand the pressure
of local convention.   This is a melancholy story, told with
great skill and completeness.

From an early age the novelist was distinguished by the
prudence and elegance of his style, which was founded on
a close study of eighteenth-century masters.   Pressed to a

confession, he admitted in after years that Montesquieu and Voltaire had been his masters. His passion for Italy had been a passing sentiment, and in the fullness of his talent he returned to what he called " the sweetness, the delicacy, the tranquil and benevolent majesty of the broad landscapes of the Loire." He instinctively repeated this serenity in his manner of writing. Curiously enough, there used to be a little complaint of want of exactitude in his style, as though it were somewhat lacking in grammatical accuracy. Nothing was heard of these censures after 1918, when the French Academy received René Boylesve among the Immortals. This is not a matter about which a foreigner may venture to speak, but perhaps the ease and fluidity of his method may have laid him a little open to the charge.

Boylesve loves the minute study of local character and manners. He is never sensational, never emphatic, but he recounts the order of events with a nonchalant grace, with a subtle notation of causes and effects. Among English novelists, the one whom he resembles most closely, in spite of immense differences, is Mrs. Gaskell. But he had, as he showed in " Le Leçon d'Amour," a voluptuous and sensuous side never revealed in the discreet authoress of " Cranford." The life of modern novels is precarious, and no one can venture to prophesy, but I hope that readers will continue to delight in the stories, so intensely French in feeling and so distinguished in manner, which René Boylesve has bequeathed to us, and meanwhile we mourn the premature cessation of a voice so melodious and so clear.

# MR.  SASSOON'S  SATIRES

# MR. SASSOON'S SATIRES

No one can question that the generation which just preceded the War was remarkable for the universality of its interest in verse. Never before, except during a few late years of Elizabeth's reign, were there so many poets alive in England in proportion to the number of inhabitants. This bardic fury has gradually cooled down, but even now we cannot with absolute distinctness perceive what will be the ultimate result. One thing we may be sure of, literature cannot endure, and will not retain, such a crowd of gifted creatures. When poets are like grains of sand upon the shore, the tide of oblivion must sweep over most of them. It is sad to think of the board schools where every child of the age of fourteen rivalled Mr. Kipling, and the suburban clubs where every maiden warbled. Can all these be forgotten? Can silence ever subdue the thunder of the lyres of Brompton? Unfortunately there is no doubt that it can—and must. There is no room in the world for such a profusion of song. It was extraordinarily, devastatingly good, up to a certain point, and was doomed from the first to be forgotten. There is too much of it, and it will die of its own tropical profusion. But among the three or four writers under the age of fifty of whom it may safely be predicted that their verse will outlive the fashion of the moment, Mr. Siegfried Sassoon has an assured place.

It is to be observed that the earliest work of writers of originality shows, when we look back upon it, signs of the peculiar faculty which is finally to be characteristic, but

which will presently be obscured for the moment by what
is merely imitative. This is what happened in the case of
Mr. Sassoon. If I am right in believing that a sarcastic
observation of life, noted in elaborate language, and rather
objective than subjective, in other words that branch of
the poetic art which we call satire, is the peculiar gift of
this poet, then it cannot but be of interest to glance at
what (unless I am mistaken) is the earliest of his numerous
publications, the little drama called " Orpheus in Dilœ-
ryum," which he brought out in 1908. This attracted no
attention, and intrinsically it deserved but little, since
the execution of it was crude and indistinct. But the
point is, that it was definitely satirical in character; that
it mocked the pomposities and affectations of " cultured
persons " in language which was ornately sophisticated;
and that it regarded objects and actions from the outside
rather than from the inside. Mr. Sassoon was not encouraged to pursue this line; and in his subsequent pre-War
volumes we find him reverting to the usual " Georgian "
tricks of introspection, amatory sentiment, and traditional
form. He performed these manœuvres with increasing
skill, but they did not lead him anywhere. He was in
danger of being lost in the throng of refined and graceful
versifiers who all wrote well, but who sang in indiscriminate
chorus.

The War broke into the lyrical conventionality, and this
poet experienced the real facts of life in Flanders. The
result was seen in the volume which first brought the name
of Mr. Siegfried Sassoon prominently before the public,
" The Old Huntsman " of 1917. The name-poem of this
collection is the monologue of a country publican, who has
once been huntsman to the squire, and has now retired to
the unprofitable management of the " Golden Fleece."
This is the longest poem Mr. Sassoon has published, and
it belongs to the class of Tennyson's " Northern Father "

in its attempt to illustrate rustic psychology in language
exactly on a level with rural experience. The influence of
Mr. Masefield is apparent in its form. It is skilful and
picturesque, but belongs to a pre-War order of thought.
In the rest of the volume, the more genuine voice of a
remarkable writer was perceived. The time has even now
hardly come when we can speak of the War with calm, or
even reconsider its aspects without repugnance. But these
poems of Mr. Sassoon's were received with more than
reluctance, even with a kind of disgust. The shouting was
over, the laurels were cut, but people at home were still
unwilling to recognise the brutalities of the real thing. In
France, M. Barbusse startled everybody with his dreadful
book, " Le Feu "; here much less sensation was caused by
the less violent poems of Mr. Sassoon, but the movement
was identical; it was an unwilling transition from a pink
world to a black one, from illusion to reality. It is not
well to waken the ghosts of ten years ago, yet I must
quote one of the poems in Mr. Sassoon's volume of
1917 to exemplify what I mean. It is the piece called
" Blighters " :—

> The house is crammed : tier beyond tier they grin
>   And cackle at the show, while prancing ranks
> Of harlots shrill in chorus, drunk with din ;
>   " We're sure the Kaiser loves the dear old Tanks ! "
>
> I'd like to see a Tank come down the stalls,
>   Lurching to rag-time tunes, or " Home, Sweet Home ! "—
> And there'd be no more jokes in music-halls
>   To mock the riddled corpses round Bapaume.

In the little volume of the next year, " Counter-Attack,"
the note of exasperation was even more vehement. Indignation never made fiercer verses than these, read at the
time with angry impatience, now for the moment perhaps
forgotten, but in the future sure of revival as a record of
observation and resentment. This intense white heat of

protestation could not be long sustained, and in the
" Picture Show " of 1919 Mr. Sassoon, without quite
abandoning his invectives, tempered them with pathos.
To the transition, or the division, of moods belongs the
exquisite piece entitled " Memory," of which I cannot but
quote the last lines :—

> But now my heart is heavy-laden.  I sit
> Burning my dreams away beside the fire :
> For death has made me wise and bitter and strong;
> And I am rich in all that I have lost.
> O starshine on the fields of long-ago,
> Bring me the darkness and the nightingale;
> Dim wealds of vanished summer, peace of home,
> And silence, and the faces of my friends.

The prayer is answered, and the mature work of this
interesting poet seems to be definitely divided between the
" nightingale " of reverie and the " darkness " of satire.
The two volumes before me to-day, one a selection of old
poems, the other a group of new ones, almost exclusively
deal with the second aspect, and I will therefore confine
my remarks mainly to the satirist in Mr. Sassoon, though
I am far from doubting that he will often return to the
delicacy of emotional analysis which gives such poems as
" Falling Asleep " and the enchanting " Conclusion " a
place among the most perfect lyrics of our time.  But it is
as a satirist that, for the moment, Mr. Sassoon seems to
present himself, and it is therefore as a satirist that we
must inspect him.

Satire is the department of imaginative literature in
which it is most difficult to make a permanent success.
The clever versifier, of whom the once-famous Charles
Churchill is the type, who simply rails at all men and all
things, may foster a temporary celebrity by the recklessness with which he indulges his passion for grumbling, but
he adds nothing to the poetic wealth of the language.  The
genuine satirist, Dryden, or, still more, Pope, achieves

excellence by rising above the mere ridicule of human error, and, as someone has put it, by " projecting his figures against a background of the infinite." Thus in the hands of the greatest masters satire becomes, in a sense, lyrical, or at least has the exultation and dignity without which verse, however smart, cannot be acknowledged as poetic. It is not enough to be angry in a good cause, it is still less to be soured by what Shakespeare calls " a poor unmanly melancholy sprung from change of fortune." There must be a habit of mind, quite independent of circumstances, which forces the observer to express himself sarcastically and even disdainfully of the scene around him and of the actors. There is always something a little suspicious in the " strong antipathy of good to bad " of which Pope rashly boasted, and temperament has more than pure rage to do with a satirist's inspiration. If we consider carefully we see that Timon of Athens could never have written satire, but that the indifferent Apemantus might well have done so. Indeed, it is not impossible that Shakespeare, in conceiving that churlish philosopher, had at the back of his mind a thought of the snarling Marstons and Halls of his own epoch.

The social conditions of the age have nowadays routed the satirist from the most convenient of his fastnesses. What the reader has always liked, and in spite of the increasing obscurity of names will continue to like, in the satires of Boileau and Pope is the insolence of personal attack, the funny rudeness of the poet to living people whom he dislikes or despises. Gravity pretends to be shocked, but what readers really enjoy is the ridicule of Dennis or Chapelain. But the humdrum law of libel has stepped in, and if the satirist is not careful his vivacity is damped by a solicitor's letter. The field of satire, therefore, has to be impersonal, and unusual talent is required in order to cultivate it with profit. The satire of

Mr. Sassoon is entirely impersonal. He does not attempt to
forge afresh the burning arrows of Pope. The difference
between his method and that of the age of Queen Anne is
exemplified in his " A Stately Exterior," where he chal-
lenges comparison with the " Epistle to Lord Burlington."
His Scutcheon Hall, where

> A gardener clicks quick shears beyond the yews;
> Red-Admirals and Painted-Ladies bask
> And float along the dahlia-brightened border;
> Sunshine performs its horticultural task,
> And ripened figs harbour the wasp-marauder,

is the twentieth-century equivalent of Timon's Villa. But
there is no Villario in it, no Sir Visto; and for the personal
anger which inspired the earlier writer, our poet substitutes
a general mockery of things in general, all the modern
world, in his judgment, being out of joint.

The main technical defect of satire is that it must always
be fragmentary. There is no example of a satirical poem
which is a rounded whole, complete in the proportion of
its parts. Mr. Sassoon has not escaped the general danger.
His volume is a collection of episodes, of instances, of
unrelated illustrations. It consists of memoranda of
things seen and detested, of admirable landscapes defiled
by human folly, of scornful picturesque scenes out of " the
fairy-tale of Flunkeydom." He looks for the arrival of a
species of millennium, where good taste—that is to say,
Mr. Sassoon's taste, which seems to be very good—shall
somehow be restored in an " epic age "—

> When boudoir beauty shall no more beguile,
> And sentiment is elbowed off the earth.

A time will come when we, " shorn of our psycho-analytic
pride," may repose on some perfection at present very
vaguely outlined. An amusing passage in " Evensong in
Westminster Abbey " describes the horror of the emotional

discords which distract and confine us, until "hosannatic Handel liberates us at last." Very good, but what becomes of the earnest worshipper of Debussy? A fragment again, pungent and entertaining, but provoking once more the question, Can a satire be a work of art?

The worst of satirical poetry is that the argument of it is uncertain, the philosophy inconsistent. Sparkling sarcasm and wandering innuendo take the place of a system of connected thought. I cannot think that Mr. Sassoon has avoided dangers which beset Juvenal himself, and will continue to make satire an unsatisfactory branch of the art. He rails melodiously and spasmodically against whatever in present-day life he dislikes. He has a proper hatred of push, of advertisement, of privilege, of what he calls "visionless officialised fatuity." He is revolted by artificiality wherever he meets with it, even at Wembley, where he was doubtless not alone in finding the antique spirit of serenity absent. He mocks at college-feasts where the Madeira is older than the oldest of the Dons. The want of intelligence shown by visitors to a public picture gallery vexes him. Yet, if everybody appreciated Il Greco and college Madeira, what a dull world it would be, and how we should long for Mr. Sassoon's recoveries! I have only one technical objection to make. There is a humorous value in the ironical use of pompous verbiage, but Mr. Sassoon sometimes over-does his Johnsonese. He is happier where he is not girding at the "psycho-co-efficient unconfessed in calm cynosural canvasses."

# MISS SITWELL'S POEMS

# MISS SITWELL'S POEMS

THE verse of Miss Edith Sitwell has been before the public for about a dozen years. At all events I became conscious of it in 1915, when a thin grey pamphlet arrived from Oxford, containing five short pieces of a tentative character. In these there was nothing to startle or to scandalise; they were accomplished exercises owing not a little to the study of Shelley. Only the final one, the fierce and tender denunciation by a mother's ghost of the son who has murdered her for her gold, had a certain individuality. Miss Sitwell then became a contributor, during four seasons, to one of those friendly miscellanies in which talent which cannot find individual outlet makes a collective appeal for attention. In " Wheels," as this medley was called, for 1916, a piece entitled " Gaiety " gave the careful reader an impression of something new intelligently attempted.

Next year, this sensation was emphatically increased by " The Satyr in the Periwig." The advantages of a social miscellany are great at the outset of a career, but they turn after a while into disadvantages, and Miss Edith Sitwell was wise to sever her connection with " Wheels " and to publish her selected poems in an independent volume as " Clowns' Houses " in 1918. Such are the short and simple annals of this author's early career from a bibliographical point of view, but they give no hint of the hubbub which the verses themselves have continued to awaken, nor of the passions they have roused in critical bosoms.

The central instinct which drove Miss Sitwell into metrical expression was, I presume, a sense of the need she had of escaping from boredom. She found herself stifled in a literary atmosphere where almost every human being, even every boy and girl at a board school, could exhale what was called " decent poetry." The torpor of style pressed upon the whole generation; she saw no great fixed stars, but a Milky Way. She felt an irrepressible desire to introduce fresh emotion, and above all to divest words of their traditional value. She deprecated the modern excessive cultivation of logic; she proposed to herself to be preposterous and prodigious. Her imagination was fantastic, and it expressed itself naturally in unfamiliar terms. In a moment I may return to the historical aspect of this attitude of mind, which gave her early critics a great deal of needless solicitude.

While being thus true to her own nature, however, she did not escape the temptation to be *outré* and extravagant. I do not think that in future years she will look back upon the highly entertaining little volume called " Facade " (why not " Façade " ?) as doing full justice to the seriousness of her purpose. The reviewers wished to blaspheme, and here she laid herself out with liberality to collect their curses. She wrote " Long steel grass, the white soldiers pass," and the critics went simply off their heads. Nothing stimulates the Muses so much as persecution, and no doubt Miss Sitwell has been appreciated sooner than she would have been had she not so wilfully laid herself open to attack. Moreover, she is " ever a fighter," and evidently enjoys the fray. But fortunately she has not been willing to satisfy her ambition by a mere ebullience of eccentricity, and her later writings have shown her to be detained no longer by the pleasant exercise of putting out a defiant tongue at her enemies. " The Sleeping Beauty " displayed a development of style which is more than confirmed by

" Rustic Elegies." Miss Edith Sitwell has only to cease being a mere " grotesque " for her poetry to become an important factor in our current literature.

Less than justice is done to Miss Sitwell's talent by those who insist on the harlequin element in her verse. By quoting extreme examples of her mannerism, it is easy to represent her as nothing better than a mountebank, screaming for personal attention without having seriously deserved it. This is entirely unfair both to her theory and practice, but it is encouraged by her admirers when they thrust upon us such extravagant pieces as the too-familiar scene of the Bishop eating his ketchup in presence of " the flunkeyed and trumpetting sea." I am ready to admit that it would be easy and entertaining to justify this and many other slightly perverse examples of a system that is pushed beyond the borders of wisdom. Of the so-called " Bucolic Comedies " of 1923 there are many which will, in all probability, lose their strangeness and ultimately prove as acceptable as many of the recognised poems of the past.

But in order that they should do so it is essential that their author, by the development of her powers, should justify readers of the next generation in returning with indulgence to her early poems. If Miss Sitwell were not prepared to advance beyond, let us say, the giddy bravura of " Beelzebub called for his syllabub," we should have to confess that, amusing as her impromptus were (I adore " Beelzebub and his syllabub "), they had in them no quality of permanence. When we had laughed once or twice at the sheer audacity of them, there would be an end of it. But if we find their author, without resigning her ambition, rising to more serious matters, with greater skill, then we not merely appreciate her advance, but we learn to look back upon her experiments and find a new value in them. In short, we make of the author what she contrives to make of herself.

s

In this spirit I invite a candid reader to examine " Rustic
Elegies " with an open mind, and without prejudice for or
against the lady's previous productions.  The book is
formed by a group of three very elaborate and artificial
studies in lyrical satire, all composed with extreme and
sometimes finicking minuteness by a writer who pretends
to have a contempt for art, but who is to her most diminutive finger-tip an artist and nothing but an artist.  The
opening poem is the best which Miss Sitwell has yet published—the most coherent, the most articulate—and we
therefore do her no injustice if we examine it.  " Elegy on
Dead Fashions " is a sustained piece of some 500 verses,
dealing, as in a vision, with the mental and social peculiarities of the much-discussed Victorian Age.  If the publication of Lady Augusta Stanley's " Letters " had preceded
it, " Dead Fashions " might have been taken as a commentary on that special revelation of the period of crinoline.

But in Miss Sitwell's picture Windsor melts into a
vaporous landscape by Watteau, disguised as Winter-
halter :—

> The nymphs are dead like the great summer roses ;
> Only an Abyssinian wind dozes :
> Cloyed with late honey are his dark wings' sheens ;
> Yet once on those lone crags nymphs bright as queens,
>
> Walked with elegant footsteps through light leaves
> Where only elegiac air now grieves,
> For the light leaves are sere, and whisper dead
> Echoes of elegances lost and fled. . . .
>
> One wood-nymph wore a deep black velvet bonnet
> With blackest ivy leaves for wreaths upon it,
> Shading her face as lovely as the fountains
> While she descended from deep-wooded mountains.

The quietness of these verses may conceal from those
who have welcomed Miss Sitwell most joyously in her
megaphonic moods the fact that the essentials of her

style remain unchanged. Another dip into the same lucky
bag :—

> Beside the Alps of sea, each crinoline
> Of muslin and of gauze and grenadine,
> Sweeps by the Mendelssohnian waterfall,
> O'er beaver-smooth grass, by the castle wall,
>
> Beside the thick mosaic of the leaves.
> Left by the glamour of some huger eves
> The thick gold spangles on those leaves are seen
> Like the sharp twanging of a mandoline.

We shall be greatly lacking in ingenuity if we permit
these lines to leave no definite impression on the mind.
The difficulties they present are of a kind which incessantly
present themselves in the poetry of Miss Sitwell, and which
claim intelligent appreciation. Whether she always suc-
ceeds or not, her aim is apparent, namely to extend the
range of impressions produced by words without losing
essential beauty. The employment of images taken from
dress, from personal adornment, from objects of common
use, is in direct opposition to the restriction of poetic
language insisted upon by the Romantics; it recurs to the
practice of the seventeenth century, when it was considered poetic to describe the trees in winter as " peri-
wigg'd " with snow. Hence, into an elegy wholly sentimental and pensive are abundantly introduced such
epithets as " swan-skin " for strawberry-leaves, while
Artemis shoots her arrows through greenhouses of vegetable
marrows, and Psyche pines away, a kitchen-maid.

The Wordsworthians saw Nature in dim and Ossianic
forms, released from the garnishing of everyday life; to
Miss Sitwell the foreground is crossed by dream-figures in
crinolines symbolical of 1850, which carry baskets of velvet
nectarines over trellised mountain-bridges. The use of
words is consistent with this defiance of the old poetic
formulas. The wind is " dark-winged " and wines are

"plumed as birds of paradise"; the rain falls in "gauze ribbands"; wild cherries "sing their madrigals." These extensions of the significance of words produce an odd effect for the moment, but they never seem, when they fulfil their purpose, to obscure the poet's symbolic intention, and until they do that, I see no reason why we should allow them to annoy us. I ask that literature should give me pleasure; I do not dictate to writers by what route they shall approach me.

The second piece in "Rustic Elegies" is called "The Hambone and the Heart." Rabelais tells us that Panurge was born of the loves of a ham and a bottle, but Miss Sitwell is not inclined towards anything Pantagruelist. She tells, or hints, a story of recurrent tragedy, and she writes it with the image of a screaming clown, brandishing a hambone in one hand and a human heart in the other. "Prelude to a Fairy Tale" seems to open with a first draught of "Elegy on Dead Fashion," and this impression is deepened by the recurrence of marked phrases from that poem. For instance, the strawberry plants have "swan-skin" leaves, and even the pool a "swan-skin" surface. I do not quite perceive what merit resides in the couplet,

> the hot wind, that little Savoyard,
> Decked them with wild flowers à la montagnard,

but I am quite sure that we do not need to find it repeated three times in one slender volume. Indeed, my main quarrel with Miss Sitwell is not that she uses violent and grotesque imagery, as she has a perfect right to do, but that she does not perceive that to recommend such extraordinary innovations as she projects, her *technique* should be faultless. This it is as yet far from being. She can write verse of exact and poignant beauty, but her ear must be defective, or she would not allow so many sudden deviations from rhythm to disturb her serious verse. This defect also seems to be passing, and she has written nothing more mellifluous than the six final stanzas of " Elegy on Dead Fashion." Yet, even here, it is strange that she should permit the dislocated syntax of the couplet " How day rolls down " to pass unamended.

An extraordinary mixture of sensitiveness and bravado marks Miss Sitwell's attitude towards the art she cultivates, and makes it extremely difficult to estimate the value of her writing. She seems as though at any moment she might break out into exquisite music, but is held back by a crochety dryness of voice, an invasion of the bull-frog into the domain of the nightingale. The main charge brought by indignant reviewers against her verse, namely, that it indulges in analogies preposterously borrowed from senses which are in no æsthetic relation (the " creaking " of light, " blunt stalactites " of rain, the " sour, unripe " wind), has no point for the student of literature, who has only to recollect Blake, Calderon, Donne, and even Shakespeare to see how daringly poets in rebellion against convention have renewed their surface by violent sensorial innovations. Nothing is forbidden to an experimenter, except failure. If Miss Sitwell does not produce the impression she aims at, her practice must be condemned, and not her theory. It would take me too far afield to explain why in certain cases, in spite of her daring and skill, she fails to hit the bull's-eye. Perhaps the reckless acrobatism of Laforgue has been something of a snare to her. But she has no need of spangled tights and a trapeze. She is full of talent and ambition, and the one thing (so it seems to me) which she lacks to carry out her vocation to the full is a firmer instinct for sober and delicate technical precision. I would have her aim relentlessly at being less funny and more human.

# THE BLACK CAT

# THE BLACK CAT

WHEN, in February, 1907, the eminent and ultra-Parisian Monsieur Donnay was received into the French Academy, he opened his discourse by a graceful apology for a certain early impertinence. He admitted, smiling as he said it, that in his impenitent youth he had clothed the waiters at the picturesque Chat Noir in the very costume of green palms and silver lace which it was now his own privilege to wear. Still older and more eminent by nineteen years, the famous playwright now recurs again to that frivolous past, and this time offers no apology at all for the revival of his wild oats.

His book of memories and verses, " Autour du Chat Noir," will be welcomed by all who remember what a feature of- artistic life the famous *cabaret* of Montmartre was in the youth of those who, alas ! are young no more. It was in 1881 that an amazing artist, Rodolphe Salis, founded in the Boulevard Rochechouart a restaurant which was devoted to the fine arts. There was beer there for all " who earn their thirst artistically "; it was a sanctuary open only to those " who live by their intellect." The sculpture of a Black Cat hung high over the front door, while a magnificent real black cat sat enthroned in an arm-chair by the fire. Poems were read, music was performed, even little plays were staged, to amuse an audience which Rodolphe Salis alternately insulted and addressed as " Vos Seigneuries et Vos Altesses Electorales."

From the beginning of its merry existence, the house was the home of all odd artistries. The earliest society which met there was that of the Hydropaths, so called not because they recognised the healing power of water, but because they suffered from the thought of it; they were of those who cannot bear the idea of using water for drinking purposes. They were followed by the Hirsutes, by the Incoherents, by the Neodecadents, who, in their turn, gave way to the Brutalists and the Symbolists. Between these warring but extremely friendly bodies there was not a penny to choose, and the Black Cat went on purring in front of the fire. The club enjoyed a huge success, so much so that in 1885 it was forced to move to larger premises at 8, rue Victor Massé in the heart of Montmartre.

The exodus took place at 11 p.m. in great public pomp by torchlight, and to an accompaniment of fifes and violins. M. Donnay does not speak of this ceremony, in which, I suppose, that he took no share, since at this moment he had not yet become part and parcel of the concern. He was a young engineer, lately emerged from the École Centrale, with a high diploma for Greek and Latin. But, as Maurice Barrès once wrote, " Où mènent les études classiques? Elles mènent au café," where " les Quat'z' Arts " were riotously enjoying themselves. M. Donnay recounts the emotion with which he gazed up at the notice over the door of the restaurant, " Passant, sois moderne," and determined that at all risks he would be modern.

Monsieur Donnay describes the odd accident by which he became the official poet of this eclectic circle. He was sitting one evening in the salon, and wondering why the room was empty, when Rodolphe Salis entered like a whirlwind, and said, " What are you doing there? Don't you know that there's a general rehearsal going on upstairs? Come and recite some verses!" Accordingly, having just written " Quatorze Juillet " (which is printed here), young M. Donnay plucked up courage and recited; he had an amazing success. He does not tell us, what

Barrès has recorded, that his personal appearance, voice, and gesture combined to commend him. With his dark eyes, long hair, and deceptive melancholy, he reminded that acute observer of an Annamite mandarin.

It became one of the principal attractions of the Chat Noir to hear Maurice Donnay recite " La Cassière " or " Les Vieux Messieurs " among the Byzantine decorations and the *ombres chinoises* of Henri Rivière. Hitherto he had enjoyed no recognition. He was always writing verses, but the editors would not print them. The only exception had been a sonnet which was inserted on the back page of a trade newspaper, in front of an advertisement of braces, the author's name being misspelt at the foot. After giving a very droll account of this adventure, he says : " Bref, je ne fus pas aussi content que je l'avais espéré ! " No wonder; but after that triumphant evening under the auspices of the Black Cat, all was ecstasy and the primrose path.

When we compare the spirit of the Chat Noir with that of the young men of the London " 'nineties," we are struck with a difference which is of race and climate, but also of education. Our Fleet Street poets who were anxious that the world should be aware that their hearts were like a music-hall, were self-consciously being as naughty as they knew how to be. They were thinking all the time of the Nonconformist Conscience in their old country homes, and wondering how the children of the manse could dare to be so daring. The passage of a maiden aunt would have snatched any one of them from the absinthe which in reality he so much disliked and would have re-installed him at the tea-table. They could never persuade us, if they half-persuaded themselves, that they liked sitting up all night drinking beer.

M. Donnay has found himself disinclined to analyse the spirit of the Chat Noir, but we may feel that it certainly was not the spirit of the Rhymers' Club. It was not the expression of a sect or of a set purpose, but was an outburst of genuine gaiety and independence, adopting forms which were simple in the extreme, and yet cultivated and jovial. The English verse of the 'nineties is wistful; it seems to confess to a lack of high animal spirits, to an absence of resolution. This is the sort of thing :—

> And then a woman passed. The hour
> Rang heavily along the air.
> I had no hope, I had no power
> To think—for thought was but despair.

There is no use in having a heart that is like a music-hall if it cannot yield you more fun than that.

The French poet—doubtless to his disadvantage in some respects—has never possessed a Nonconformist Conscience. He inherited from his Latin forbears a wealth of fantastic sensation. He had never trembled under Isaac Watts, but he had laughed aloud with Rabelais. And to comprehend what we may almost call the necessity of a Chat Noir, we must recollect that France had just gone through a dark time. The realists, with Zola at their head, had denuded the life of imagination of all its charm. There were political factions and social intrigues which robbed the southern sunlight of its warmth.

The declared aim of the Chat Noir was to discredit naturalism and to reawaken idealism. It was welcomed not merely by the idle public, but by the leaders of feeling, for the young poets were strengthened in their effort by the intelligent sympathy of a generation which looked further back than the war of 1870. Among those who generously welcomed their amusing extravagance were Jules Lemaître and M. Paul Bourget. It is remarkable as emphasising the difference between French and English habit in these matters, that in spite of the wild note of the

Chat Noir, and the audacity of its crackling and screaming mirth, it was astonishingly "cultivated." Its poets remembered their Greek philosophy and their Latin lyrics. Almost all the most popular verses contained allusions which would be lost over the heads of a London cinema audience, but which were seized in a flash by the infatuated public which crowded, as by privilege, into Rodolphe Salis's vibrating halls. M. Maurice Donnay was not merely the most farcical of wits, but he was a scholar-poet like Lionel Johnson. The 'nineties, with us, if we can imagine them streamed upon by sunshine and fed with warm Gallic blood, may be taken as a rough conception of this imaginative gaiety of the Chat Noir.

In later days, M. Paul Bourget remarked that M. Donnay would do well to take for his motto what Beatrice says in " Much Ado about Nothing "—" there was a star danced, and under that was I born ! " Those who have had the happiness of being beguiled on the stage by the recurrent triumphs of the author of " Amants " will not be surprised to find running through the verses printed in this merry little volume a saltatory movement. M. Donnay has always had a spirit in his feet which leads him to dance where other poets walk or run :—

> Ainsi qu'une belle Fatma
> Dedans la boutique où l'on entre
> Pour voir quelque danse du ventre,
> Le poète qui vous aima
> Blonde, châtaine, rousse, brune,
> Qui vous aima comme la lune !
> Le poète qui vous aima
> L'autre tantôt et tantôt l'une,
> Par devant votre chœur moqueur,
> Va danser la danse du cœur.

The lyrical pieces of M. Donnay's youth are not to be taken too seriously. They were widely quoted and discussed when they were originally recited at the Chat Noir.

The typical bourgeois, M Gorgibus, of whom it was said
that—

> Ne pouvant prendre la Bastille,
> Il en prend du moins l'omnibus

was a universal butt;

> Je songe, en remerciant Dieu,
> Qu'ils n'en ont pas en Angleterre

was a couplet which gave general satisfaction;

> Il était laid et maigrelet,
> Ayant sucé le maigre lait
> D'une nourrice pessimiste,
> Et c'était un nourisson triste

escaped the shipwreck of memory which awaits all popular
rhymes.   But no one could any longer recall what it was
that roused M. Gorgibus on July 14, nor what the particular dainties were that do not exist in England, nor
what was the life's history of the sad youth whose name
was Adolphe.

The poems themselves, after having passed from mouth
to mouth, had disappeared, with the shadow theatres, and
the great black cat, and the lithographs guarded by thin
pink paper.   M. Donnay has done well to collect these
fallen rose-leaves in a pot-pourri where the romance of
youth is mingled with the musk and spice of a wit that
has not yet evaporated.   There is something of Théophile
Gautier, more of Verlaine, in the texture of these sparkling
lyrics.   Nous n'en avons pas en Angleterre, but Calverley
might have written something like " Les vieux Messieurs "
if Mrs. Grundy would have given him his head.   But a
reading of these innocent (although extremely frivolous)
Chat Noir rhymes makes us realise what a chasm yawns
between the British and the French ideas of being funny.

Two short plays—or poetical farces or saynètes—complete our excursion " Autour du Chat Noir."   Of these

" Phryné " was performed in the Shadow Theatre in January, 1891, and " Ailleurs " in November of the same year. It was between the two dates that Théodore de Banville died, and although there is nothing in the present preface to justify the conjecture, I cannot help believing that M. Donnay, perhaps unconsciously, offered his little dramas as a tribute to the delicate author of " Riquet à la Houppe." They present to us, tenderly and sensuously, with impish peals of laughter, conceptions of antiquity which are modern in the extreme.

It is very notable that in the midst of all his hirsutes and his brutalists, M. Donnay remained severely traditional in form. " Ailleurs " is a series of Aristophanic scenes, exhibiting the adventures of a Dante and a Virgil who are Voltaire and Terminus. When the latter sings (why? Goodness only knows !) the hymn of the Birth of Moses, he does it in rhythms and rhymes of the most classical exactitude. This severity of style adds greatly to the entertainment of the reader, and was doubtless appreciated by the audience at the Chat Noir. " Passant, sois moderne," but do not deviate into the errors of the Dadaists and the Decadents ! The Black Cat allows you to say (almost) anything you like, but you must say it in correct verse, with alternate masculine and feminine rhymes. The prosody which was good enough for Racine is good enough for you. So much for the form ; as to the substance, Passant, sois moderne !

# GISSING

# GISSING

If any legitimate disappointment is felt by the reader of the collection of George Gissing's "Letters to His Family," it will be due to the suggestion that this is in some way a continuation of "The Private Papers of Henry Ryecroft," Gissing's most mature and least tormented work. The correspondence here published has nothing whatever to do with "Henry Ryecroft," and it would have been wise not to put it forward in rivalry with that book. If, as the editors surmise, Gissing intended to expand what they call "that classic of self-revelation," the project was quite certainly not planned in the form of these letters, which do, indeed, reach the final period of serenity in the author's life, but are mainly and essentially occupied with the years of intense intellectual effort which saw the production of his early novels. No one who is acquainted with the character and adventures of George Gissing will expect these domestic letters to contain much that is cheerful or facetious. We do not go to George Gissing for that kind of entertainment, since he never, as he admitted himself, grew "tired of noting the monotonous and ignoble days." But he was pathetically mistaken in supposing that his "solitude was a wearisome topic." It was so to him, and yet he perpetually recurred to it. The proverb says, Laugh and the world laughs with you, weep and you weep alone. The life of George Gissing was the saddest, and also the most solitary, of any modern author of eminence, but it does not repel attention, perhaps because of its pensive intensity. The sadness of it was inevitable, and presents to us a spectacle which is genuinely tragic, because it is seen to have been beyond human ingenuity to alter.

The career of George Gissing offers a complete commentary on Dr. Johnson's famous line :—

> Slow rises worth by poverty depress'd.

The novelist had reached the same age when he published his first successful novel, " Demos," as the moralist had when " London " appeared.  Each was just keeping body and soul together by the ceaseless labour of a journeyman author.  But the parallel ends with the circumstance of their penury, and Samuel Johnson was sustained by a passionate vitality which Gissing entirely lacked.  The one could " pause awhile from letters, to be wise " ;  the other realised no aim save, by clinging desperately to literature, to escape " toil, envy, want, the garret and the jail."  No one must expect the familiar letters to members of his family, which are here arranged by their piety and care, to produce fresh " revelations " of the life of George Gissing.  Very soon after his death in 1903 ample particulars were forthcoming, and were disseminated with a freedom which it is not for me to censure or applaud.  Nothing, in any case, was left unrevealed, and it may well be argued that such a character as that of George Gissing is not worth discussing if the truth is not told.

In his case, certainly, it was promenaded in complete undress by a succession of biographers.  Nothing is now added to all the troubles of early youth, and the few letters dated from Manchester and the United States do not hint at the incidents of those doleful years.  The correspondence really starts in October, 1877, when the world-worn lad was just twenty, and had already gone through a nightmare of adventures.  His friend, the late Thomas Seccombe, in his valuable account of him, pointed out that these are

described with the utmost fullness in " New Grub Street."
We may leave them there.

The new letters do, however, throw considerable sidelight
on the intellectual character of Gissing, and on his essential
aims. The popular view of him, as a companion of the
poor who was moved by extreme pity to expose in an
attractive form the sorrow and injustice of their life, is an
incorrect one. We have always suspected, and the confessions to his family confirm the doubt, that no irresistible
instinct of philanthropy urged the author of a long series
of gloomy stories to express himself in the form of fiction.
Gissing was a novelist made, and well made, but not born;
nor were his personal instincts proletarian, but aristocratic. With the least encouragement to make a living
otherwise, there would have been no " Demos " and no
" Thyrza." He described " The Nether World " not
because he had any curiosity about crime, but because he
was forced to earn the bread and dripping on which he
kept his indignant body alive. He says to his brother, in
1880, after the publication of " Workers in the Dawn,"
which his family had thought gloomy, " If you knew much
of my daily life you would wonder that I write at all, to say
nothing of writing cheerfully."

At the same time, he was writing with desperate sincerity,
" for thinking and struggling men," by whom he unconsciously meant himself. His books were ground out of
him by the contemplation of his own misery, and nothing
but his fine artistic conscientiousness kept them from being
openly egocentric. He wrote, again in 1880, " I mean to
bring home to people the ghastly condition, material,
mental, and moral, of our poor classes, to show the hideous
injustice of our whole system of society, to give light upon
the plan of altering it." But it was his own " ghastly
condition " which inspired him, and in this he is sharply
to be distinguished from the Balzacs and Zolas who

gathered all their material from outside. Gissing's life
was not spent in collecting facts, but in stimulating a
keen intuition by means of intense and unmitigated self-
contemplation.

The real bent and bias of his mind are revealed in these
letters with more distinctness than ever before, and this is
what gives the collection a value which its slight colourless-
ness may seem to belie. We perceive, in the first place,
that the genius of George Gissing was thwarted from his
first entrance into competition with the world. He was,
in boyhood, a prodigy of acquisition. At the age of fifteen
he came out first in the country in the Oxford Local
Examinations, and prize after prize succeeded. These
preliminary laurels were all gained in classical accomplishments, mainly by direct proof of erudition in Latin and
Greek. Gissing had been born in Wakefield, and it is an
odd coincidence that the one other leading man of letters
native to this Yorkshire town should be Richard Bentley.
Whether Gissing remembered, or had indeed ever heard of,
this fact I doubt; but I like to think that it stimulated his
studies to know that he and the great Master of Trinity
learned their Latin at the same local school.

Gissing was by instinct a critical humanist, and if fate
had been but reasonably kind, and if the extreme penury
of his early years could have been modified so far as to
allow him an entrance to Oxford or Cambridge, it is hardly
to be doubted that he would have become an eminent
scholar. Like Bentley, he should have gone from Wakefield
with a scholarship to St. John's. Ensconced in college
rooms, with his texts around him, his oak sported and his
wants unconsciously provided for, Gissing might have
attained as much happiness as his fluttering spirit desired.
He might have become celebrated for his criticism of
Byzantine texts, and have done for Cassiodorus what Bentley
did for Manilius. There was something in him of Casaubon,

nothing of Dickens; he was a humanist whom poverty pressed into the mould of a novelist. That his novels are so interesting and so well written is merely the result of his intellectual force, which was prodigious, but they were composed against the grain, and the writer's heart all the while was not in Grub Street but on the shores of the Ionian Sea.

Gissing was supposed to be saturated with his particular subject as a " realist." Henry James defined him as one who "reeked with the savour, was bowed beneath the fruits, of contact with the lower, with the lowest middle-class," about whom, in the later 'nineties, he was accepted as the one trustworthy authority. But we do not begin to understand the temper in which books like " The Year of Jubilee " and " Born in Exile " were written until we read these letters to his family and realise that Gissing's attitude to democracy was not that of a lover but of a hater. Circumstances forced him, as he believed, to concentrate his attention on the vast cohorts of the lower middle class; but it was not admiration, it was hardly sympathy, which the " vulgar blatant scoundrels," as he calls their spokesmen, excited in him. He observed, he dreaded, he despaired, as with fascinated and terror-stricken eyes he watched the advance of democracy. He had the instinctive fear of alteration which is the birthright of the timid, and in this Gissing is the opposite of the great bluff Dickens—his only rival in this peculiar field—with his robust confidence in the benefits of change and his high practical optimism. Gissing's natural temper was aristocratic, and his attitude was that of a man forced by conditions to speak an alien language and to live in a Leyden jar. He writes to his brother in 1885, when his work as a " realistic " novelist had just begun :—

" What advantages of civilisation have I ? I live a very hermit's life; weeks pass and I do not exchange three words with a soul. I cannot afford theatres, for the gallery and pit have become loathsome to me. I have not time really to visit the museums; I pay an enormous rent for the privilege of living in barracks. I would give a year of my life for six months of true country, with the rest of autumn soberness, with leisure to read Homer under a cottage roof."

The reader is conscious of what is almost physical relief when the poor man gets his partial release at last. In 1888, on board a collier bound for Naples, Gissing sailed for Italy and plunged into sight-seeing. But the excitement of travel and the agitation which invariably disturbed him amid unfamiliar surroundings spoiled the pleasure, and he was surprised to find himself, in a Florence January, regretting the English fireplaces. The real revelation came much later, when, in 1897, he worked his wandering way to Calabria, and discovered the true bent of his temperament. He had wasted his energy in endeavours to appreciate Tuscany and the middle art. " I have, I am sorry to say, comparatively little interest in the Renaissance. On the other hand, I shout with joy whenever I am brought very near the old Romans. Chiefly I am delighted with the magnificent white oxen, with huge horns, which draw carts about the streets. Oxen and carts are precisely those of Virgil." At Cotrone he plunged deeper still, and was brought very near the old Greeks. The result was " By the Ionian Sea," the most satisfactory of all his books, because the one most fully in harmony with his character. In the eastern Italy which had once been Greece the querulous isolation of Gissing melted into a restful communion with his beloved antiquity.

The letters collected in this volume do great credit to George Gissing's natural affection. Very good letters, in the technical sense, they cannot be said to be, for they lack, in a strange degree, the hallmark of language which we expect from a writer so gifted as Gissing. They are unaffected to the verge of baldness, though not stinted in expansion. He says in them, with deliberate fullness, what he thinks will interest, or, still more often, benefit the brothers or the sisters to whom he writes. Those who have learned to think that George Gissing was cynical and bitter will be surprised at his almost childlike appreciation of such faint pleasures as come to his lot. Oddly enough, he has no adequate expression for what he feels, and only one adjective. Everything is " glorious," but nothing made live for the inward eye by any definition of the glory.

It is proper to say that in the later letters the expression of pleasure becomes less and less tongue-tied. In every capacity it was Gissing's fate to do himself less than justice. He was thought to be sullen when he was merely shy, and sinister when he merely lacked the power to communicate his sympathy. His was, in fact, a very gentle, sensitive, and appreciative mind, tied fast to a temperament the most unfortunate that could have been devised. His notorious inability to do what was sensible and plain, his exasperating practical incompetence, were shadowed in the intellectual order by a speech which did perpetual injustice to his thought. In spite of all this, which made of him a sort of social cripple, George Gissing remains a figure of increasing prominence and attraction in the literature of his time. His books will continue to be read and he himself to be talked of when many more dignified and sententious authors are forgotten.

MALLARME

# MALLARMÉ

THE existence of the magnificent edition now published by M. Eugène Montfort, nearly thirty years after the author's death, is proof, if proof were needed, of permanent interest felt in Mallarmé's work. As a matter of fact, no poet of the second half of last century, with the solitary exception of Baudelaire, has been so often reprinted and so extensively analysed as Mallarmé. His poems have the very curious quality of attracting two classes; they fascinate the most distinguished and are a trap for the silliest. If all the vain and foolish things said in praise of Mallarmé were collected, we should shrink affrighted before such a mountain of imbecility; and yet he has provoked some of the most illuminating eulogy of our time. Mallarmé's poetry is difficult to formulate. He consistently refused, like Robert Browning, to explain anything that seemed obscure in his writings, and he smiled with an agreeable irony when indiscreet admirers asked questions. He turned the tables on his inquirers, for he possessed the Socratic manner, and he asked *them* to say what was the meaning of his poetry. If they were so rash as to respond, he said that their interpretation, whatever it might be, was perfectly correct, and he congratulated them, though he deprecated the waste of their time. His modesty was extreme, his personal urbanity impregnable; he was never angry with anyone, he pushed his hermetic poems on nobody's attention; in his anxiety to please he would not wrangle with an opponent. But the world of letters has found him, what Rémy de Gourmant said long ago, " le plus merveilleux prétexte à

rêveries," and literary snobs have raved over what it was
impossible that they should appreciate.   Let us see what
we can make of this cryptic genius to-day.

Etienne Mallarmé (who called himself Stéphane) was
born in Paris on March 18, 1842.   His family were *bourgeois*,
but the boy had leanings to aristocracy, and was nicknamed
at school the Marquis de Boulainvilliers.   When he was a
child he met the aged Béranger at somebody's house, and
secretly determined to be the Béranger of the age to come.
It was as though Charles Doughty had determined to be the
Eliza Cook of his time.   He was trained to be a schoolmaster, and at the age of twenty came to England to learn
our language, which he subsequently taught in a succession
of French colleges for thirty years.   As a result of his
English studies, he formed an infatuation for Edgar Poe,
and he translated all the poems of the author of " The
Raven " into French prose.   This is one of the most
faithful and exquisite translations ever made, and in connection with the obscurity of Mallarmé's own poetry the
fact should be noted.   He was between thirty and forty
when he made his earliest attack on publicity by issuing
" The Raven " in a folio illustrated by Manet, then hardly
better known than himself.

I have described elsewhere how, in 1875, I found the little
brown, gentle person trotting about in Bloomsbury with the
elephant version in his arms, and how I took him off to see
Swinburne, who was mystified by Manet's designs.   But the
moment was a critical one in Mallarmé's career; for he had
now determined to devote himself seriously to verse, and to
break away from the Parnassian tradition.   It was at this
time that, at the invitation of the elder Coquelin, he composed " L'Après-Midi d'un Faune," which, however, was
not then performed, and, indeed, on being printed, was
received with ridicule.   It is now the best known and the
most articulate of Mallarmé's compositions.   He very

gradually, through a shower of poisoned arrows, reached
the fortress of fame, and sat entrenched there as " le type
absolu du Poète," until his sudden death from bronchitis
in 1898. How he seduced and bewitched a bodyguard of
admirers is well known, for, having been laughed at and
told that he did not know how to write, he lived long enough
to be greeted as the only Frenchman of his day who possessed
the gift of style.

The inspiration of Mallarmé was fragmentary and
episodical. In consequence he finished, or at least published, very little, his works in verse taking up no more
space than those of Malherbe or Gray. He wrote, of course,
vastly more than he printed, and we hear of an epic " Igitur
d'Elbemone " which occupied him for seven years at
Avignon. It is earnestly to be hoped that this incomprehensible monster may never see the light. The greatest
enemy of such a writer as Mallarmé is the editor desirous
of collecting " the Complete Works." The genius of this
poet depended on the skill with which he seized and per-
petuated a momentary impression. This was often so
slight as almost to evade detection, and it had to be projected against a background of hyperbole. There will be
found in the poetry of Mallarmé an absence of subject, and
of interest in subject; he is not easily moved, and when he
is, it is by something that moves nobody else. " Don du
Poème," a very characteristic piece, is a case in point; it
has extraordinary technical perfection and a wayward
beauty of phrase, but it is not *about* anything whatever.

The early poems of Mallarmé are composed under the
influence of Baudelaire. They are precious, artificial and
musky, with the particular distinction that they are radiant
with a species of spiritual purity. From the first we detect
in them the Mallarmean peculiarities, a determination to
cultivate the Absolute, and an individual conception of the
value of words. The youthful Mallarmé was bred among

the Parnassians; he admired Théodore de Banville and attempted to rival Heredia; he was the early friend and among the first supporters of Verlaine. But he was of another race than they, and from the beginning we can observe his passion for discovering unfamiliar services for words. Quite early, he isolated himself from all his companions by his rejection of what he called the " santé facile et sûre " of their use of language. He did not wish to be graceful and easy, and still less to be transparent. He scorned the logic oī the poets, their " Ovidian touch." Mallarmé reacted against the classic style in a new and peculiar way, defying the rules of construction and order, while preserving a technical discipline of his own so severe that, for long periods, it paralysed his own power of composition. Yet, although his method in writing was rigid to excess, it involved a tendency to anarchy.

That Mallarmé is a " difficult " writer it would be childish to deny, although admirers have been found to assert that the difficulty exists only in the inattention of the reader. Let us therefore be intensely attentive to the closing stanzas of " Prose pour des Esseintes," and say firmly what idea they convey to us :—

> L'enfant abdique son extase
> Et docte déjà par chemins
> Elle dit le mot : Anastase !
> Né pour d'éternels parchemins,
>
> Avant qu'un sépulchre ne rie
> Sous aucun climat, son aïeul,
> De porter ce nom : Pulchérie !
> Caché par le trop grand glaïeul.

There is scope here, surely, for limitless commentary ! Mallarmé was forty years of age when he first became famous through a passage in Huysmans' much-discussed novel, " A Rebours." The hero of that book, Jean des Esseintes, broke out into a passionate eulogy of the author of " Hérodiade," from which latter he borrowed a sumptuous passage. This made a sensation among the younger French authors, and inspired the response from which I have quoted above. It also, I think, determined Mallarmé on a still more furious and uncompromising eccentricity, his poems subsequent to 1884 bring much more obscure and fantastic than those which preceded them, almost diverging into " wings " and " altars," like those of our divine poets of the Commonwealth, and drifting into mere typographical experiment. Perhaps he himself felt that he had gone too far, since in the collection of his " Vers et Prose," which he published the year before his death, the most extravagant later effusions are not included.

But, even in the clearest of his early poems, such as " Les Fenêtres " and the celebrated " Après-midi " itself, Mallarmé is always difficult, though seldom entirely incomprehensible. His admirers said that there are too few obscure authors in French, and that it is cowardly to insist on lucid writing. Tired of the nudity of logic, they welcomed a figure swathed in the robe of Isis. Mallarmé, in essence, offers less difficulty to an English than to a French reader, because we are used to obscurity. The easiest way for us to approach Mallarmé is to think of him as a belated Elizabethan, somebody like Lodge or Greene, not inspired by the sinister passion of Donne, but luminous and gentle, depending for his effects solely upon the symbolic oddity of his language. The well-known " Brise Marine "—which contains Mallarmé's most popular line :—

> La chair est triste, hélas ! et j'ai lu tous les livres—

is an example of what I venture to call Elizabethan simplicity of thought combined with elaborate subtlety of language. If the reader will examine this piece, he will perceive that the idea in it is not at all remarkable, but that it is an intensely ingenious harmony of such sensations as

U

a rather rudimentary idea can call up. This makes
Mallarmé an exceedingly dangerous writer for others to
imitate. It is not enough to invert language, to dislocate
syntax, to employ sumptuous images, in an unprecedented
style; the poet must also possess the intangible charm which
enabled Mallarmé, in spite of all the dangers into which he
wilfully ran, to emerge a pure and sometimes an almost
perfect artist.

No criticism can equal the actual impression left upon
the senses by the finest verse of Mallarmé, and therefore I
quote " Soupir," which is one of the shortest, but one of the
most highly finished, of his early compositions :—

> Mon âme vers ton front où rêve, ô calme sœur,
> Un automne jonché de taches de rousseur,
> Et vers le ciel errant de ton œil angélique,
> Monte, comme dans un jardin mélancolique,
> Fidèle, un blanc jet d'eau soupire vers l'Azur !
> Vers l'Azur attendri d'Octobre pâle et pur
> Qui mire aux grands bassins sa langueur infinie
> Et laisse, sur l'eau morte où la fauve agonie
> Des feuilles erre au vent et creuse un froid sillon,
> Se traîner le soleil jaune d'un long rayon.

Here we have most of the attributes of Mallarmé's mannered
verse, its exquisite delicacy, which is music itself, its veiled
dimness of outline, its temerity of language, its abstraction.
Here we have his most characteristic word, " Azur," which
recurs incessantly in his poetry, and have also more than
a taste of the frigidity of his ornament. His style is cold
and jewelled, incapable of touching even the surface of
passion, as we may see very curiously exemplified, with dim
splendour and vain mystery of dialogue, in his sole dramatic
fragment, " Hérodiade," where mistress and maid converse
in sumptuous alexandrines without producing the smallest
effect either of heat or movement. All life is " still life "
to Mallarmé; his genius, profoundly veiled, haunts a chilly
region of glaciers, lilies, swans, and diamonds. There are
grand single lines, even in such a cold abstraction as " Toast

Funèbre," but also a general impression of sterility and ennui from which the author never even attempts to escape.

What will be the duration of Mallarmé's influence, which has extended beyond the confines of his own speech? In England imitation of such enigmas as " Le Tombeau d'Edgar Poe " has produced strange results that do not seem to possess much lasting value. But in France there has been a definite encouragement of the production of poetry in which, in the poet's own phrase, words take the place of ideas, and this seems directly due to Mallarmé. His fame, which had died down a little, has been of late revived by the popularity of his most brilliant disciple, M. Paul Valéry, and by the wide discussion of " pure poetry " as somewhat cloudily defined by the Abbé Brémond. It must always be remembered that Mallarmé was not merely an artist, but a theoretician, an involuntary leader in a school of artistic expression. His explanations of the theory of poetry prepared a whole army of young writers to accept at his own valuation what their elders, like Brunetière, flung aside as an incoherent series of sonorous rhymes.

The curious part of the situation was that Mallarmé never ceased sincerely to deprecate the idea of discipleship. He was followed by a crowd out of the gates of Hamelin, yet all the while protesting that he did not pipe for his followers but for himself. There was a paradox in the whole situation, since the teacher would listen but would not teach, had, indeed, nothing to impart, and yet was incessantly besieged with inquiries. He lacked the element of rhetoric sufficient to correct his individualism, but this, instead of being a weakness, strengthened his position in a circle of young men sick of oratory. Perhaps the chief source of his influence was his extreme integrity of purpose. He lived in and for literature with all his heart and soul. He had no other aim in existence than to uphold and to extend the dignity of the written word.

Quite recently (June 1927) fresh light on the methods of Mallarmé has been thrown by the discovery and publication of a collection of four *Contes Indiens* hitherto unknown. His son-in-law, M. Edmond Bonniot, who has unearthed them, thinks that they were written late in Mallarmé's life. The subjects of these four tales are taken from Indian folk-lore. It is interesting to observe that they are written in a prose which, although voluptuous and subtle, is without the least obscurity. They are stories which give the reader no more trouble to peruse than do the tales of Mother Goose. It is curious to see that the most cryptic of all known authors could be perfectly lucid if he chose to be.

# SAMUEL BUTLER'S ESSAYS

# SAMUEL BUTLER'S ESSAYS

THE temperament of Samuel Butler was unattractive to the nineteenth century, but when he died in June, 1902, it was evident that the chrysalis of his dark fate had already opened, and had released a butterfly. During the subsequent quarter of a century Butler has enjoyed a vogue as shining as his previous obscurity was complete. He has been accepted by the current generation as a main contributor to its instruction and enjoyment. He has been praised to the skies, he has been discussed with endless volubility, he has been edited in a dozen forms and sold in thousands of copies. He has been celebrated in a massive biography, in which his friend Mr. Festing Jones has displayed a talent for the reproduction of characteristic detail comparable with that of Boswell. Nothing about Butler has been neglected, although something may have been concealed. Every element of notoriety, even a touch of the mysterious, has been summoned to the service of the once-despised and rejected author of " Erewhon."

In the face of all the panegyric which is now poured on the genius of Butler, it may seem overbold on my part to suggest that violent reactions lead to slow reactions, and that the appreciation of that genius, having reached a pitch beyond which it would be difficult to go, is now certain to give way gradually to calmer reflection. Previous to the war (which had a considerable influence on the admiration of Butler) one of his soberest critics said of the " Essays " re-collected in the very handsome volumes before me, that " each was a masterpiece of idiosyncrasy." I have been reading these essays over again, and it seems to me that, although several of them are interesting and all are ingenious, not one is quite what can be called a " masterpiece." I think that when the temperature of fashion, now so high in Butler's case, begins to go down, it will sink steadily, and perhaps reach again a point much lower than his deserts. We ought to be prepared for the change, and the first step towards preparation is to examine what have been the causes of his extreme popularity.

It is plain, I think, that we cannot any longer admit his universality. The thoroughgoing idolaters of a year or two ago claimed for Samuel Butler advantages which, if logically pursued, would have placed him with Leonardo da Vinci, Bacon and Erasmus, a touch of Beethoven being generously thrown in. His mental activity covered an immense area, and he wrote with contemptuous assurance on religion, biology, painting, sculpture, music, philosophy, and family prayers. He was like Aurora Leigh, who " brushed with extreme flounce the circle of the sciences." A Handelian oratorio, entitled " Narcissus," betrayed his confidence in his own judgment as an authority on finance.

His interests were very wide, and he drifted, as De Quincey did, into dictatorial statement about a vast variety of themes. He treated life as if he were " playing a violin solo in public and learning the instrument as one goes on." As he was portentously clever, he dazzled a large number of hearers who had even less capacity for fiddling than he had, but the game could not last for ever. Very unwillingly, the circle of his admirers is beginning to realise that Butler was not really a first-rate Jack-of-all-trades, and I perceive that the adorers now concentrate on saying that he was a great biologist. On this I should like to have the opinion of a real biologist. But that Butler's encyclopædic authority is not unassailable is, after all, unimportant, because that is not actually the matter on which his recent popularity has been founded. Let us examine what that quality is.

What has attracted so much attention to Samuel Butler is the fact that he is the most complete interpreter, for example, of that " pyrrhonism " which more than anything else distinguishes popular thought to-day from the dogmatism of the nineteenth century. Everyone who reads Pascal knows how formidable a foe to traditional complacency is the quality of incessant questioning. To attain truth nothing must be taken for granted—indeed, " le pyrrhonisme c'est le vrai," Pascal admitted in what seems a strange moment of partial illumination. But the spirit in which Butler started on the pursuit of truth would have alarmed the author of the " Pensées " in the highest degree, since the modern philosopher acknowledged no bases of traditional truth at all. He was confronted by certain established verities in religion, morals, art, and philosophy which were being taken for granted at the outset of every inquiry. The verities taught by science were, in particular, regarded as beyond question, as being solid stepping-stones to higher things. Wisdom, therefore, recommended the Victorian mind to waste no time in reconsidering these obvious certainties, but to use them in making further advances in knowledge.

But Samuel Butler was unwilling to take this advice, and early in life he briskly set about undermining these primitive certainties and at the same time his own foundations. His great aim was to think precisely, even when the subject of his thoughts was a matter universally defined, since of all men Butler was by nature most the enemy of definitions, which he thought either superfluous or mischievous. Like Zeno, he was " an assailer of all things." He set himself throughout the wide circle of his intellectual interests to vivisect every proposition which presented itself to his intelligence, to take nothing for granted, and to subject

the most settled convictions to fresh examination.    If
things were universally held to be above question, that very
fact showed that it was time for Butler to inquire into their
constitution.   He was, above all else, a house-breaker, and
it is this which has principally endeared him to a generation
of iconoclasts.

If the entire body of Butler's work is taken into con-
sideration, it will be seen that this " pyrrhonism " of his
not merely underlies all his writings, but gives it a purpose.
He was a seeker after truth, and believed that it existed,
but his real aim in life was to disturb erroneous impressions
of truth.   He fought against the phantom with far more
zeal, and more effectively, than he embraced the reality.
For this reason his works have had an irresistible fascination
for those whose temperament urges them rather to exposure
than to confirmation, rather to destruction than to edification.   This, it can hardly be questioned, is the mood of the
twentieth century, which is tired of the bondage in which its
precursors lived, and is little careful of the future if only it
can cast off the shackles of the past.

In various departments of faith the Victorian age had
discouraged the use of eyes, and had instituted blinkers,
so at least Samuel Butler assured a juvenile public, only too
ready to be persuaded.   In his irony he said that " to insist
on seeing things for one's self is to be an ἰδιώτης, or, in plain
English, an idiot."   Come away into the wilderness, he
cried; leave your universities and conventicles, and be an
idiot with me.   In this way, by deep sophistication, he
appealed to the unsophisticated mind.

He has been rewarded by a response which has made
him one of the most effective of recent writers, but which,
in my opinion, will soon, by the very nature of things,
exhaust itself, and leave the reputation of Samuel Butler
sadly diminished.   I cannot see in the author of " Erewhon," amusing and penetrating as he is at his best, a

permanent force in English literature. It is not enough to take away; something must be given in return, and Butler, who snatches the nuts out of our hands so deftly, can but hold out a cold paw when we ask for compensation.

The twenty-two essays which take their final place in these two volumes exhibit very clearly the quality of " pyrrhonism " which I have indicated as Butler's central attribute. With one or two exceptions, they are not " essays," in the sense of Montaigne or Charles Lamb, but they are fragments of the author's controversial activity, specimens of or offshoots from his implacable protest against tradition. Butler's lucidity and humour are rarely long absent in these pieces, and they are welcome as relieving the tension of his thought, which is ever on the stretch, and is apt to be exasperating when once these attractions are relaxed. Occasionally, like Voltaire, of whom Butler cannot fail to remind the reader, he allows the argument to lapse into sheer frivolity, and that lack of taste, of a sense of proportion, which was the besetting sin of Butler, makes itself disagreeably apparent. For instance, in the essay called " How to Make the Best of Life," which in the main is a stimulating and pleasing chain of reflections, all is spoiled by the rigmarole at the end, with its irrelevant attack on Lord Balfour's " Foundations of Belief." Butler enjoyed undermining those foundations, but he resented the use of any dynamite except his own.

More than half of the essays contained in these volumes are new, being either transcribed from the author's manuscript or retrieved from the pages of forgotten periodicals. Among the latter is a group of letters contributed to the " Examiner " in 1879, and printed here under the general title of " A Clergyman's Doubts." That interesting newspaper was then on its last legs, William Minto having resigned the editorship, or being on the point of resigning. But, unless I am much mistaken, he had bequeathed Butler to his successor. The expiring " Examiner " was looking out for a " real representative of the School of Modern Thought," and I well remember Minto's conviction that he had found such a representative in the author of " Erewhon." But in the meantime he had been puzzled, as everyone was puzzled, by the excessive and (as I shall always think) the unjustifiable irony of " The Fair Haven." I do not believe that the editor, or indeed anyone else, detected the hand of the enemy in all these strange letters purporting to come from sincere but troubled Evangelical clergymen. They are sixteen in number, and they answer one another in the voice of the mother of Sisera. I hesitate to differ from Mr. Festing Jones, who thinks that Butler composed them all, but I fancy that in one or two cases unsuspecting incumbents were actually deceived, and wrote in good faith, as " Cantab " or " Oxoniensis." In the letter signed " Lewis Wright " I can discover no trace of Butler's style, which was not easily concealed.

The zeal of editors is sometimes unkind, and I do not think that Samuel Butler, if he was alive to-day, would thank his devoted disciples for fishing up out of oblivion those rash essays on sculpture and painting which are here printed, or reprinted, for the first time. What is named " L'Affaire Holbein-Rippel " is a very characteristic example of Butler's inability to let anything alone. It deals, in very tedious detail, with the authorship of a Holbein drawing in the Berlin Gallery, which merely purports to be a copy by a Basle glass-painter of the seventeenth century, but which Butler, with incredible pertinacity, persisted in attributing to the master himself. There are also what may be called appendices to his odd, though often very fascinating, " Ex Voto " and " Alps and Sanctuaries," but even here fate seems to be pursuing the critic. Butler's great aim was to distinguish a sculptor whom he had discovered, named Tabachetti. To this artist he confidently attributed copious work which, as has since been discovered, was finished before Tabachetti was born. This does not militate against the amusing vivacity of Butler's dialectic.

The most durable part of Butler's writing, indeed, will probably prove to be its humour. He wrote in a reckless mood which gave elasticity to his periods. No one ever approached the citadel of tradition waving a merrier pickaxe, or flung himself upon the task of demolition in higher spirits. Whether he is attacking Darwin or evangelical religion, whether he is proving that a woman wrote the " Odyssey " or is ridiculing the protoplasmists, Butler is always sprightly. His style brightens with his own crackle of laughter, and I think he will long be read with pleasure as a humorist. As a " serious seeker after truth," I am sadly afraid that future readers will turn with apathy from a writer who does nothing but break down doors which they themselves will long have found wide open.

# A  BLIND  POET

# A BLIND POET

THE sad disability of blindness has always been held, by sentimentalists, to be favourable to poetic frenzy, and to encourage the inner light. But it is more than doubtful whether any " inner light " exists unless the flame has been kindled from without. We are told about the poetic feats of " blind Thamyris and blind Mæonides," but even the tradition shows that they had been long in possession of sight. I learn about Thamyris (it is all I know, yet nothing to what Apollo knows) that the Muses broke his lyre and put out his eyes because he challenged them to a contest. He was therefore mature in audacity before he got mixed up with those formidable females. Blind Harry I leave to the piety of the Scotch, but I am unable to discover a poet, not traditional, who was born blind. The " inward eye," of which Wordsworth speaks, has to be nurtured on memory before it can expand in imagination, and I think it will be found that all the blind poets have seen long enough to have garnered impressions. Coleridge speaks of—

> that blind bard who on the Chian strand,
> By those deep sounds possessed with inward light,
> Beheld the Iliad and the Odyssey
> Rise to the swelling of the voiceful sea,

but internal evidence makes it certain that Homer saw long enough to store his mind with an infinity of impressions, which " deep sounds " alone could not possibly have given him.

In English literature we possess several pathetic instances

X                   305

of loss of sight, but none of prenatal deprivation of it.  I
do not believe that any laborious education could enable a
person born blind to describe scenes or distinguish colours
with real originality.  The trick may be learned, as it was
by Thomas Blacklock, who described how he saw Aurora
emerge in rosy-fingered morn from the eastern gate, but this
was mere verbal imitation, and, moreover, even Blacklock
was six months old before he lost his sight, and some
glimmering may be retained of what is seen in infancy.
Milton, on the other hand, who is the typical poet of blindness, kept hold of the visual world until he was over forty,
by which time he had completely stored his memory with
images.

The writer of whom I speak to-day was unique in presenting the problem in a form which made it almost impossible
to decide what in his impressions was genuine and what was
derived.  Philip Bourke Marston was born with normal
eyesight (although probably with deficient general vitality),
but at the age of four his eyes were permanently injured.
Mr. Obsorne attributes this to an accidental blow, but I
think he is mistaken.  I understood long ago that the
injury was due to an overdose of belladonna taken to ward
off an attack of scarlatina.  Whatever the matter was, it
was blunderingly treated.  The principles of optical sur-
gery were not what they are now, and the unfortunate child
developed a glaucoma which gradually deprived him of all
commerce with the external world.  But the process was
slow, and no doubt permitted him to become familiar with
the general features of earth and sky.  When I saw him
first he was still able " to see the sunshine, the firelight, and
the waving of the trees in the wind."  Soon afterwards, at
the age of twenty-two, he was plunged into impenetrable
darkness.  But in this melancholy case, no less than in that
of Milton, there could not be complete visual vacancy,
because there had once been sight.

Preraphaelite memoirs of fifty years ago make frequent reference to a writer whose circumstances were so tragical as to sound almost melodramatic. It was said of Philip Bourke Marston, and without exaggeration, that " his whole life was sorrow." Fashion changes so rapidly that it is probable that his name, which was once constantly recalled, is now mainly forgotten, and it is therefore well that an old and faithful friend, Mr. C. C. Osborne, should revive the memory of a delicate and gifted spirit. Philip Marston was born in 1850 ; his father was the playwright Westland Marston, a follower of Sheridan Knowles in the tinsel art of blank-verse tragedy, in which he attained some position. His highest level was reached the year before his son Philip's birth, in the then successful and now quite unreadable " Strathmore."

Westland Marston was a man of high culture, enthusiasm, and gusto ; he had a remarkable gift of critical discernment. He was one of the earliest critics to perceive the genius of Swinburne and Rossetti, and he sought their acquaintance before they were famous. The family consisted of his wife, two daughters, Eleanor and Cicely, and the afflicted son, who was the darling of the house, very gentle, amenable, and intelligent. He could have no regular teaching, but his parents instructed him in poetry, and his mother was his only too willing slave. By this I mean that his powers do not seem to have been disciplined or expanded, so that when his misfortunes crowded upon him, he had none of the self-reliance which has lightened the load of blindness for many ingenious patients. In later years he was remarkably deficient in the manual cleverness which relieves many blind persons.

The death of his mother in 1870 was the first of a series of blows which fell upon him during the next ten years, in dreadful succession. Her death affected his health, and his sister Cicely, who assumed her place as his peculiar guardian, took him to Italy for a month, and here his spirits revived. At this time the Marstons were living in an agreeable house, near the Regent's Park, where they entertained their literary friends with liberality. Here might be met Browning, the Rossettis, Swinburne, Madox Brown, and the younger members of the *cénacle ;* it was a nest of the newest, the most modern imaginative society, and Philip was the indulged and the fairly happy centre of attention. Since 1867, or earlier, roused by the choruses in " Atalanta in Calydon," he had been writing verses, curiously accomplished in form, and these were passed from admiring hand to hand.

Meanwhile, a flash of happiness crossed his path. A charming girl, Mary Nesbit, had become attached to him, and they were now betrothed, to the delight of all who knew them. It was at this moment of respite that I first saw Philip Marston, in the studio of Ford Madox Brown, in 1871, whither he was conducted by his sister, Cicely. His appearance was striking, and has left with me a lasting impression. He sat, a pale anæmic youth, preternaturally grave and silent, with a mysterious look of expectancy; his hair copious and ruffled over the high white forehead. He had not yet grown the full beard of dark chestnut brown which afterwards concealed his worst feature, the rather weak and pouting mouth. On that occasion I noticed that he never spoke until he was addressed, when he replied in a deep, slow, rather unearthly voice, and resumed his silence.

Misfortunes now began to rain upon him. In the winter of that year Miss Nesbit died of a galloping consumption. Philip Marston found what solace he could in composing verses of a heart-breaking melancholy—" God knows I had no hope before she came." A certain distraction was caused by the publication of his earliest volume, " Song-Tide," which was received with considerable favour, and

not least warmly by Marston's most eminent friends, w
rejoiced in comforting him with their praises. He foun
new friend in the youthful Oliver Madox Brown, and in
attentions of a number of men who formed the outer cir
of the worshippers of Rossetti.

Of these, Arthur O'Shaughnessy was the most
tinguished, and in 1873 he married Marston's sist
Eleanor; I have described in another place the ext
ordinary ritual of the wedding, which was a sort of flo
manifesto. The marriage was happy in itself, but at o
attended by discomfort. For some reason which esca
me, Westland Marston, who had been comfortably off, n
lost most of his money. The house had to be given v
Philip and Cicely went into lodgings in Notting Hill.
poet's history now became a catalogue of premature deatl
Oliver Madox Brown, a youth of genius, died of blo
poisoning in 1874; the O'Shaughnessy family was wi
out, first their two infant children, then the motl
then the father. Worst of all for Philip, his devo
guardian-sister, Cicely, died of apoplexy in 1878, leav
him and his aged father desolate. By a happy chance,
1877 (not 1867 as incorrectly stated in her Memoir), a n
friend had appeared, the American writer, Mrs. Lou
Chandler Moulton, who watched over the poor solit
poet till his death in 1887. She could not, howev
protect him against the jars of poverty, which distressed
later years, nor transplant him from the miserable lodgir
where his insomnia was exasperated by the "lacerati
noises" of Euston Road, and by the rudeness of a neglige
landlady. In 1881 the blind poet, to whom life spared
distressing circumstance, was visiting D. G. Rossetti wh
that artist had his first paralytic stroke, and in 1882 he w
alone with James Thomson when the author of "The Ci
of Dreadful Night" succumbed to a fit of delirium tremer
From 1880 until the end the hospitable friendship

Mr. and Mrs. Osborne was invaluable to Marston, and
provided him with occasional escapes into country air.

When D. G. Rossetti wrote that Philip Marston's
" Garden Secrets " were " worthy of Shakespeare in his
subtlest lyrical moods," he employed the language of extravagant hyperbole. Swinburne, a saner critic, never spoke
so violently, but both friends, and all who surrounded the
patient and pathetic blind bard, instinctively tried to
comfort him by excess of praise. He was not easily to be
comforted, for he rejected " literary sentimental slobber-
ing," as he called it. In spite of his lack of all cynicism
or revolt, he was not to be patronised, and anything like
pity he repelled with dignity. Mr. Osborne makes large
quotation from unpublished letters, and they present Philip
Marston in a new light. Hitherto he has loomed, in his
rather monotonous verse, a monument of suffering and
sorrow, stoically endured; but the letters show vivacity
and even humour. They display excellent taste, and with
their simplicity of manner, considerable acuteness. When
a critic, not pre-eminent for sincerity, presses his praise
upon him, Marston comments on the man's unfortunate
manner of " mumbling and meditating." A well-meant
eulogy is " a little too much of a good thing," and the blind
poet's appreciation of certain darlings of the Press is
distinctly pointed.

Forty years will, in the course of a few days, have passed
since Philip Marston's body was accompanied to the tomb
by the laudation of all his contemporaries. His grave is,
as Elizabeth Browning might say, " a place where poets
crowned may feel their hearts decaying," since whatever
vogue his verses once possessed has entirely passed away.
The only examination of his work, so far as I know, which
has appeared of late years, is a brief essay, published in
1918, by Mr. John Drinkwater, whose catholic taste has
always urged him to recall the beloved who are no longer

loved. Mr. Drinkwater expatiates on the beauties of the sonnets, but even he has to admit that Marston, true poet as he was, never got quite inside the charmed circle of greatness.

His blindness, I cannot doubt, was the cause of his arrested development, since his early work is his best; although he continued to give expression to a susceptibility so rare that it should have inspired the most individual accents, it never did, because he was forced to get from books what a poet ought to get from nature. He was the most abundant sonnet-writer of his time, and his sonnets have great technical excellence, but their expression seems third-hand; they render the tradition of the Italians as reflected in the verse of Rossetti. The poignant monotony of Marston's verse is another cause of the lassitude with which we read the exquisitely polished records of his unhappiness. The indifferent spectator wearies of a muse that is such an incorrigible Niobe. Yet, after all, the real reason why Marston is forgotten is that he represents to excess methods and artifices which are diametrically opposed to such as are in fashion at the present moment. But as a figure, as an exquisite human being with whom life sported as a cat does with a mouse, the sad blind poet of " The Rose and the Wind " will never be quite forgotten.

# A VICEROY AND HIS
NOTE-BOOK

# A VICEROY AND HIS
# NOTE-BOOK

THE more diverse and even contradictory are the
qualities of a human character the more likelihood is
there of a false aspect of that character being presented
to posterity. Our habit in contemporary biography has
now reached a parlous perfection in falsity. We have two
classes of portraiture, the one displaying the deceased
personage as practically faultless, as a bust if not moulded
in wax at least carved out of polished marble; the other
indulging in diatribe or even in scandalous innuendo.
Between these the living man escapes, and from the
cautious piety of friends and the spite of enemies no appre-
ciable portrait emerges. Truth appears to be the last
thing which either writers or readers desire, and we are
mystified by a white figure or else by a black one, neither
of which reminds those who were well acquainted with the
subject of his moral or social features. The error seems
to arise partly from the fear that any acknowledgment of
imperfection will be thought spiteful or ungenerous, but
most of all from the absurd convention that a human
character is unaffected by external influences. This is the
line taken, almost universally, in fiction. The personages
in our novels, if they are brave, are always brave; if they
are quixotic, they do nothing but tilt at windmills. If
they are humane, their tenderness never abates; if they
are mean, generosity fails them on every occasion. Our

biographers have slipped into the convention of treating their themes as characters in a novel.

But this, as anyone who reflects on experience may see, is not the truth in real life. Actual people, although they possess certain fixed characteristics, possess them elastically, and are affected by all manner of circumstances in their exercise of them. I am tempted at this moment to dwell on the matter, not on account of any immediate instance of the common error, but because I am afraid lest it should affect impressions of the eminent and extremely interesting man whose posthumous work comes before me to-day. Of all prominent persons of our age, I know not one who would be likely to suffer more severely from the conventional scheme of biography than Lord Curzon. He was so various in his public and private actions as to challenge and at the same time to defy analysis. No one whom we have known has been more complex, in no one have the acts and manners been more contradictory. He is to be the subject of biography, and I sincerely hope that his extraordinary figure may be approached without timidity and with a proper sense of its peculiarities. Lord Curzon was loved and admired; let us be courageous enough to admit that few men have been more hated.

Why was this? It is the duty of the biographer to explain why, or at least to recognise the paradox. Lord Curzon was often kindness itself, but he could be cruel. He was distinguished and high-minded, but his speech was sometimes coarse and paltry. His pomposity of manner was balanced by his delicate simplicity, his occasional density by the quickness of his intelligence. He was generous, and could be jealous; considerate, and overbearing. He was a bundle of contradictions, so wise, so silly; so profound and so superficial; so remote and so affectionate. All this—and in saying so much I avoid altogether the tribute that everyone, even his enemies, must pay to his statesmanship, his passion for work, his public spirit—all this should incite a conscientious and intelligent biographer to produce, not a faultless ivory bust, but a portrait of intrinsic value.

These considerations are, I hope, not quite out of place in view of the posthumous volume of Lord Curzon's writings which his executors have now placed before us. The diversity of the author's character is here largely displayed. Here is the customary divergence between the head of gold and the feet of clay. The editors of the volume have evidently been hampered by the conditions of their trust in this instance, and what they say in their interesting preface is not wholly illuminating. Lord Curzon's " Tales of Travel " seemed to be complete in itself, but the editors have found a collection of essays, more or less finished, " which were intended by [the author] to form the sequel to his ' Tales of Travel.' " It is not quite clear whether Lord Curzon left any direction to this effect, but we are told that he " was not spared to arrange the chapters and to correct the proofs."

The editors are afraid that there will be " detected " here and there " a partial lack of that final polish which was so characteristic of everything that Lord Curzon wrote." That is generously expressed; it is even somewhat excessive. " Final polish "—that is to say, a classical perfection of phrase—was never characteristic of Lord Curzon's style, which was highly coloured, felicitous, and personal, but liable to extraordinary lapses. It was always a little Corinthian, and would suddenly become barbaric. Lord Curzon was really an improvisatore, and " final polish " are words strangely inappropriate to describe his exuberant language. I detect in the pages of the present volume nothing which leads me to think that the author, if he had been spared, would have made any essential corrections.

We may therefore take it that " A Viceroy's Note-Book "

is exactly what it would have been if Lord Curzon had seen it through the press, and we need not be surprised that it exhibits that strange complexity of temperament to which I have drawn attention. Nothing could be more odd than its diversity of attitude, at one point so dignified, at another so trivial; so handsome in praise, so reckless in blame; so grave and charming at one moment, and then so childish. For students of the character of one of the most interesting men of our time it is invaluable. It presents us with evidence of his chameleon-like diversity, but if that evidence is to be disregarded, the result will be negligible. Let us examine of what elements the volume consists, and here it is proper to bear in mind the candid confession of the editors that it fell to them to " arrange the chapters." I see no reason to suppose that the author would have arranged them otherwise.

The book, then, opens with a series of twelve little essays on odd experiences of Oriental travel. These are lively in a high degree. The tone is natural, even conversational, and many survivors, in reading them, will recognise the voice of a charming and convivial host. These pages from a note-book are in an easy, even in a light key; everything bombastic, serious or educational is strictly banished. They are followed by very serious, rather densely composed, monographs on Indian frontier geography; and these by fresh and delightful recollections of juvenile journeys in the Far East made long before the author dreamed of being, or at least was expected to become, a Viceroy. And then the playful tone of the opening of the book is resumed in more or less facetious recollections of " Greece in the 'Eighties."

With regard to the little chapters dealing, at the beginning of the " Leaves," with those oddities of Eastern life and language which Lord Curzon observed during his viceroyalty, I find it very difficult to form an opinion.

They are, often—not always, but often—exceedingly diverting.  The amusing incident is told with almost as much
verve as the noble author was accustomed to exercise when
he gathered his cronies about him.  But the reader is
haunted with an uneasy doubt whether it was always
perfectly tactful to recount these mirthful incidents.  How
does the " Acting Commander-in-Chief "—not named,
indeed, but easily identified—how does he like this high-
spirited account of his being " laid on his back on the
parade-ground in full sight of all the troops at P——r " ?
Was it quite kind to tell the public how a veteran of the
Mutiny applauded his own praises at a Delhi banquet,
" when I was Viceroy " ?  Will the Portuguese have
sufficient humour to enjoy the roaring farce of Lord
Curzon's official visit to Goa ?

I am like Miss Rosa Dartle—I only ask for information,
and having lisped my question, I am free to read these
pages again with unabated amusement.  But I am not
quite sure of being so easily silenced when it comes to
Rabelaisian tales of the indiscretions of maharajas and to
absurdities of Baboo English.  It is characteristic of Lord
Curzon to have been excessively entertained by the inscrip-
tions and petitions of which he received so copious a
stream.  Many of them are indeed very laughable, although
it is impossible not to recollect that excerpts of a like
correspondence are frequent in the funny columns of our
own newspapers.  Many are perfectly harmless, and the
student who wrote to Lord Curzon suggesting that the
standard of passing examinations " should be reduced to
such a level that nearly all the candidates may get through "
deserves immortality.  At the same time, at the risk of
seeming prudish, I cannot be quite sure that all this local
merriment is tactful in a Viceroy.  A large number of
His Majesty's Indian subjects read English.

The author rises abruptly to a height of dignified eloquence in his defence of the extension of British influence in 1895. He describes Chitral, and appropriately styles it one small chink in the mountain palisade which Russia at that time was showing such a feverish desire to penetrate. The year before the famous siege, which will always be remembered as one of the romantic incidents in our Indian history, Lord Curzon visited Chitral, then almost unknown to Western travellers, and was fascinated by the strangeness of its scenery and the picturesqueness of its inhabitants. His account of this journey is in his best manner, sober, minute, and yet full of colour. It is written to show how important a fragment of the Empire may be if it holds a unique strategical position, and it is a complete apology for the mode in which the Indian Government after the remarkable events of 1896, instead of abandoning the field, so consolidated it that it became an integral part of the northern edge of British suzerainty along the entire Hindu Kush frontier. As Lord Curzon aptly puts it, " Little Chitral, for a short space, shook the quiet of the great world, and will have its place in the history of the Asiatic continent, while, now that it has again relapsed into obscurity, it remains both a lesson and a type." In the close *résumé* of events, the name of Sir George Robertson is just mentioned, but it seems odd that it should not once be said that it was he who conducted the gallant resistance which closed in the retreat of the Chitrális on the 18th of April. This is a little like " Hamlet " without the Prince of Denmark.

A chapter on the Indian Frontier extends the tale. The traveller takes us from Kashmir and Srinagar to Gilgit, and on the journey reveals a curious bibliographical fact :—

" In 1904 I passed through [Srinagar] on my way to the outer frontier of the Indian Empire. I afterwards wrote a book about the latter, which though it was already in print and had been sold for a considerable sum to an enterprising publisher, I was never allowed to bring out; for, when I had actually corrected the final proofs and my photographs had been engraved, I was appointed Viceroy of India; and the Prime Minister, Lord Salisbury, declared with, I believe, quite unnecessary punctilio, that a new Viceroy ought not to publish anything about the country which he was so soon to rule. So my plates were put away, the cheque was returned, and my proof sheets reposed, as they have done ever since, in a tin box from which they will now never emerge."

They will, then, never be enjoyed by the "wandering sinner," who wrote to Lord Curzon long afterwards to assure him that he found in his writings "sermons on stones, books in the running brooks, and Good Gracious God! in everything."

From Gilgit we are taken on to the Pamirs, through scenery of awful magnificence, and to the remarkable mountain-valley of Hunza, whose inhabitants hold the Aga Khan for their spiritual head. The Hunzas were ruled by a hereditary monarch styled the Tum, who announced in 1891 that he "cared nothing for the womanly English, as he hung upon the skirts of the manly Russians." This ruler, who had quarrelled with and murdered his father, the late Tum, "took the initiative and settled the matter, and placed himself on the throne." These are the parricide's own words, written to the Maharaja of Kashmir. It was necessary to deal very sharply with this Playboy of the Hunza Valley, whom Lord Curzon calls "a peculiarly bloodthirsty ruffian," reigning over a "nest of mountain-wasps." A chapter entitled "The Old Persian" is, in reality, a review of that fine fruity classic, the "Haji Baba" of James Justinian Morier, which, after more than a century, retains its authority as a portrait of

Y

Persian manners and life, or, as Lord Curzon puts it, of
" the salient characteristics of a singularly unchanging
Oriental people."

Not less sound, but more uncommon, is the picture
which fills the next chapter of that still unfamiliar country,
Annam, and Hué, its capital. Lord Curzon travelled here
in the winter of 1892, when he was received in audience by
the young Emperor, Thanh Thai. The moment coincided
with the troubles of the French Government in its penetration of Indo-China, and with those reforms by M. de
Lanessan which the revelations of Pierre Loti had made
imperative. On all this, however, Lord Curzon does not
touch, but dwells on those wonders of Annamite architecture
on which Pierre Loti himself was to expatiate at a later
date.

Our Viceroy, whose cousin Robert Curzon, Lord Zouche,
had written in 1837 a famous book on " The Monasteries
of the Levant," shared with his distinguished relative a
curious fondness for monks. He studied them in several
parts of the world, and they inspired some of his most
vivid pages. In Korea, an abbot stole his gold watch and
chain, and is described by his indignant guest as " a
swarthy vagabond." He is more indulgent to the hegu-
menos of the Iberon monastery, who confessed, " with a
pathetic twinkle," that he had sometimes an " anamnesis "
of the beautiful ladies of Tiflis. The Buddhist monasteries
of the Drum, in China, were filled with fraternities of the
most ascetic demeanour, but unfortunately idiotic in facial
expression, and far from being as responsive as the two
thousand yellow-robed monks whom it was Lord Curzon's
privilege to address at Mandalay. He specialised in monks,
and described them, after close attention, as " saints and
profligates, bon-vivants and ascetics, gentlemen and vaga-
bonds, men of education and illiterate boors." So that the
diversity of character of which I ventured to speak just

now appears to extend to the monastic class, which might be expected to be particularly exempt from it. In these brief descriptions of visits paid to some of the most out-of-the-way places in the world, always in friendly company, the Viceroy is at his best. His vivacity of observation, his amiable self-consciousness, his application and resource, are patent throughout. He is no longer the stately representative of imperial Government; he is a gregarious undergraduate of unusual power and accomplishment, hunting for intellectual entertainment. For George Nathaniel Curzon was both things, and many other things. He was Proteus, and when we try to hold him, he slips through our fingers.

# " CUMMY "

# "CUMMY"

THE theory that authority has left the seats of the Mighty and that nobody pays any regard to the once popular Victorians seems to be belied in the case of Robert Louis Stevenson. Editions of his books are multiplied so often as to suggest that publishers are unable to meet the demand. His style and his personal character are still the objects of violent praise and blame. Volumes are continually issued to prove that he was a plaster saint, and are replied to in volumes that declare him to have been a particularly squalid sinner. Metaphysical critics issue manifestoes to show that he was not worth thinking about, and teach us to believe that they are thinking about nobody else.

Meanwhile, to the very few of his intimate friends who survive, the Real R. L. S. seems to evade all these investigations, which (in fact) do not matter one peppercorn except in so far as they prove the tenacity of his appeal. It is strange that a nature so gentle as his, so un-revolutionary, in a certain delicate and charming way so superficial, should hold its own in the hurly-burly of opinions. But it does, and the very violence with which, in certain quarters, it is attacked merely shows how broad a surface lies open to attack.

These reflections are torn from me by the appearance of a massive tome which illustrates a corner of the early life of R. L. S., namely a tour on the Continent which he took at the age of thirteen, in company with his nurse, Alison Cunningham. Here, surely, is an instance of the persistency of fame. Who would care to read the diary of a female attendant who accompanied, let us say, the infant John Stuart Mill to the Hebrides, or packed the luggage of George Eliot on a trip to Coventry? A famous novelist of the younger school has asked, with snorts of defiance : In what did the supposed " charm " of Stevenson consist? Well, the fact that, more than thirty years after his death, curiosity about him remains so strong that the diary of his nurse, kept for a little while when he was thirteen years of age, is presented to an avid public, and is snapped up at the price of a guinea and a half, merely because he is occasionally mentioned in it—this fact alone seems to me to be evidence of mysterious and perennial " charm."

There are excellent persons, as I am told, who " collect " everything that regards R. L. S. They will add to their library " Cummy's Diary," we may be sure, although they may be a little put out of countenance by the swagger of it. The book is rather too splendid for its substance. The paper, the binding, the " format " generally, are enough to give our modest " Cummy " the nightmare, and it is " dedicated by gracious permission " to a Royal personage ! Bless my soul; and bless the soul of R. L. S., and of Miss Alison Cunningham, so simple and so easily abashed as we knew her long ago !

The editor of the " Diary," in his short preface, labours under the disadvantage of not having seen the author until she was eighty-nine years of age. This is rather late in the life of a lady to make her first acquaintance. Mr. Robert T. Skinner's brief memoir is probably accurate, but is bound to be perfunctory; it is definite only in some beautiful passages of tribute quoted from Stevenson himself, and already familiar to all his readers. When I had the privilege of seeing Cummy first, she was a mere girl of fifty-nine, and this gives me a great advantage over Mr. Skinner. I remember Louis telling me that she applied to herself the dictum (I know not whether this has ever been published) that in her youth she was "no what you would exactly call ' bonnie,' but pale, penetrating, and interesting." She was certainly all that when I had the rather alarming honour of being inspected by her (as one of "Lew's" questionable English friends) at Braemar in 1881. She had a certain searching austerity of manner, allied to extreme kindliness, and to a faint jealousy of outside influences acting upon her "lamb." She was shy, and resolute, and extremely Scotch; and she was severe towards evil-doers. The tattle-mongers who now talk Freudian non-sense about Stevenson's early "sins" do not know Cummy; her bright eye was fixed on his goings out and his comings in. But enough—for the moment—about this.

Miss Alison Cunningham accompanied Mr. and Mrs. Thomas Stevenson on a journey which they took in 1863 to what unsympathetic schoolboys call "the beastly abroad." She travelled with them in the capacity of nurse to their only child, the interesting R. L. S. At the age of thirteen many young gentlemen have dispensed with the services of a nurse, but Robert Lewis (not yet Louis) was so delicate as to be almost an invalid. His mind was active enough, and his attitude towards "the abroad" was far from being unsympathetic. He had read much, and he was fired with curiosity. The admirable Cummy had been a pillar of the household ever since she came into the family in 1852. She was well fitted to take care of the future genius as having been, so we are quaintly told, "nurse in the Free Church Manse at Pilrig." More impressive to the Southron imagination is the fact that from the very first she made herself essential to the happi-ness of the Stevenson family. She was, indeed, in the strictest sense, a "treasure," and in surroundings which were not always comfortable, "Kinnicum," as she was also called, provided a cosy corner and a feather bed for her

often agitated little charge.   When R. L. S. dedicated to
her " A Child's Garden of Verses " he called her

> My second Mother, my first Wife,
> The angel of my infant life,

and he remained, until his very latest weeks in Samoa,
her " laddie, with all love."

Stevenson once used a very odd phrase about Alison
Cunningham.   While acknowledging in his unvarying style
all the good she had done him, he prayed that God would
" mercifully forgive her all the evil."   I do not know that
any of his commentators have noticed this.   What could
he mean?   I think the only possible " evil " that the
devoted Cummy could have done was to oppress the boy's
conscience with the discipline of her rigid Puritanism.
But that this was " evil " may be seriously questioned.
Neither his father nor his mother, both of them in their own
way delightful, had exactly the character required to soothe
and guide such a fantastic little soul as the child Robert
Louis.   Each of them possessed too much the same nervous
and highly-strung temperament as their son.   Their likeness
led to differences, and when the boy began to grow up there
were electric storms in the family life which once or twice
threatened to be serious.   The influence of Cummy, who
was more like an aunt than a servant in the house, was
steadying and calming; she was a miracle of common-
sense and homely tact, and she protected her nursling
against all the shocks of life, even against the nerves of his
loving, fidgety parents.   This, at least, is how it seemed to
me in the old days long ago.

The tour in 1863 was quite a considerable affair.   The
travellers started from Edinburgh on January 2, and did
not return until May 20.   They spent nearly two months
in Mentone, whence, in the old comfortable way, in a
carriage, they proceeded to Italy, penetrating that country

as far as Naples, and returning through Germany. The route was exactly that of the seventeenth-century travellers who embarked upon the Grand Tour. " Cummy's Diary " was kept for the benefit of Cashie, a nurse in another Stevenson family, a great friend of Cummy, and slightly patronised by her, as being untravelled and inexperienced. Stevenson fanatics will be thrilled to read how, at the very beginning of the trip, " Lew took me for a walk round the walls of York by moonlight, and round by the River Ouse."

But London reserved a nasty shock for Miss Cunningham, who could hardly believe her eyes when she saw vessels plying up and down the Thames on Sunday. " O Cash," she exclaims, " how sad it makes one to see such things ! How God's holy day is dishonoured ! " This did not augur well for travelling through Popish countries, but things turned out better than might be feared. She found Paris " enchanting," and she records the goings-on in the churches without severity. But at Marseilles the Protestant awakes again, and she finds it awful to think that the beautiful land of France, " and very nice people too," are " under the reign of the Man of Sin." The context leaves it doubtful whether she refers to Napoleon III. or to the Pope of Rome.

At the hotels she did not like the publicity of the table d'hôte. Sitting among so many people, and all so grand, made her feel " like a bogle." At Nice she took refuge from the Carnival in the Scotch church of Dr. Watson of Largs, and was refreshed by hearing two good Scots sermons :—

" The people here have been going on at a fearful rate to-day, men and boys dressed in all conceivable costumes, having false faces on and playing some kind of music. How sweet it was to leave this toolery and great rabble of people, and go into the House of God and listen to the words of

Jesus ! It is awful to see the dozens of priests going about
and allowing such wickedness to go on unchecked, but I
suppose the priests will sanction the festival. They are
dark, mysterious-looking men, going about with their
long gowns and cocked hats, professing to be the true
servants of God; verily they have their reward."

It would be particularly interesting to know whether
Lew was permitted to enjoy the Carnival, or whether he
was hurried away in the middle of it to the ministrations
of Dr. Watson of Largs. On this the " Diary " throws no
light. Cummy was consoled by the discovery that there is
scarcely a plant mentioned in Scripture which is not found
at Nice. There was white heather also, but not so good as
" that of bonnie Scotland." Mr. and Mrs. Stevenson were
not in good spirits, and Cummy thought that they would be
much happier if they would look at the silver lining. She
herself was very gay, and developed a sudden desire to
climb to the top of the highest peak of the Alps. This was
not encouraged, but she was heartlessly told that she might
go to Confession if she liked ! We learn with unfeigned
satisfaction that " Lew is a very good bit boy, no trouble
indeed." They walked in a lemon-orchard, and Cummy
had a great desire to " pull " a lemon, " but Lew said, in his
old-fashioned way, that, though it was allowed, yet he did
not think it altogether right," so Cummy refrained. Thus
was the biter bit ! I seem to recognise my R. L. S.

In face of that sustained public interest in Stevenson of
which I have spoken, it is important that his character as
man and writer should be illuminated. It is obscured by
the sensational efforts of volunteer biographers whose only
aim is to truckle to the taste of the moment. It is not by
picking up gossip in the ambiguous billiard-rooms of Edinburgh that light is to be gained, but by studying the written
sources of information. Anyone who really wishes to

understand the adolescent Stevenson may find the story
written clear in " The Adventures of John Nicholson." At
his worst R. L. S. was but one of that " convention of
unhappy young asses " who beat for admittance at the
house of Collette. But the psychologist who sincerely
tries to fathom the not very deep or dark well of Stevenson's
youth will find that " Cummy's Diary," slight and even
laughable as it may be, helps him in its search. It helps
him to understand what pressure was gently brought to
bear upon the moral life of this boy of genius, and what the
atmosphere was which he continued to breathe. Be it
remembered, moreover, that he was frail and sensitive in
physique, unprepared for those riots of the flesh which
scandalous journalists foist upon his memory. There was
no time, in the Edinburgh winter nights, when Cummy
would not see him to bed with a hot bottle.

There has been more nonsense written about Stevenson
than about any other author of our time. He has been
ridiculously travestied, for evil and for good, over-praised
for virtues which he did not possess, over-advertised for
faults which he never committed. It is high time that some
sound critical pen undertook to brush aside all this stuff, and
I therefore rejoice to see that Mr. Robert Lynd, in whose
taste and judgment everyone has confidence, is engaged on a
" Life." I hope he will read " The Adventures of John
Nicholson " with care, and that he will not disdain to study
the artless " Diary " of Alison Cunningham. It is the
atmosphere that is wanted, an examination of the delicate,
cold soil out of which the warm, frail blossom shot. Nobody
could render this more subtly than Mr. Lynd, and I hope he
will not delay, since I want to read a really good book
about Robert Louis (or " Lew ") before I die.

# A GREAT LADY

# A GREAT LADY

IRRESISTIBLY, in reading this agreeable record, the mind goes back to July 6, 1786, when Court journalists informed the fashionable world that " Miss Burney, daughter of Dr. Burney, is appointed Dresser to the Queen." It was on March 17, 1853, that Miss Mary Bulteel, gay, intelligent, and independent, was captured, at the age of twenty, and caged, or, at least, enclosed, for the rest of her life, in the gilded prison of Court routine. Fanny Burney was thirty-four when she was tempted to embark on what she found " the wearisome life of attendance and dependence "; she has made it familiar to us in her " Diary." Her character was more set, her horizon more narrow and prudish, than those of her successor, while the atmosphere which surrounded Queen Victoria was never that of the intellectual and moral Leyden jar in which Queen Charlotte stagnated.

Still, in reading the letters and journals of the very lively subject of Miss Ponsonby's compilation, it is impossible not to be reminded of a woman of some genius whose peace of mind was shattered by the " prodigious risk of giving the gown before the hoop, or the fan before the neckerchief." In her sense of fun, in the sharpness of her censures, in the wariness of her discretion, the later courtier equals the earlier, but here the resemblance ceases; and there is no reason to believe that Lady Ponsonby, whose duties were infinitely lighter than those of the author of " Evelina," felt much of that tedium under which Fanny Burney languished. At the same time, there is a noticeable

z                                337

parallel between the adventures of the two " confidential companions," and each had her moments of longing for freedom and repose.

Miss Mary Bulteel was the grand-daughter of the Prime Minister Earl Grey, who carried the Reform Bill in the year of her birth and who survived until she was thirteen. She moved in the great Whig world, formed friendships with some of the most interesting people of the day, and was elegantly but moderately Puseyite. As a young girl she interested herself, to use her own words, " in matters of thought, speculative, philosophical, ethical, religious," combining them with special study of music and French literature. Her uncle was General Charles Grey, Prince Albert's private secretary, and it was while paying him a visit at Windsor that she was presented to Queen Victoria, who became instantly attracted by her intelligence and charm. Miss Magdalen Ponsonby, who has put together their memorials, is of opinion that in almost abruptly choosing her as her new Maid of Honour, the Queen was guided by the fact that Miss Bulteel was " decidedly unlike the usual type of courtier." It may be so, of course, but this was not the Queen's customary impulse. Whom else did she ever appoint who was not more or less of the usual type of courtier? What I should suggest as probable is that the very clever and sympathetic girl contrived unconsciously, through music, perhaps, or through conversation, to fascinate the Queen, and to make her, in this solitary instance, break through the punctilious conventionality of Court relations. The subsequent record of Miss Bulteel's external life is brief. After eight years of service as Maid of Honour, her connection with the Court was not severed, for she married General, afterwards Sir Henry, Ponsonby, the Queen's Private Secretary, who died thirty-four years later, whereupon his widow was appointed Extra Woman of the Bedchamber in 1895. She ultimately retired to a house at Ascot, where she died in 1916, in her eighty-fifth year.

Young as she was, and thrown upon her own resources in an entirely unfamiliar element, Miss Bulteel immediately began to form an independent idea of Court life. She perceived that the one interesting feature of it was the Mistress, and that those who were associated with herself in service were unable, and perhaps unwilling, to form any idea of the Queen's inner feelings. Very tactful and cautious in expression, the intelligent girl kept open her ears and her eyes, and formed views which were not in accordance with the tradition of the Court. In particular, she observed the infatuation of the Queen for the judgment of Prince Albert, whose opinions roused in Miss Bulteel's mind "the most fierce antagonism." Writing long afterwards of the period which began in 1853 and ended in 1861, she said of the Prince :—

" He was without a spark of spontaneity, and this often made him put the commonest everyday occurrence into an abstract form, stating it as a proposition and treating it logically, whereas by the rapid application of common-sense, Cookerson would arrive far nearer the truth in half the time. I have always thought the Queen possessed an instinct and a quick appreciation of people (without being able to reason about them) in a far more marked way than the Prince. But in more abstruse questions, her want of knowledge and her prejudices, when the conditions of the problem were not discernible at first sight, told against her."

This frankness and lucidity gave Lady Ponsonby (as it now becomes convenient to name her) an advantage over all who in those early years came under the spell of Windsor. Her published estimate of the character of Queen Victoria is an elaborate analysis of a temperament which was forced

by circumstances and by a strict conception of duty on to a
higher plane than nature intended it to fill. Lady Ponsonby speaks with unvarying loyalty of the fine con-
stituents of Queen Victoria's nature, but she does not
encourage the customary courtly illusions. She shows her
to us as rather kind than thoughtful, rather earnest than
amusing; the dinners at Osborne were " insufferably dull,"
and the other Court ladies drew upon themselves the
unspoken scorn of the keen-eyed girl for " foolishly cringing
to all the little miseries of etiquette." She sees that the
Queen is usually badly dressed, and she notes Victoria's in-
sensitiveness to all impressions drawn from literature or art.
She is enchanted when Lady Mt. Edgcumbe, greatly daring,
tells Her Majesty at the piano, " Dear Madam, you really
must do that passage again; it is impertinent to Mozart
to libel it so ! " But all this frankness of observation does
not prevent her from responding to the genuine affection
which the Queen extended to her, or from perceiving and
doing ample justice to the monarch's sterling qualities of
heart and will. Perhaps no one of the countless individuals
who were brought into relation with the Queen understood
her so well as Lady Ponsonby.

Yet, unquestionably, the one member of the Royal
Household with whom Lady Ponsonby was most completely in sympathy was the Empress Frederick. The
letters which passed from the one to the other through a
long stretch of years are particularly interesting. Lady
Ponsonby had not been greatly pleased by Prince Frederick
William, " a good-humoured, taking lieutenant, with large
hands and feet, not in the least clever." But his wife was
" clever " enough for a bunch of princes, and Lady Ponsonby had, all through her life, a penchant for cleverness.
On the Princess's first arrival in Potsdam she wrote to her
friend in Windsor : " You cannot think how dull and
melancholy and queer I feel." Her letters to Lady Pon-

sonby were frank to the verge of indiscretion, and the outcome of a great seriousness determined not to be warped by the pressure of alien circumstances. She was not always modern enough for Lady Ponsonby, whose daring flights into speculation threw over the Princess's face that " second-century look " which her correspondent amusingly deprecates. But they were much more in intellectual sympathy with one another than with anyone else in the two Court circles.

The letters written during the Emperor's last illness, in 1888, are of a poignant intimacy, and those after the Empress's bereavement testify to the loneliness and unhappiness which surrounded her widowhood. In 1898 she confesses, " I see very, very little of my son, who rarely, if ever, comes to see me, even when I am ill." She confesses that it is only to Mary Ponsonby that she opens " the flood-gates of all the pain and bitterness, the stinging regrets " that fill her soul. The tragedy came to its slow end at last in 1901.

Royal relations, however, were far from absorbing the whole of this intelligent and inquisitive Court lady's mind. We find that her sympathies extended over a wider field, and even impinged upon topics which Queen Victoria might consider, in her favourite phrase, not quite " discreet." There is some difficulty in following Lady Ponsonby in these excursions, for though the volume is in some respects well edited—there are good notes and an excellent index —the material is presented to us in a curiously disjointed fashion. There is no development in the story, but we read in successive chapters about unrelated persons and things. This is probably due to the fact that the keeping of records by individuals was not encouraged at Windsor, and also in part to the fact that Lady Ponsonby was not careful to preserve other people's letters or to date her own. She was acquainted with a vast number of persons, some of the most interesting of whom are not even introduced in this memoir. For example, our curiosity is roused by learning that she was at one time much under the influence of John Stuart Mill, and, again, under that of Herbert Spencer, but they hardly appear, the latter only on an occasion when he was " grim and unsympathetic." Her initiation into the principles of Socialism is dwelt upon in a series of letters addressed to her son, Mr. Arthur Ponsonby. By the way, will not the colleagues of that ardent statesman be shocked by a picture here given of Her Majesty, incredibly bedizened, marching forward with her train held up by the future M.P. for the Brightside Division of Sheffield?

Lady Ponsonby reveals in her correspondence a curious tendency to reproduce the peculiarities of the friend to whom she writes. In this respect she is a chameleon of style. The letters which pass between Sir Henry and herself are examples of this local coloration, since it is often necessary to glance at the initialled signature to be sure whether husband or wife is speaking. The most amusing instance is the interchange of letters with George Eliot, with whom Lady Ponsonby became acquainted in 1894 and later on almost intimate. It is admitted that George Eliot was one of the worst of letter-writers, pompous, didactic, and without a spark of humour. Quite a phenomenon that the author of "Silas Marner," when she took a pen in hand to address a friend, sinks like a plummet into an abyss of dullness! But what is particularly odd is that Lady Ponsonby, who, when left to her own devices, was a transcendent letter-writer, no sooner has to correspond with George Eliot than she falls into her friend's fault, and discourses about Divinity and the Enchainment of Causes. The phenomenon, no doubt, was due to that almost excessive instinct of sympathy which made Lady Ponsonby the rarest and most enchanting of companions.

In 1875 she chaperoned a party of five friends to Düsseldorf, and this episode is commemorated in letters to Sir Henry and in fragments of a journal. The company included Mr. A. J. Balfour, whom Lady Ponsonby seems to have now met for the first time and who much excited her interest. She gives repeated impressions of his appearance and manners; these seem a little intimate for publicity in Lord Balfour's lifetime, but I presume that after more than half a century he looks back upon his old self with equanimity. We are admitted to see him sitting on his large soft felt hat at the rehearsals of the Musical Festival, and wearing " a long black coat which makes him look like a disreputable Archdeacon." The sketches of Mary Gladstone and of Spencer Lyttelton are no less lively; to an elderly reader the effect is that of walking through a deserted gallery. Comparatively few will still remember that Everard Primrose, the reckless writer of inimitable fun from Vienna, was Lord Rosebery's brother. In one instance only, I think, the editor has been indiscreet, or, at least, unkind. I know not what induced Lady Ponsonby to write down the horrid description of Renan on page 142. It is like one of M. Rouveyre's terrific caricatures, and might have been cancelled. She had a kind of volcanic tendency to be delightfully preposterous, as when she electrified the sedate Royal family, who were vapouring at dinner about Sir William Wallace as the hero of Scottish history, by asserting that he never existed at all. The Queen was scandalised at such temerity.

The reviewer must now retire for a few moments to give place to the friend. To have known Lady Ponsonby through her leisurely and ripe old age was to have been admitted to the presence of a rare and elected spirit. Her temperament was of that happy sort which combines the sanguine with the nervous; she was ardent without sentimentality, and critical without venom. Her conversation, interlarded a little to excess with French phrases, had an eighteenth-century distinction, high-toned, humorous, and slightly revolutionary. Her face, a rather narrow oval under a cupola of forehead, would be palely fixed upon her interlocutor, who did well not to be taken in by her apparent excess of candour. She excelled in retort, and was apt to follow up her quick riposte with disconcerting laughter. A cheerful philosopher, she had no patience with mental timidity, but was ready to accompany a friend on any voyage of speculation, at least part of the way. When she was very old, she appeared to retain her hold on life through her cheerfulness, her curiosity, and her sympathy. To know her, as the hackneyed quotation says, was a liberal education.

# BODLEY AND THE BODLEIAN

# BODLEY AND THE BODLEIAN

WHEN, in the year 1605, King James I. of England paid a State visit to Oxford, he was taken to the newly fitted Bodleian Library, where he " did break out into noble speech," and declared, with evident sincerity, " If I might have my wish, I would desire to have no other prison than this Library, and to be chained together with so many good authors." The sentiment did credit to a monarch whose behaviour was not always what his great successor used to call " discreet," but who did genuinely love learning as he understood it. It is well to add this final clause, since literature did not appear to learned men in 1605 as it does to us to-day. If James I. had been chained to a desk, and left among his manuscript companions, their converse would have been of a kind intolerable to our ears. Far into the night they would have quoted Tremellius in Hoseam, and discussed Rabbi Shelomoh Jarrhi, and refuted Ockham in his quodlibets; and if the name of Shakespeare had been uttered, they would have received it with disdainful bewilderment. If we had intruded on their company we should have found no point at which they and we were intelligible to one another. The splendid bibliography of Mr. T. J. Wise approaches the completion of its last volume, and it is significant to point out that it contains not one single entry of a book which Sir Thomas Bodley would have admitted to the Bodleian, while, on the other hand, the Bodleian originally contained not one single book which Mr. Wise would care to possess or describe. The difference between bibliography as it was in 1600 and what it is to-day could not be more vividly exemplified.

Sir Thomas Bodley was a public servant of great activity and resource, but we should know little and care less about him if it were not that at a moment of sharp disappointment he abruptly withdrew into private life and began to endow the University of Oxford. By repudiating all ambition to be famous, he became far more celebrated than his gratified ambition could have made him. He enjoyed the extreme of involuntary success through having determined to be a failure. Were it not for the Library, the name of Sir Thomas Bodley would long ago have ceased to awaken curiosity, and curiosity itself could hardly have been satisfied unless he had written what he called his " Life." This document he preserved in the Bodleian, and there it was found nearly a hundred years later by the most punctilious of antiquaries, who printed in 1703 an invaluable little octavo, called the " Life, the First Draught of the Statutes of the Public Library and a Collection of Letters to Dr. James." This volume bore no editor's name, but it was the work of Thomas Hearne, the non-juror, who was himself to learn the bitterness of libraries and the ingratitude of dons. The fate of Hearne has always roused me to an indignation which I must curb in this place, merely saying that he was a man after Bodley's own heart, and well deserving the honour of revealing his predecessor to the world. The " Reliquiæ Bodleianæ " of 1703 is a delightful little book, and it includes practically all that is known, or ever will be known, about the early history of the famous Library. Hearne made one mistake; he printed the letters higgledy-piggledy, in no chronological order. Mr. G. W. Wheeler demands warm thanks for having removed this disability. With patient ingenuity of conjecture he has arranged the letters in proper sequence, and the Clarendon Press has issued them in a handsome volume.   So far, however, as the text goes, a comparison of Mr. Wheeler's pages with the analogous ones of the " Reliquæ " (such as I have in several cases made) merely shows what an accurate pen the much-libelled Hearne possessed.

The autobiography of Bodley is quite brief, but it gives us all the principal points in his career up to his absorption in the work of the Library.   He was born at Exeter in 1544, was originally intended for a parson, and trained in divinity at Magdalen College, Oxford, where he became a Fellow when he was nineteen.   He held a variety of University offices, but in 1576 grew tired of the life, and started on a Grand Tour, pervading Europe for four years, during which he became proficient in all the usual vernaculars, but particularly, no doubt, relied on Latin for communications, since he shows no interest in any modern literature.   He came back enriched with every elegant accomplishment, and was appointed Gentleman Usher to Queen Elizabeth.   Burleigh became his patron, and " would always tell the Queen that there was not any man in England so meet as myself to undergo the office of Secretary " of State.   Unfortunately, Bodley was equally attractive to Essex, who made " prodigal speeches " to the Queen regarding Bodley's superiority to Burleigh.   The Queen became angry, and Bodley fell between two stools, being, according to his own account, the victim of jealous intrigue.   Perhaps we may conjecture that he was not quite loyal to Burleigh, to whom he should have stuck as to his best friend.   Bodley was removed from " the throng of Court contentions," and made Ambassador to the Hague. Coming back to England, he found new conditions and another monarch.   His account of what happened is not very clear, but he retired abruptly from public life, concluding " to set up his staff," as he says, " at the Library-door in Oxon."   He determined, for the future, to devote

all his money, leisure, and influence to the foundation of
such a public collection of books as had never before been
seen in Europe.

Having determined that the foundation of a Library at
Oxford should be the "greatest of his worldly cares,"
Bodley settled in that city, which he describes (I do not
quite understand why) as in 1599 "in every part ruined
and waste." Perhaps he means, indifferent to the claims
of disciplined learning. He looked about for a helper, and
he found Thomas James, a young fellow of New College, who
was like-minded in his passion for books and for the care
of them. James was in Cambridge, whither he had gone
to study the state of the college libraries, of which he gave
a bad report. Meanwhile Bodley was examining the state
of things in Oxford, and he found them deplorable. A
hundred years before the birth of Sir Thomas Bodley,
Duke Humphrey of Gloucester, one of the few bibliophils
of his age, had bequeathed his books to the University, and
that collection was supposed to be the Library. But
when Bodley came to set up his staff at the door of it, he
found nothing but "a great desolate room." There had
been no endowment for the maintenance of the Library,
and no care in preserving the books, which had been stolen
or dispersed until there was nothing whatever left but
the empty shelves. Two facts were accordingly borne
in upon the retired diplomatist : first, that books without
endowment formed a worthless gift, and secondly, that
every precaution should be taken to prevent dispersion.
These two ideas became a fortunate obsession, and they
fill his correspondence, the latter to a degree which is almost
absurd.

Bodley's zeal was appreciated by Convocation, and he
was empowered to restore and fit up the shell of Duke
Humphrey's building. Merton College presented timber
for desks, shelves, and cases. The Vice-Chancellor ex-

pressed an eager interest in the selection of the books. Bodley made arrangement of a capital sum for the purchase of volumes, for the payment of salaries, and for all that would be needful to ensure the permanence of the new foundation. There were long delays, but no serious obstacles, and on December 24, 1599, he writes that—

" Within this fortnight, I trust, I shall have ended with my carpenters, joiners, carvers, glaziers, and all that idle rabble; and when I go in hand with making up my bars, locks, hasps, grates, chains, and other gimmoes of iron, belonging to the fastening and rivetting of the books."

Bodley's anxiety for the safety of the books was extra-ordinary. He would allow no visitor to enter the building until every volume, manuscript or printed, was completely fastened to the shelves. His letters expatiate on chains and locks, and the aspect of the Library when at length it was finished must have been penitential in the extreme. On no pretence whatever was a single volume to be allowed to leave the building. Books too small for chains were to be locked behind wire grating. This painful solicitude was overdone, and Bodley himself admitted in 1602 that " the multiplicity of chains " was interfering with " the sight and show of the books." But he was taking no risks; the book-thief was stalking through the colleges, and he would have no repetition of the disaster by which Duke Humphrey's Library of 129 volumes were all stolen or strayed.

The collection of books went on slowly. Sir Thomas Bodley gave many, but had to depend on the generosity of donors, and he seems, like many noble public benefactors, to have been a sturdy beggar. He made those who gave volumes pay for the binding also, and he insisted on important gifts. When Dr. James was appointed Keeper, one of his duties was to deal with donors, who were to be wheedled, urged, and squeezed. All were to be thanked, but in terms proportionate to their benefaction. When Tobias Matthew, Bishop of Durham, after presenting some books, visited the Library, Dr. James was instructed to give him " a short, sweet welcome." In the course of the correspondence, Bodley, writing from his houses at Burnham or in London, eagerly desires to know what is said by visitors, who were not admitted even for inspection until the end of June, 1601, when there was a kind of private view. The Library was still closed to students. Bodley now lived mostly in college rooms, so as to hold his darling creation under personal watch and ward. Dr. James was an excellent Keeper, but he had his limitations. He was bold enough to wish to marry, which filled Bodley with apprehension, and there was a battle royal about this, until James said he should resign unless he was allowed to have a wife, whereupon Bodley, lamenting, yielded. But James had an even more dangerous weakness. He wanted to *read* the books—a monstrous pretension! Sir Thomas Bodley had to remind him that this was an unworthy ambition in a librarian. It upset Bodley very much, and we find him writing quite sharply to remind the peccant James that the " perusing of titles and authors is not void of profit," and indeed much more suitable for a bibliographer than idling his time away in reading. No wonder that James, who was a bookworm born, grumbled that " in a place of some eminency for books " he had no opportunity to study them.

Many little points may be collected from the letters to complete the picture of the infant Bodleian. The admirable Founder, and his hardly less praiseworthy Keeper, learned by experience the tricks of their trade, for they had no previous experience to go upon. It cannot be too emphatically said that their Library was an unprecedented institution. Europe had seen large collections of books brought together, and in particular the Bibliotheca Orientalis had quite lately been sumptuously housed in the Escorial by Philip II. of Spain. But nowhere had there been instituted and endowed a great representative public library until the patience and generosity of Sir Thomas Bodley were rewarded at Oxford. Hence the founders of the Bodleian were thrown back upon theory and experiment, and their delays were many and exasperating. They were learning all the time. The Library proved stuffy, and casemates had to be fitted in. The floors grew dirty, and had to be cleaned and scented with rosemary. The transmission of things which we think of to-day as matters of course was difficult and uncertain. For instance, no good ink was available in Oxford, and the carrier from London declined to carry what might break upon the journey and ruin all his goods. Bodley was equal to the occasion; he told his servant to assure the carrier that the bottles contained nothing but distilled water, a pious fib. A plague of " little worms " began to break out among the folios, and this required drastic treatment.

Why has the famous " book-worm " ceased to trouble librarians? It was the scourge of the seventeenth century. Small books—which Bodley disliked—gave trouble by gaping. They had to be fastened by strings, and placed in rows, the fore-edges outward. Dr. James was given but little latitude, and Sir Thomas from a distance ruled the Library with a rod of iron.

The right of using the Panbiblion, as Richard Haydock called it, to Bodley's delight, was confined to the superior dons, to the exclusion of undergraduates and even B.A.'s; gradually " gentlemen strangers," that is to say, foreign students of position, were admitted. In 1605 came the first printed catalogue, which roused Sir Thomas to great wrath with Dr. James and the printers by its Hebrew misprints. Bodley was as sly as he was firm; when King

A A

James paid his official visit, the Keeper thought that the works of His Majesty ought to be bound with regal splendour in preparation. Bodley, who probably rated the prose and verse of the King at a moderate value, refused to have any difference made between these and the writings of other authors. Accordingly, Dr. James was instructed to hide them, and if the King should happen to ask for them, to say that they had gone to London " to be bound in velvet." All these things, and many others, will be found in the admirable volume which Mr. Wheeler, with a pertinacious intelligence which Bodley himself would have appreciated, has prepared for the delight of all to whom the Bodleian is a Mecca of the intellectual life.

# THE PROSE OF DR. JOHNSON

# THE PROSE OF DR. JOHNSON

INTO the study of Samuel Johnson there enters something
which resembles the miracle of the loaves and fishes. We
cannot exhaust the interest awakened by this writer and
this man about whom a hundred volumes have been written.
Something always evades us, and beckons us on; the more
we are told the more we want to hear; and to go over the
old familiar ground is to discover new charms at every
turn. Johnson is the type of the author whose character
transcends his writing, and whose writing incessantly
throws fresh light upon his character. We cannot know
one without the other, and both together leave us with
dark spaces for speculation and wonder. In his own lifetime, the writer was seen to preponderate, especially during
the last four years of it, when he reigned as the despot of
letters. But with his death, the man almost instantly began
to assert a prominence, of which the successive biographies,
with Boswell's triumphant at the end, were the visible
evidence. It then grew to be the fashion to say that Dr.
Johnson was the most fascinating of human beings, but
that his writings were naught. Who could waste time over
" The Rambler " or be idle with " The Idler? " Could
anything be more insipid than " Thoughts on the Falkland
Islands "? No, no; Dr. Samuel Johnson was a very great
social prodigy, but a writer only by accident. That was
the judgment of critics half a century ago.

The question of his position in English letters frequently
occupied the mind of Johnson himself, and he regretted, in
his pathetically ineffectual way, that he had pursued his

profession with so little concentration. "The chief glory of every people," he bravely declared, "arises from its authors," and he knew not, in 1755, whether he had been able to add anything to it. There was excuse for doubt, since, at the age of forty-six, when most writers have plainly shown what they can do, Johnson had published vigorously, though briefly, in verse, but in prose practically nothing except a group of anonymous essays. If he had died just before the conclusion of the "Dictionary," he would be remembered only as one who determined that England should "no longer yield the palm of philology to the nations of the Continent." He was to live nearly thirty years more, and to produce, occasionally with profusion, illustrations of his remarkable genius.

But if we think of the apparent emptiness of the first half of his life, and of that singular indolence which never ceased to frustrate his intentions, we may understand how it comes that for a long period the conviction prevailed that the writings of Johnson were, what a great authority called them, "scanty and inadequate." The genius of Boswell positively threw so dazzling a light on the personal habits and conversation of his friend that it plunged, by contrast, the writings into darkness. There has been again a reaction ; the "Works" are once more the objects of sympathetic study, but here again let us beware of excess. It does not seem possible that the famous twelve volumes can ever take a place on the toilet-tables of the fair. I think that no one has dared to reprint them in full since 1825.

There is, however, nothing unusual in the fact that a large portion of Johnson's writings has become unreadable. When I admit that "The False Alarm" and "Taxation no Tyranny" are unreadable to-day, it by no means follows that they will not be read to-morrow. The dead works of great authors have a marvellous aptitude for throwing off their cere-clothes. As a fact, however, a very large portion of Johnson's prose is at present dead, or in a swoon. But, if we come to that, so is much of the prose of his most eminent contemporaries. What of Bolingbroke, and what of Samuel Clarke? Who can read the "Divine Legation"? Who dares to plunge into the Bangorian controversy? Yet these were precisely the rivals with which Johnson's genius in its youth languidly and unconvincingly contended. He was sure that they had added to "the chief glory" of this country, and he was not sure that he himself would ever do so. Mr. S. C. Roberts, who published an excellent selection from "The Idler" some years ago, and who is a convinced Johnsonian, has answered the question in the skilful little volume before me, where, in two hundred and fifty pages, the best passages from the great author's works are separated from what seems to have become superfluous or tedious, and are presented to us for our profit and diversion. The task must have been a laborious one, but it has been performed with elegance and taste. No one could have a more advantageous introduction to Johnson as a writer than is given him by Mr. Roberts in this delightful little book.

Mr. Roberts adopts the chronological method, and, after giving selections from Johnson's poetry (omitting, however, "London" altogether), he starts the prose with "The Rambler" of 1750. It is to be noted that by this time Johnson had well passed his fortieth year, and it is strange to find a great master of prose opening his special office so late. How came it that one who read with such omnivorous gusto, and who had such an impulse to impart his knowledge, made no effort to write until his youth was nearly past? We cannot solve a riddle which puzzled Boswell himself, The biographer learned that Johnson "furnished some numbers of a periodical Essay" published in Birmingham in 1732. After "very diligent inquiry," Boswell was unable to discover these early specimens. We are therefore

thrown back upon " A Voyage to Abyssinia," issued in
Birmingham in 1735, when Johnson was twenty-six years
of age. It has been Mr. Roberts's design to represent
his author always at his best, and he must therefore
not be blamed for not including an excerpt from the
" Abyssinia."

That book is not a direct translation (or paraphrase)
from the Portuguese of the Jesuit Father Jerome Lobo, but
from a translation into French, attributed to a shadowy
" Mr. Legrand," which Johnson had found at Pembroke
College. Johnson knew many things, but he did not at that
time read Portuguese. The fact that this is a translation
has prevented due attention being given to its style. But
there is a letter to the editing bookseller, followed by a
preface, and these, though unsigned, are manifestly the
independent work of Johnson. Here, then, we have the
earliest specimens of his prose, and as " Lobo " is a rare
book and not easily consulted, I will (without disrespect to
Mr. Roberts) give a quotation from the preface. The
translator defends his original :—

" The Reader will here find no Regions cursed with
irremediable Barrenness, or bless'd with Spontaneous
Fecundity, nor perpetual Gloom or unceasing Sunshine ; nor
are the Nations here described either devoid of all Sense of
Humanity, or consummate in all private and social Virtues.
Here are no Hottentots without Religion, Polity or Articulate Language ; no Chinese perfectly Polite, and com-
pleatly skill'd in all Sciences. He will discover, what will
always be discovered by a diligent and impartial Enquirer,
that wherever Human Nature is to be found, there is a
mixture of Vice and Virtue, a contest of Passion and Reason,
and that the Creator doth not appear Partial in his Dis-
tributions, but has balanced in most Countries their
particular Inconveniences by particular Favours."

In this passage, as in others in the " Lobo " paraphrase, we have the complete idiosyncrasy of Johnson's prose revealed. Here are the determined cultivation of discipline in the arrangement and construction of sentences, the love of antithesis, the indulgence to the ear in rhythm, and, above all, the contrast cunningly introduced between solemnity and familiarity. No doubt, from early times, the conversation of Johnson displayed these features, but it is remarkable that at the very outset, and after very little practice, he should have secured this individual manner of writing. I can see nothing immature in the preface to " Lobo "; its descriptions might come out of " Rasselas," its morality out of " The Idler." We may wonder that, while his early verse owes so much to the teaching of Pope, his early prose shows no tincture of Steele or Swift. It goes back, over the head of Addison, to the end of the seventeenth century, with the addition of qualities entirely modern and novel. We smile at the formality of this stately mode of writing, but it was really a vivid reaction against the triviality into which English prose had fallen after 1730.

Having thus supplied himself with an instrument, our surprise is considerable to find him neglecting to use it. We are told that " reviews, prefaces, biographies, essays and catalogues " filled Johnson's working hours. If so, what has become of them all? We have the very unsatisfactory " Life of Savage," but what else? It is difficult to understand how the work of all these years can have disappeared, and how nothing solid remains in prose until we reach " The Rambler." On this collection of essays critical opinion has usually been severe; it is said to mark the culminating period of Johnson's worst qualities of style. It is blamed for its pompous language and morose morality. I think this censure too severe, and I hold that the reader who has the courage to turn the pages of " The Rambler " will be rewarded by much that is simple and entertaining. But it is quite true that the formal mechanism of Johnson's sentences and his hortatory weight are here as prominent as in any part of his writings. We must regard him here as taking up the task of a lay-preacher, and as deliberately competing with the popular theologians of his youth. The sermon in the hands of the great churchmen of the beginning of the century had been as popular as the novel is to-day. Of Sherlock's " Treatise on Death "—a lugubrious disquisition—it was said that it had been " a nation's food," so incredibly had it proved a " best seller." It was Johnson's aim, as an essayist, to combine the spiritual force of the preachers with an æsthetic allusiveness, above all with a stately grace of style unknown to any of them, even to Butler. In " The Idler " he grew less " wordy," and the advance of taste in ten years found him freer in fancy and lighter in hand. But it is always the same sententious Samuel Johnson.

The student of Johnson's prose is bound to concentrate his attention on " Rasselas." Written when the author was fifty years of age, this unique romance displays in their maturity the character and style which a long habit of study and of reflection had polished to a height of perfection. If it is not too much to ask of a giddy generation, I would beg that those who are interested in the art of authorship should test their appreciation by reading " Rasselas " *aloud*. They may be surprised to find in it a richness of expression and a harmony of sound. They may be struck by the symmetrical arrangement of the sentences, which flow without a discord, wave after wave of full and balanced music. They may be persuaded that no little of the praise justly conceded to Goldsmith and Gibbon and Burke should be transferred to, or at least shared with, the author who preceded them all. For it should never be overlooked that the influence of Johnson upon style, which was prodigious, was of two distinct orders, one wholly good, the other wholly disastrous. His sterling merits of order and discipline were reflected in all that was elegantly formal in the prose of the next hundred years, while his pomposity, his love of loudly-tramping elephantine words, his didactic morality, were travestied in the works of a set of ridiculous imitators. Anyone who wishes to see what the degenerate study of Johnson's prose could result in may open the pages of Madame D'Arblay's "Wanderer."

At the very close of his life, a new Samuel Johnson burst upon the world, a juvenile sprightly spirit in whom we hardly recognise our Idler and our Rambler. Our estimate of his prose needs to be altogether revised when we take up "The Lives of the Poets." Here the report of Boswell, which we might have thought suspicious, is justified by a body of writing that is simply conversation in its rarefied form. Dr. Johnson talked, and we listen; he talked about the poets, and on what subject could he be more varied and more diverting? The logical and didactic elements seem to have passed away, and we find a very human companion holding forth on a theme which had a peculiar fascination for him. If I had any reproach to bring against Mr. Roberts it would be that his quotations from the "Lives of the Poets" are too scanty. Above all, I can scarcely forgive him for having omitted the Gilbert Walmsley digression from the life of Edmund Smith. Johnson had practically nothing to say about that most ineffectual poetaster, and so he turns upon us, and expatiates on what has nothing whatever to do with the author of "Phædra and Hippolytus." His voice breaks, he almost falters, and in slow melodious accents he reveals to us what he himself owed to the converse and the hospitality of a man little known to the world. His voice takes a deeper pathos, and he murmurs the immortal reflections about the " stroke of death " and the eclipse of the gaiety of nations. If I had to choose the passage in which the genius of Johnson is more characteristically revealed than anywhere else I should be tempted to point to this page in the " Life of Edmund Smith."

On the general subject little can be added to the estimate made by Austin Dobson more than thirty years ago :—

> Say, where is there English so full and so clear,
> So weighty, so dignified, manly, sincere?
> So prompt to take colour from place and occasion,
> So rich in expression, conviction, persuasion?
> So widely removed from the feeble, the tentative;
> So truly—and in the best sense—argumentative?
> You may talk of your Burkes and your Gibbons so clever,
> But I hark back to him with a " JOHNSON for ever ! "

# THE EMERGENCY
## THE BIRTHRIGHT OF THE PEOPLE

# THE EMERGENCY
## THE BIRTHRIGHT OF THE PEOPLE

THE very existence of a World of Books depends upon
the liberty of the Press. It was a great republican, a man
whose life was devoted to the cause of Freedom, who
declared three hundred years ago that those who " spill
that seasoned life of Man which is preserved and stored
in books commit a kind of homicide." The man who kills
the printed expression of his fellow-men might almost kill
a man more innocently, " since he who kills a man kills a
reasonable creature, God's image; but he who destroys a
good book kills reason itself, kills the image of God, as it
were, in the eye."

It is a topical reflection that three centuries after the
grim Puritans fought with success for what they called
" the Liberty of Unlicensed Printing," a tyrannous minority
should now be able to gag the thought and speech of the
nation, to forbid the free circulation of ideas, and to
silence the voices which sway opinion in the untrammelled
intercourse of citizen with citizen.

" Milton, thou shouldst be living at this hour." So
Wordsworth cried in 1802, when he feared that England was
ready to forfeit her ancient English dower of personal
liberty. Everyone knows the magnificent sonnet, but not
everyone recollects why Wordsworth wrote it. It marks
the moment when, after the Treaty of Amiens, Napoleon
demanded from the English Government the suppression
of English newspapers and pamphlets hostile to his new-

born Consulate. Wordsworth sang back to Milton, " England hath need of thee ! " He should have had more faith, for the pretensions of Bonaparte were scornfully rejected by a public opinion not so " stagnant " as the poet feared, and in fact the incident strengthened the liberty of printing, which had several times since 1694 been threatened with censorship. For more than a hundred years, we have believed that all things which are honest and of good report, even though they may be contrary to the convictions and prejudices of others, may be printed, and, as it were, publicly exhibited on the broad table of publicity.

Strange it is that those who invade our liberties and do not hesitate, after so many generations of open discussion, to slam the doors of public writing, have not had the intelligence to reflect that they are using a knife which cuts both ways. If they have the power tyrannically to stop their opponents' pens to-day, how is it that they do not realise that their own may be snatched from them to-morrow? Once let the sacred rights of publication be tampered with, what is to prevent the weapon successful to-day from being used in the opposite sense when the tables are turned?

I can imagine nothing more lamentable than that the Press of this country should be used, on one side or on the other, in causes ticketed white or black, no less than red, as a monopoly for the distribution of political authority. The general prerogative, enjoyed by the Church and then by the Crown, of stopping open discussion and refusing informa- tion to the people was gradually, painfully and grudgingly relinquished by those who established it. We gained our liberty with blood and tears. It stands, it has long and without question stood, firmly inscribed on the national Bill of Rights. It is an integral part of the birthright of the nation. As the great Puritan master said in 1644,

" Give me liberty to know, to utter and to argue freely
according to conscience, above all other liberties."

Confined, a willing prisoner, inside the palisades of a Park,
the kind Government has vouchsafed me a ticket-of-leave
for my going out and my coming in. On this pass, the
First Commissioner states that it is for my domestic use
" during the Emergency," by which he means the General
Strike. This euphemism pleases me greatly. It is so
guarded, so tactful; it reminds me of the scruples of the
poet Crabbe, who hoped that there was nothing in his verse
which could give the least offence to any person, however
foolish or wicked. " The Emergency " covers all opinion ;
it foresees all contingencies. I cannot doubt that it will
become historic. In future times children will cluster
round aged knees, and when they have asked, " Grandpapa,
tell us what you did in the War," they will start another
question, " And now, Grandpapa, tell us what you did in the
Emergency."

What an elderly person, for action all unfit, is doing in the
Emergency can interest very few readers. Nevertheless,
for those few, I will confess that I fall back upon the
consolations of literature. " Stone walls do not a prison
make," nor Clarence Gate a cage so long as my silent
sentinels stand round the room in rows. Industrial
despotism may prevent the manufacture of new books, but
I, for one, can do without them very well. If anybody cares
to know it, I am deep in " Don Quixote." It is full of tags
appropriate to the situation, and although it might be
injudicious to proclaim them aloud, the thought of them
makes me laugh in my fastness. " Hamlet," too, is comfortable reading ; it is a pity that we know it all by heart.
But have we ever done full justice to " Tristram Shandy " ?
Now is the time for " The Canterbury Tales." Depend upon
it, in hours of suspense, the old books are the best books.

B B

Accordingly, I venture to advise all those who are good enough to look to me for counsel, if in troublous times they are not so fortunate as to be serving their country actively, to console themselves with the best authors. Liberty will always come back to us, and we ought never to doubt that as England won the War, she will win the " Emergency."

*May* 9, 1926.

# INDEX

# INDEX